A TECHNOMORAL POLITICS

A TECHNOMORAL POLITICS

GOOD GOVERNANCE, TRANSPARENCY, AND CORRUPTION IN INDIA

Aradhana Sharma

UNIVERSITY OF MINNESOTA PRESS
MINNEAPOLIS · LONDON

The University of Minnesota Press gratefully acknowledges the generous assistance provided for the publication of this book by Wesleyan University.

Portions of this book are adapted from "The Righteous and the Rightful: The Technomoral Politics of NGOs, Social Movements, and the State in India," *American Ethnologist* 43, no. 1 (2016): 76–90; copyright 2016 by the American Anthropological Association, all rights reserved, doi:10.1111/amet.12264. Portions of chapter 3 are adapted from "State Transparency after the Neoliberal Turn: The Politics, Limits, and Paradoxes of India's Right to Information Law," *Political and Legal Anthropology Review* 36, no. 2 (2013): 308–25; copyright 2013 by the American Anthropological Association, all rights reserved, doi:10.1111/plar.12031. Portions of chapter 5 are adapted from "New Brooms and Old: Sweeping Up Corruption in India, One Law at a Time," *Current Anthropology* (2018): supplement 18, S72–S82; copyright 2018 by The Wenner-Gren Foundation for Anthropological Research, all rights reserved, doi:10.1086/696070. Portions of chapter 6 were originally published as "Good Governance," in *The People of India: New Indian Politics in the 21st Century,* edited by Ravinder Kaur and Nayanika Mathur (Gurugram: Penguin Random House India, 2022), 170–81.

Excerpts from Hamraaz's poetry are reprinted with permission of the author.

Copyright 2024 by the Regents of the University of Minnesota

All rights reserved. No part of this publication may be reproduced, stored in a retrieval system, utilized for purposes of training artificial intelligence technologies, or transmitted, in any form or by any means, electronic, mechanical, photocopying, recording, or otherwise, without the prior written permission of the publisher.

Published by the University of Minnesota Press
111 Third Avenue South, Suite 290
Minneapolis, MN 55401-2520
http://www.upress.umn.edu

ISBN 978-1-5179-1807-1 (hc)
ISBN 978-1-5179-1808-8 (pb)

A Cataloging-in-Publication record for this book is available from the Library of Congress.

Printed in the United States of America on acid-free paper

The University of Minnesota is an equal-opportunity educator and employer.

Contents

Acknowledgments — vii

Introduction. The Will to Improve Governance: Setting the Stage for a Technomoral, Translocal Politics — 1

1. The Indian Right to Information: An Exceptional Tale — 25

2. Rightfully Worded: A Law, a Petition, and a Few Stories — 55

3. Where the State Goes to Hide: Bureaucracy, Bureaucraft, and the Limits of Transparency — 87

4. Whose Law Is It Anyway? The Common Man as Subject of Rights — 119

5. "A River That Starts Small and Grows Big": Corruption, State, Culture, Law — 153

6. On Good Governance Populism — 185

Epilogue — 223

Notes — 233

Bibliography — 247

Index — 267

Acknowledgments

Funding for this research was provided by the American Institute of Indian Studies and Wesleyan University.

This project would not have been possible without the support of the activists associated with Parivartan, India Against Corruption, and Satark Nagrik Sangathan, with whom I worked closely. I especially want to thank Anjali Bhardwaj, Arvind Kejriwal, Ashok ji, Neeraj, Pushpa ji, and Ram Ashray ji for opening their worlds to me. No acknowledgment would be complete without mentioning Santosh Koli, the fearless face of Parivartan and then India Against Corruption from whom I learned so much, and who was killed in a road accident in 2013.

Deep gratitude for my mentors, John Clarke, Inderpal Grewal, Akhil Gupta, Betsy Traube, and the late Gustavo Esteva and Sally Merry. What I have learned from them goes beyond ideas and words. This book would not have been completed without collaborators and friends Erica Bornstein and Jennifer Curtis, who made sure I logged on Zoom day after day for our writing sessions during Covid-19, and who encouraged me to think in new ways. Indeed, the idea of technomoral politics, which I probe in this book, emerged out of conversations with Erica Bornstein and first appeared in our coauthored article, "The Righteous and the Rightful: The Technomoral Politics of NGOs, Social Movements, and the State in India" (*American Ethnologist* 43, no. 1 [2016]: 76–90). I am grateful for a fabulous posse of New York City–based South Asianists and feminists, especially Tejaswini Ganti, Jinee Lokaneeta, Ritty Lukose, Vasuki Nesiah, Rupal Oza, and Dina Siddiqi, for commenting generously on chapter drafts and for their camaraderie. Nausheen Anwar, Kathy Coll, Saida Hodžić, Arzoo Osanloo, Mridu Rai, and Gina Ulysse are sisters and fellow travelers extraordinaire. I don't know where I would be without their wisdom, brilliance, warmth, laughter, and reminders to take care of myself.

My students at Wesleyan are a joy to be around and learn with. Their creative, out-of-the-box ways of comprehending, being in, and transforming their worlds push me to do things differently and imagine otherwise.

I have received excellent feedback on sections of this book that I presented at Wesleyan University's Center for the Humanities, New York University, Cornell University, University of Copenhagen, University of Göttingen, the Institute of Business Administration (Karachi), and University of Oslo. Participating in three stellar workshops helped me gather ideas about the state and governance, populism, and welfare rights: thank you to Ravinder Kaur and Nayanika Mathur for organizing "The People's State"; to Srirupa Roy, Paula Chakravartty, and Gianpaolo Baiocchi for assembling "Lineages of the People"; and to Keir Martin for putting together "Dependence, Gender, and Kinship." Being a part of the Wenner-Gren Foundation Symposium led by Akhil Gupta and Sarah Muir in Portugal in 2016 was a truly rewarding experience where I got to think alongside some of the sharpest minds working on the issue of corruption.

I finished writing this manuscript as a Think Tank fellow at Bailey College of the Environment at Wesleyan University, where I worked in community with a transformative and inspiring group of scholars: Raquel Bryant, LaToya Eaves, Justin Hosbey, and Marguerite Nguyen. I want to thank Barry Chernoff for giving me this opportunity, and Menakka and Essel Bailey for their support of the Think Tank.

This book would not have taken final shape were it not for the fantastic comments received during the review process, as well as the enthusiastic support of Jason Weidemann, my editor at the University of Minnesota Press, and his entire team. A special shout-out goes to Frances Revel for reading through chapter drafts with a sharp and careful editorial eye, and to my former student, Jack Swansey, for research assistance.

My mother, Versha Sharma, and my uncle, Vijay Dhawan, have always been my pillars. For them, my deepest love and *shukriya*.

Introduction

The Will to Improve Governance
Setting the Stage for a Technomoral, Translocal Politics

On June 5, 2010, Narendra Modi, then chief minister of Gujarat, gave a speech on *suraj* or *su-raj*, literally "good governance."[1] The occasion was the Bharatiya Janata Party's (BJP) national convention in Mumbai. That Modi was selected to give the keynote address was no coincidence. He had branded himself as a good governance guru who had made the necessary political and administrative changes to help Gujarat develop. Upholding Gujarat as a model to emulate, Modi urged his party colleagues to pledge their commitment to suraj.

He described good governance as an idea that had "come of age." However, as a "modern mantra of development agencies," it had been rendered "apolitical." Modi called for its transformation from an international "buzzword" into "a political reality" and its inclusion in party manifestos in India. "'Suraj' (Good Governance) or 'Sushashan' (good administration) is not new to us," he declared, offering "the concept of Ram Rajya and the advice given by Lord Krishan to Arjuna in Gita" as examples.[2] Even as Modi collapsed India into Hindu and history into mythology to claim suraj's native, holy pedigree, he also borrowed elements from the global development industry's discourse on good governance.[3] Using policy language promoted by the World Bank and the Asian Development Bank, and referencing the work of David Osborne and Ted Gaebler (1993), Modi conjured a neoliberally hued picture of an entrepreneurial, efficient, law-bound state that demonstrates, at least nominally, accountability, transparency, participation, and equity. For him, good government was "catalytic," "competitive," "customer-driven," "decentralized," and "market-oriented," aimed at "steering rather than rowing" and "empowering rather than serving." Importantly, it was also a "weapon in the fight against . . . [the] alarming growth of insurgency and terrorism"—a mechanism, contra neoliberal orthodoxy, not for "downsizing" the state so much as "rightsizing" it to make it more powerful against enemies within and without.

Notably, this version of suraj for twenty-first-century India was neither purely local nor merely religicomoral; rather, it was a churning of Hindu mythological references with marketized, technical, neoliberal ones to promote a strong nationalist agenda.

Soon after Modi gave this speech, another individual emerged on the national good governance platform, who also used vocabularies culled from translocal sources to pitch his agenda for change: Arvind Kejriwal, currently the chief minister of Delhi. Then a well-known bureaucrat turned activist in Delhi who ran Parivartan, a nongovernmental organization (NGO) that advocated for the proper implementation and wide use of India's right to information (RTI) law, Kejriwal went on to gain countrywide prominence as an anticorruption movement leader and then a politician with a mission to clean up governance.

Indeed, it was the brutal killing of Amit Jethwa, a transparency and anticorruption crusader in Modi's home state of Gujarat, on July 20, 2010, that set off a cascade of events as Kejriwal expanded his political horizons beyond grassroots RTI work to a wider, law-driven, good governance agenda on the national stage.[4] At a rally in Delhi on July 26 to protest the murders of Jethwa and seven other RTI activists in 2010 alone,[5] Kejriwal vociferously condemned the killing of "ordinary people . . . for simply asking for some records, for raising their voices against the powers that be." Criticizing unreliable and politically co-opted police and vigilance agencies, Kejriwal asserted the need for a whistle-blower protection law and a new anticorruption law that would create "an independent body [to end] corruption within the political system—a *Lokpal* [ombudsperson]."[6] I was at this rally alongside Kejriwal's colleagues at Parivartan, with whom I had been volunteering for nearly two years to understand the political and social life of the RTI Act. Passed in 2005, this law overturned the colonial-era Official Secrets Act in force since 1889. It was hailed as India's "actual independence"[7] from colonial rule and the most significant step in governance reform in over five decades. But its active thwarting in both spectacular and everyday ways—from deadly attacks on its users to routine denial of information requests—had made it clear to Kejriwal that this act alone could not ensure clean, accountable, democratic governance. "What India needs is a progressive legislation package to implement *swaraj*," he had told me months before the rally, referencing Gandhi's idea of decolonized, ethical self-rule to pitch good governance. In fact, he had been experimenting with governance reform laws, like the Nagar Raj, or city governance, bill as part of his swaraj goal when news of Jethwa's murder broke. This would serve as the last straw.

In August 2010, Kejriwal convened a meeting of activists, civil society leaders, ex-bureaucrats, and legal experts in Delhi to consider measures to stop the killing of RTI crusaders and of the RTI law itself by governmental forces and to propose a new law to end state corruption. By 2011, he was spearheading the India Against Corruption (IAC) campaign alongside Anna Hazare, a well-known Gandhian activist. Celebratorily dubbed the Indian Spring by the media, this national movement undertook a Gandhian-style public *satyagraha,* or struggle for truth, to pressure the Congress Party–led government to enact the Jan Lokpal (People's Ombuds) law to end state graft and improve governance. Borrowing from Gandhi's repertoire of moral protest—staging hunger strikes and courting arrest—Kejriwal and his peers argued that punishing graft and purifying state institutions were necessary for saving the nation and its democratic institutions as well as empowering the *aam aadmi,* or common man (Sharma 2014). Despite massive public support, however, they failed to get their draft of the new law passed.

The IAC campaign disbanded in 2012, but Kejriwal pledged to intensify his mission to improve governance, this time from within. He founded the Aam Aadmi Party, or AAP, in late 2012, declaring it a morally upstanding alternative to mainstream parties and dirty politics. Represented by a broom symbol, AAP has won elections and formed a government in Delhi three times since 2013, in addition to contesting in other states and on the national electoral stage. Transforming from a squeaky-clean civil servant in the Indian Revenue Service with a reputation for emptying his own garbage, to a prominent face of activism against state opacity and corruption, and finally to a broom-wielding politician who claims to represent all ordinary citizens and promises swaraj, Kejriwal currently heads the Delhi state government. His meteoric political rise puts him on par with Modi as a national icon of good governance.

At first glance, Modi and Kejriwal are political rivals with little in common. Modi is a right-wing Hindutva ideologue who endorses a hardened, virulent form of Hindu majoritarian rule and is accused of choking democratic institutions and freedoms. Kejriwal is a technocrat who repudiates ideology for idealism and supports democratic, participatory rule. However, both are populist leaders who promote a technomoral politics[8] using technical reforms to achieve their moral objectives of suraj and swaraj, respectively. Good governance is a malleable and roomy enough concept to accommodate very different political projects; that is what makes it at once intriguing and disquieting.

This book offers an ethnographic meditation on good governance politics in India today, which, I argue, is a technomoral, translocal assemblage— that is, it is a complex, shifting blend of charged ethical vernaculars about goodness and technical expertise about laws and policies on the one hand, and local imperatives and global standards of neo/liberal governance on the other. This politics takes judicialized and populist forms brimming with potential, paradoxes, and dangers. I parse this politics for what it reveals about statehood and bureaucracy, citizenship and rights, the social life of laws and liberal activism, and populist authoritarianism in democratic contexts.

To do so, I examine two of the most important governance reform– focused Indian social movements of the past three decades: the first seeking to legally end state secrecy and the second venality. There have been other law-focused and state-facing movements in recent times, notably the 2019 mass protests against the restrictive and discriminatory Citizenship Amendment Act and the National Registry of Citizens (Bhushan 2021), and the 2020 farmers' movement against laws meant to neoliberalize the agricultural sector (Jodhka 2021). However, what distinguishes the RTI and anticorruption campaigns from these other movements is the activist imperative to improve governance and empower people by fighting for new laws rather than opposing existing and proposed laws. In this book, I center the befores, in-betweens, and aftermaths of the RTI and IAC campaigns that share a "striking resemblance" and lie on the "same continuum" (Sharma 2015, xix) of good governance.

I follow the twists and turns of a group of activists led by Kejriwal over six years as they morphed from a small protransparency NGO to a mass movement against corruption to a populist party that promises swaraj and as they fought for state reform on the streets, in courts, on the electoral stage, and over social and conventional media. Good governance is the thread that sutures this shape-shifting, kaleidoscopic politics aimed at manifesting a clean, accountable, participatory, and empowering form of rule through administrative laws and policies. Although seemingly banal, these laws and policies are profoundly consequential in shaping the political field on which battles over democratic statehood and citizenship are fought.

To be clear, this book is not about Arvind Kejriwal as a political figure. Rather, it is about the style of good governance politics he iconizes, which combines transparency, anticorruption, and swaraj, and which turns on laws and populist ethical vernaculars to reshape democratic statehood in the name of the ordinary public. This form of politics in Delhi is my ethnographic "particular" (Abu Lughod 1991), which helps me consider the implications, risks, and possibilities of good governance at large, for good governance is not restricted to Delhi or even India but rather is a global phenomenon.

Today, institutional actors at all scales, including the World Bank, the United Nations, Transparency International, local NGOs, civil society organizations, and social movements, endorse good governance. So do politicians of all ideological varieties, who deploy this discourse to take an antiestablishment stance on behalf of "the people." From Modi in India, who pledged "minimum government, maximum governance" on coming into power in 2014, to Donald Trump in the United States, who made a campaign promise to "drain the swamp," to Hugo Chavez in Venezuela, who implemented a new constitution, the list of good governance populists is diverse and growing. My Delhi-based ethnography has critical relevance for understanding the dynamics of similar processes unfolding across the globe and opens avenues for comparative conversations.

I begin by providing some historical and theoretical context, and thickening the terms I use.

Assembling Good Governance Politics

Good governance politics in India is translocal. While it consists of demands from within and below—demands that stem from a postcolonial history of justice-based movement activism—it also takes shape in a local context traversed by powerful international trends. Indeed, if place-based governance everywhere today is "'multiscalar' rather than limited to one jurisdiction or one scale" (Valverde 2012, 14), then so too are governance reform efforts. I bring into view a dimensional diorama, which includes a transnational backdrop against and in contentious articulation with which a local politics unfolds. This backdrop consists of the neoliberal discourse of good governance purveyed by development agencies like the World Bank and the International Monetary Fund (IMF), which is technically and legally oriented but also culturally adaptable. This sets the stage for a technomoral political comingling.

Good governance became established as a development buzzword during the 1990s at a particular historical conjuncture. Structural adjustment policies of the 1980s had largely failed, especially in Latin America and Africa, and wrought widespread misery (Ferguson 2006; Stiglitz 2007). Instead of faulting their own policies for producing a "lost decade," global development institutions blamed the failure on corrupt and clientelist (read: bad) governance in the Global South (Abrahamsen 2000; Horton 2012; Tidey 2022).[9] Then the Berlin Wall fell, announcing the triumph of capitalism and liberalism. The Cold War's end augured the decline of centrally administered, ideologically encumbered, inefficient states. Whereas the structural adjustment disaster demonstrated good governance to be vital for development success, the lifting of the iron curtain proved that ideal political organization meant nothing other than Western-style liberal democracy and the rule of law. This conjunctural unfolding provided fertile soil for establishing good governance as a rubric for neoliberal restructuring and a conditionality for development aid, affecting debtor nations.

Good governance also posed a challenge. How would development agencies, as "legitimizers of scientific capitalism [and prone to] scrupulously distanc[ing] themselves from any explicitly moral or 'value-laden' claims" (Ferguson 2006, 80), not to mention politics, confront the cultural and political issues that goodness and government unmistakably raised? How would they account for good governance's messiness while also operationalizing it as a policy mandate and a prerequisite for lending (Doornbos 2001)?

The World Bank's annual conference on development economics in 1991 provides insight into how experts arrived at a universally applicable definition of good governance that did not stray far from their technocratic common sense (Doornbos 2001; Summers and Shah 1992). The conference report documents a vibrant discussion about good governance's political and cultural entanglements and how to square those with the Bank's extant history of avoiding culture and politics entirely (Ferguson 1994).

Conference participants agreed that governance is unmistakably political; it describes "the manner in which power is exercised in the management of a country's economic and social resources for development" (World Bank 1992, 1). They parsed its "two distinct but intimately intertwined dimensions that must be tackled simultaneously: one is political (and relates to the commitment to good governance), and the other is technical (and relates to issues of efficiency and public management)" (Landell-Mills and Serageldin 1992, 307; Boeninger 1992). At issue was how to account for the political nature of governance and turn it into a condition for development lending without appearing to challenge the principle of nation-state sovereignty and without flouting the Bank's statutes that disallow political intervention in client nations (Landell-Mills and Serageldin 1992; Summers and Shah 1992).

The Bank's general counsel advised that the agency could engage governance issues if they were limited to "good order and discipline in the management of a country's resources" (World Bank 1992, 5). Ostensibly order, discipline, and resource management were technical matters separate from politics. The Bank could not interfere in a country's "partisan politics" or consider "political factors that do not have a preponderant economic effect" (5). Here one observes the discursive decoupling of economics and policy from politics. Policy prescriptions to allow free markets to function unhindered were considered technocratic and apolitical (Ferguson 1994, 2006). Bank experts agreed that they could offer technical advice on institution and capacity building, and that they could "provide decisive support to local reformers in achieving progress . . . [toward] political liberalization" (Boeninger 1992, 279).[10] The Bank thus resolved the problem of politics by technically tempering it and reducing it to a neutral administrative-managerial and "'a-political' conception" (Doornbos 2001, 99). Even as "policy [came] to replace politics" (Randeria and Grunder 2009, 15), the ground-level effects of technical apolitical good governance are anything but depoliticized, as I elaborate in this book.

Culture proved to be thornier. Bank experts argued that "the state cannot be separated from culture ... [and] governance cannot be considered without reference to its cultural context" (Martin 1992, 325). Neither could "goodness," given the "various conceptions of 'good' and 'bad'" that exist in a world of "moral pluralism" (Martin 1992, 332). This diversity made it hard to pin down a universal definition of good governance, raising practical concerns for development policy experts who "worry that cultural relativism will invade our research program like a computer virus" (Klitgaard 1992, 343). Indeed, Robert Klitgaard (1992) blamed anthropologists for their relativistic sentimentality and lack of rigor in defining the concept of culture and declared it too "mushy and risky" a term for technocrats (347).[11] That said, he and others conceded that culture mattered in the calculus of governance "as a dependent variable, an independent or moderating variable and a giver of meaning" (347).

Bank experts harmonized the universality of good governance with cultural variation by settling on a "minimum core of characteristics" (Landell-Mills and Serageldin 1992, 306), which could allow the Bank and other multilateral lenders to pursue their liberalization agenda without appearing to impose Western political and cultural norms across the globe (Doornbos 2001; World Bank 1992). The Universal Declaration of Human Rights of 1948, seen as "representing the moral consensus of the international community" (Landell-Mills and Serageldin 1992, 306), served as a guide for a broadly agreed-on notion of good governance. It already included globally ratified core values of state accountability, transparency, legitimacy, and responsiveness to public demands, as well as legal measures to secure citizens, contracts, and freedoms. "Unless a society progressively absorbs ... [these] values ..., the institutions of that society will not reflect universal concerns" (Summers and Shah 1992, 350). That this declaration emerged from a particular place and time, and that it reflected a fragile and contested "transnational normative pluralism" (Goodale 2007, 3), were not questioned by these experts. This is hardly surprising; development discourse has always coded as "universal" what are in fact "provincial" (Chakrabarty 2000) standards, goals, and worldviews that emerge out of Euro–North American contexts (Escobar 1995).

Ultimately, while acknowledging the cultural variability of good governance, the Bank settled for a standardized definition: "Conceptually, it is almost impossible to reduce . . . complex social, cultural, political, legal, economic and other interactions . . . into a single measure . . . [but] in general terms the notions of freedom, transparency, participation, and accountability are key ingredients for good governance" (Landell-Mills and Serageldin 1992, 305). Eschewing a singular metric for list of components, this donor-driven discourse emphasized "state structures designed to ensure accountability, due processes of law and related safeguards. . . . that have been characteristic for Western liberal-capitalist systems" (Doornbos 2001, 96).

This broad rubric of good governance took hold across the development industry and allowed agencies to do two things: first, to implement political liberalization without doing politics, and second, to mitigate "the risk of ethnocentric and cultural bias" (Landell-Mills and Serageldin 1992, 311) by adhering to minimalist norms capable of being "indigenized" (Martin 1992, 326). The idea was to allow good governance to strike local roots rather than appear as an externally imposed diktat, making it more effective in the long run (Boeninger 1992, 308; World Bank 1992, 12).

～

Good governance is a "flexible carrier" (Doornbos 2001, 95) that bundles together political strategies of rule, technical means of securing lawful rule efficiently, and cultural ideas about good and bad. Its self-evident desirability and deliberate plasticity allow room for different moral and ideological notions of goodness. This makes it a ready ground for technomoral and translocal articulations, un/settlings, and re/makings at once paradoxical and dangerous.

Although the top-down strictures of the regime of global governmentality (Ferguson and Gupta 2002; Hindess 2004) materially affect how states demonstrate their commitment to political liberalization on the international stage, their policymaking agendas must also respond to citizens' bottom-up demands for justice, accountability, and survival in contexts of neoliberal precarity. As a global development standard, good governance cannot but encounter local calls for state transformation that are differently anchored and articulated, and this process involves translation and "friction." "Through friction, universals become practically effective," writes Anna Tsing (2005, 8), getting "transformed in translation" and given "new genealogies of thought and action" (224). Sally Merry (2006) uses the term "vernacularization" to denote this complex "localization" of international norms. Therefore, global good governance discourse does not determine national policies in any simplistic fashion. Its trajectories across borders are uneven and disjunctive (Ong 2006), articulating kaleidoscopically with local histories and worldviews to produce a translocal, technomoral political assemblage (Ong and Collier 2005).

I illuminate this assemblage in India, focusing on the activist will to improve governance that spins around laws and moral symbolism—Gandhian swaraj and satyagraha, or the ideal of the wronged common man fighting a venal state, for instance—and shapes a politics that is antiestablishment and populist (Laclau 2005). While the global aid industry promotes technocratic good governance as a weapon to counter bad populism (Summers and Shah 1992; World Bank 1992), and some critics view the current global wave of populism as a reaction against neoliberal policies (Mishra 2017; Mudde 2015), I argue that neoliberal good governance reforms in fact invigorate a populist politics that is moralizing in tenor and judicialized in practice.

Scholars use "judicialization" or "juridification" to denote the expansion of laws and legal cultures in recent times such that they affect people's lives in ever more intimate ways (Couso, Huneeus, and Sieder 2010; Randeria and Grunder 2009; Sieder 2020). This includes the widening scope of human rights consciousness (Merry 2006, Moyn 2014; cf. Goodale 2022a).[12] Costas Douzinas (2009) declares that we are witnessing the "triumph of rights, which have mutated, expanded and been turned into a vernacular touching every aspect of social life." Eckert et al. (2012) discuss the "increasing juridification of social and political protest worldwide" (1) as individuals, communities, civil society groups, NGOs, and social movements in the Global South turn to national laws, constitutional rights, international covenants, and human rights languages to demand recognition and entitlements. These forms of judicialized politics, moreover, relate "to factors external to courts, such as processes of socio-legal mobilization, 'rights revolutions,' and the transformation of social and political conflicts into legal disputes" (Sieder 2020, 160). They play out in the streets, legislative spaces, NGO offices, and homes as much as in conventional legal settings, as my book chronicles.

To account for the "variety of social processes entailed in the proliferation of law" (Eckert et al. 2012, 2), scholars turn to both global and local forces. Many connect intensified judicialization with neoliberalism, arguing that "pressure from international agencies such as the World Bank, the IMF . . . [has enabled the] transnational spread of legal norms, institutions, and practices" (Sieder, Schjolden, and Angell 2005, 2; Sieder 2020).[13] They document how local communities use these languages of laws, institutional norms, and human rights as "moral leverage against neoliberal developments" (Moyn 2014, 151; Douzinas 2013), challenging the socioeconomic marginalization caused by liberalization policies and demanding restitution from their governments and international agencies (Keck and Sikkink 1998; Randeria and Grunder 2009).

Neoliberal good governance is an important piece of this story because it makes the rule of law a centerpiece of political liberalization. The 1991 World Bank conference participants averred that an "effective rule of law is as fundamental for a free market as it is for the effective exercise of human rights" (Boeninger 1992, 278), and it is therefore inseparable from good governance. They acknowledged that Western systems of laws have a checkered history in postcolonial settings, where they can be seen as an imperialist force and where other mechanisms of resolving disputes have always existed (Martin 1992, 336–37), but they argued that a proper vernacularization of laws would overcome this obstacle. Thus, dominant good governance discourse positioned the rule of law as a universal container to be filled with local content and meaning relating to moral goodness, fairness, and justice. This has led to a noticeable spike in law-focused activist and state politics in the postcolonial and postsocialist worlds, as constitutions are written and revised; laws regarding transparency, anticorruption, and electoral reform are debated and passed; and survival is recoded as a human right to life.

India has witnessed a flurry of activity around laws and rights in the past two decades. Information, education, livelihood, food, forests, and whistle-blower protection, among others, are all rights today, evidencing increased judicial activism. My point is not that global neoliberal policies have caused this recent spate of new rights in India; rather, I view this as a product of the uneasy articulation of global shifts with local trends and imperatives.

The history of judicialized politics in postcolonial India is rich. Citizens, activists, NGOs, and social movements have long used constitutional and other legal means to challenge authority and right wrongs. Their relationship with the law, however, is complicated by its colonial entanglements; it is at once a source of oppression and a means of fighting that oppression.[14] After India's independence, for example, nationalist leaders saw the law as a tool to consolidate the authority of a fragile state, but also as a tool to expand the freedoms and rights of a people emerging from under the yoke of colonialism (Chatterjee 2014). Indeed, they claimed that what distinguished them from the colonizers was respect for the rule of law (De 2014), and they used it to construct a just and developed society. Once the constitution came into effect in 1950, people from various classes began using legal mechanisms to protect fundamental rights and contest state authority (De 2018; Shani 2022).[15]

Indira Gandhi's declaration of a state of emergency in 1975 proved critical for judicialized activism and for Indian politics broadly (Kaviraj 2011; Prakash 2019). This exertion of sovereign power, which curtailed civil liberties and quashed dissent, was aided by the Indian Supreme Court (Bhuwania 2016).[16] To undo its surrender to the executive branch during the Emergency, the court introduced public interest litigation (PIL) in the late 1970s. PIL was understood as "an attempt by the post-Emergency Supreme Court to restore its image in the public eye after the crisis of legitimacy created by its ignominious role during the Emergency" (Bhuwania 2016, 25). This instrument allowed the court to claim an interventionist, populist ground as a "people's court" (Bhuwania 2016, 17) and to influence policymaking in the name of redistributive justice and compassion (Baxi 1980). It also "enabled the court to extend a unique invitation to journalists, activists, academics and anyone else who may be a witness to constitutional neglect and lawlessness to participate in the judicial process" (Bhuwania 2016, 2). PIL expanded the sphere of judicialized activism substantially in the 1980s as social action groups, movements known as "non-party political formations" (Kothari 1984; Sheth and Sethi 1991), and other actors began using it as a tool to question the state, make policy interventions, and do grassroots political work.[17]

The mushrooming of people's laws in India since 2005, many of which transform welfare entitlements into rights and enact state reform, builds on this history of judicialized activism and PILs in India. These new rights talk back to neoliberal restructuring and address its devastating outcomes. However, they also intersect, albeit uneasily, with global good governance discourse despite activist attempts to consciously distance themselves from neoliberal orthodoxy.

The Indian good governance politics I elaborate on is liberal in that it does not seek to overthrow the state but to make it work better. It challenges the illiberal excess as well as the neoliberal violence of the liberal democratic state through lawful means. Put differently, it uses "liberalism to disturb the assurance of what was supposed to be a liberal state . . . to vitalize the legal system . . . [and] to push the state to live up to its laws" (Tsing 2005, 219). As enabling as this might be, Nandini Sundar (2011) reminds us that the liberal strategy to "make law, not war" also carries the "risk of an over-judicialisation of resistance and aspirations." State-facing, legalized activism to reform rule and secure citizen empowerment and survival expands mechanisms of governmental accountability and the scope of rights and entitlements. Might it also crowd out other modes and sites of struggle, as well as visions of political change? This book probes the contradictions and limits of good governance politics.

Locations and Arguments

I take a deep ethnographic dive into the paradoxical dynamics and effects of good governance as an assemblage of legal and policy mechanisms and populist, virtuous vernaculars. I follow the social life of reform laws—both enacted and proposed—for how they are interpreted and experienced by citizens, state actors, and movement activists and how they instantiate technomoral struggles over the meanings of citizenship, democratic rule, and ideal statehood. Thinking with interdisciplinary ideas culled from the fields of political and legal anthropology, political theory, and postcolonial studies, I offer insights into statehood (as an enclosure), citizenship and rights (as fractured), bureaucracy (as enchanted and crafty), and transparency and corruption (as contentious problematics), as I illuminate the neoliberal and illiberal entanglements of judicialized liberal politics. Although located in Delhi, my analysis has relevance for understanding good governance politics as a globally prevalent though differently translocalized assemblage.

My work joins a growing body of anthropological scholarship on legal and policy reforms undertaken in the Global South and North to improve governance and empower the public. Prashant Sharma's (2015) book, for instance, paints a complex picture of the making of the RTI Act in India and what it means for democratic deepening. It provides a backdrop against which my granular ethnography of the RTI law's social and political dynamics and afterlife—the emergence of the anticorruption movement and AAP—proceeds.[18] Nayanika Mathur's (2016) work on the right to livelihood in India is close in spirit to mine in that it examines how this law alters bureaucratic practices and explores the limits of progressive laws to enact the change they promise. Kregg Hetherington's (2011) book on the politics of transparency in Paraguay is also adjacent to my work, although his analysis of peasant transparency activism unfolds against a history of militarism and land-based rural struggles, whereas my context is democratic and urban. I channel Marianne Valverde's (2012) sociolegal insights about multiscalar measures to improve city governance in Toronto, Canada, and their failures (Valverde and Moore 2019) while adding an ethnographic dimension with activist, citizen, and bureaucratic perspectives on state transformation. Sylvia Tidey's (2022) book on the ethical force and paradoxes of good governance reforms in post-authoritarian Indonesia speaks to my concerns directly; it shows how liberal democratic anticorruption efforts disconnected from local moral practices of relationality and care may "actually make governance worse" (5). Where Tidey focuses on the antagonism between good governance as anticorruption and ethics of care primarily from the vantage point of civil servants, I engage a wider set of actors and themes.[19] My book is unique in examining transparency, corruption, and populism together as part of the good governance ensemble, and drawing out its antidemocratic leanings and technomoral dynamics.

Scholarly analyses of global good governance discourse largely view it as set of rationalized and technical top-down interventions (Doornbos 2001) that are depoliticized and demoralized (Ferguson 2006). Conversely, I argue that good governance allows the yoking of legal technicalities of governance with moral vernaculars about goodness to provoke Manichean battles of right versus wrong (Mouffe 2005) and of a morally upright "us" against a corrupt, statist "them" (Laclau 2005). This perilous, technomoral, and populist politics is at once democratic and authoritarian, liberatory and reactionary, inclusive and hierarchical.

By situating good governance as a technomoral assemblage, I knot together morality, law, and politics. Morality and law, of course, are overlapping fields of inquiry. Moral anthropology, as Didier Fassin (2012) delineates, has focused on Durkheimian studies of social norms and obligations, Foucauldian analyses of ethical subject making (Mahmood 2005) and practices of freedom (Laidlaw 2002), and, more recently, on sharing economies, notions of a good life, humanitarian care, hope, and mercy (Osanloo 2020; Robbins 2013; Widlok 2016). Moral anthropology has explored the realm of the ordinary (Das 2012) as much as it has transcendental values. The law is a central concern within this field, given that it is seen as a mode of subject formation and a mechanism through which dominant moral codes manifest and are enforced.

Although anthropologists have long studied how morality is instantiated in local sociolegal traditions, they no longer take the local to be a hermetically sealed site of study (Merry 2006; Moore 2005). Moreover, rather than seeing the law as either fully continuous with or autonomous from morality and society (Latour 2010, 264), they explore how morality is delegated through more-than-human legal mechanisms and practices (Latour 1992). Anthropologists have also acted as moral critics of the law as a modality of power through which inequalities are both challenged and maintained (Greenhouse 2012). The law is less a singular and reified arena than a complex, shifting social formation (Moore 1978). It extends beyond the formal boundaries of judicial institutions, encompasses expert techniques and hegemonic moral beliefs, and involves a range of subjects who struggle with and against it for power, recognition, and justice. It is this understanding of the law as a technomoral force field and its intersection with politics that interests me.

Whereas the anthropology of morality and law has tackled politics largely through the scope of human rights and humanitarianism (Fassin 2012; Mattingly and Throop 2018; Ticktin 2006), my work exposes a different interface between politics, legality, and morality. I focus on the politics of state governance, global neoliberal governmentality, and judicialized activism, all of which pivot around law-based liberal democratic reform deemed good. Therefore, I work with anthropological studies of the law that attend to the increased dispersion of lawfare under neoliberalism and follow the social, political, and bureaucratic life of laws. My focus is not on court-level functioning or judicial decision-making and reasoning regarding administrative laws (Latour 2010), or lawyers, or judges. The key actors in my stories are activists, citizens, and state officials who demand, use, and apply (or obstruct) laws meant to improve the government's functioning and accountability. This constellation also includes "lively" nonhuman matter (Latour 2010)—such as petitions, signatures, notifications, legal texts, files, workshop materials, and discussions—that manifests the law as well as the state (Sharma and Gupta 2006). I draw on anthropological studies of bureaucracy as an affectively charged realm of materials and practices (Bear and Mathur 2015; Navaro-Yashin 2012) and of corruption (Gupta 2012; Haller and Shore 2005) to tease out the ethics of everyday rule (Tidey 2022) as well as the (re)making of statist ideals. Although these subfields do not necessarily name themselves as doing moral anthropology, they tackle deeply moral issues about state work.[20]

The core of this book concerns the complexities of movement-based activism to both morally condemn and outlaw state venality and secrecy in an effort to transform democratic governance in India. My arguments are grounded in events and processes that largely unfolded in Delhi. What is the significance of Delhi as a site for examining good governance from activist and statist perspectives? As the politicoeconomic heart of a highly centralized democracy, Delhi occupies a hegemonic place in the national imaginary. It is the hub of political power, elite judiciary, central government bureaucracy, law- and policymaking, license and permit raj, and powerful news media toward which parties, citizens, capitalists, NGOs, and activists must remain oriented. A megalopolis with a long history of migrants, and where different social classes rub up against each other, Delhi is a national microcosm that provides an intense and variegated view of political projects aimed at transforming governance, citizenship, and rights from the bottom up and top down. What happens in Delhi reverberates nationally, and important regional happenings, like the RTI movement, tend to crosscut Delhi to gain broader visibility and impact. This city is also where the encounter between global and national political imperatives plays out most starkly, given that key international development and rights organizations are located here. Delhi represents a critical knotting of governmental and political scales—local, national, and transnational—and is therefore an appropriate site to study good governance ideologies, technologies, and struggles in their translocal dimensions.

The narrative arc of my book tracks the recent activist history of governance reform in chronological order. Beginning with the movement for state transparency and the RTI Act's passage and usage, it works its way through the anticorruption campaign that arose in reaction to the statist subversion of the RTI law but failed to force the government to pass a new anticorruption bill; it ends with the emergence of AAP, a populist party with an agenda to change the face of politics and governance forever. In this chronology, I highlight the interplay between transparency, corruption, and swaraj as ineluctable aspects of democratic good governance on the one hand, and between messy material practices and idealized understandings of bureaucracy, governance, law, citizenship, and activism on the other. Indeed, attending to the dynamic between materiality and ideology allows me to unravel the paradoxical terrain of good governance. I elaborate on its openings and constraints, in theory and in practice, by anchoring each chapter in a specific tension.

The first chapter settles on the "local" framing of the Indian RTI story as a parable about a grassroots movement led by marginalized peasants and workers (Sharma 2015), and the political work this moral tale does. Many activists I spoke to acknowledged the influence of international development conditionalities on the passage of transparency laws in other countries, but they positioned India as an exception, where the impetus for RTI came from within and below. I retell this powerful local story, as narrated to me by prominent information movement activist Aruna Roy, before widening the scope to paint a translocal picture of legalized transparency in India that illuminates a complex articulation of spatial scales (Ferguson and Gupta 2002). I also consider what a discursive split between the local and global in the RTI narrative evinces affectively and politically, arguing that it is a form of tactical position taking, at once proliberal and antineoliberal, to call out the illiberality of a liberal democratic state.

Chapter 2 centers on information petitions as a particular aesthetic genre of writing to tease out the tensions and slippages between people's thick narrations of their moral complaints against the state and their straitjacketing into thin, standardized bureaucratese (Cody 2013); between rich storytelling as parole and abbreviated information requests that mimic the langue of the state and law; and between expressive personhood and generic patterned citizenship. I describe my experience of filing an RTI petition on my grandfather's behalf, moving between his oral life stories and my written condensation of those stories into his petition, and juxtaposing both against ethnographic vignettes about activist work and official interactions. I construct a complex picture of the everyday life of the RTI law in middle-class and activist circles. Thinking alongside Walter Benjamin (2007), Michel Foucault (1995), and anthropologists who position written documents as actants (Latour 2005) with generative capacities of their own (Riles 2006), I probe the forms of communication and citizen-subjectivity that RTI petitions stifle and produce, as well as the cultures of judicialized activism and audit they spread.

Chapter 3 shines light on the statist life of the RTI law to explore the contradictory relationship between transparency and bureaucracy (as ideal and as craft). Drawing on interviews and interactions with officials across various tiers of the state apparatus and anthropological literature on bureaucratic artifacts, practices, and power, this chapter does two things. First, it enlivens ethnographically what is commonly seen as a rationalized machine composed of disinterested rules and disaffected cogs (Bear and Mathur 2015). I use the Indian transparency law to "enchant" bureaucracy (Bennett 2001) as an ensemble of people, practices, and materials; formalities and informalities (Visvanathan 2008); visibilities and invisibilities (Ballestero 2012); and rational calculations, ethical dilemmas, and structures of feeling (Williams 1977). Second, it shows how this ensemble accommodates an RTI regime, and how bureaucratic hierarchy and ordinary bureaucraft (James 2012)—formal rules as well as customary practices regarding the production of government records—work in tandem to maintain illegibility and hide things in plain sight. Indeed, I argue that secrecy lies at the heart of state sovereignty—that backstage, illiberal enclosure of the liberal state fortified by innocuous, routine bureaucraft that cannot be breached by the public.

In chapter 4, I unravel a fractured, tension-ridden arena of urban citizenship and rights by examining who uses the RTI law, how, and to what effect. I enquire into an oft-repeated truism I heard during fieldwork: "The RTI empowers the common man." I ask who this empowered common man or ordinary citizen is and whether this status is as universal and equal as it declares itself to be. I explore disjunctive understandings of citizenship, rights, and governance by juxtaposing the narratives of two individuals involved in RTI-related good governance activities: Ravi, an upper-middle-class man residing in a gated community, and Pushpa, a working-class woman living in a Delhi camp or slum. My analysis is scaffolded by Partha Chatterjee's (2004) idea of civil and political society politics but goes beyond seeing them solely as classed spheres of life, with one elite and lawful and the other subaltern and governmental. They are also different modes of doing politics (Menon 2010) and forms of position taking vis-à-vis the law and the state. I think with scholars working on the intersections of urban studies, law, and class in contemporary India (Baviskar and Ray 2011; Liang 2005) to expose a fractured field of citizenship made up of proprietoriness (Roy 2014) on the one hand and laborious rightfulness (Das 2011) on the other. What lies behind the "common man" moniker is not an evened-out political ground, sutured by neutral and universal laws meant to improve governance and empower the ordinary citizen. It is instead a riven landscape where "meta" governance rights, like RTI, are masculinized and naturalized as the property of privileged auditor-citizens, and welfare rights, like food and education, are feminized and mapped onto dependent state subjects.

Chapter 5 explores contentious public debates about corruption in India and deliberates on the (im)possibility of ending it through the law, the preferred strategy of good governance. Drawing on interviews, observations, personal experiences, and media commentaries, I reveal a discourse teeming with disagreements about what counts as real corruption, what its source is (state, society, or culture), and how to contain it. Vernacular understandings about which acts are good or bad, excusable or criminal, vary widely, complicating legal resolution. I build on insights from the anthropological literature on corruption (Das 2015; Gupta 2012) and informal networks (Lomnitz 1988), as well as postcolonial studies scholarship on the liberal public–private dualism, to approach corruption as a problematic that resists consensus and closure. This chapter ruminates on corruption as a limit phenomenon and a category of transgression (Muir and Gupta 2018) that troubles the public–private boundary enforced by law. If law and corruption are inverted mirrors of each other, as I contend, and if law produces corruption as its constitutive outside, then using laws to dismantle corruption becomes a paradoxical undertaking bound to fail at its limits.

Finally, chapter 6 examines good governance populism as an apparent contradiction in terms. By arguing that good governance promotes a populist politics, I make a counterintuitive move. Global neoliberal orthodoxy positions liberal good governance as a remedy to counter the irrational and illiberal excesses of populism and authoritarianism. Meanwhile, critics tend to view the current worldwide wave of populism as a reaction against neoliberal restructuring that has proliferated inequalities. My claim is different. Populism today is neither merely a reaction against economic liberalization nor easily stymied by political liberalization efforts. Rather, good governance as a state-making project and populism as a people-making one (Chakravartty and Roy 2017) share a discursive affinity. Good governance offers an opportune vehicle for a populist politics that can take authoritarian forms as easily as pluralist ones. To tease out these dangers, I delve into Kejriwal's technomoral good governance strategy; although popularly cast as an alternative to Modi's style of good governance, it can veer in the same direction of patriotic and patriarchal authoritarianism. I explore these risks and contradictions as they manifest affectively among Kejriwal's AAP volunteers, narrating the frictional push and pull, desire, dedication, disappointment, and betrayal—in other words, the cruel optimism (Berlant 2011)—produced by the will to improve governance.

Ethnographic Craft and Self-Positioning

This book represents research conducted from 2008 to 2014, which included interviewing people from different social backgrounds; participating in routine activist work and special events; observing rallies and sit-ins; studying legal and legislative documents; and following media and social media commentary. My ethnographic ground shifted over time. As the people with whom I began working in 2008 transformed their shape and strategy—from a protransparency NGO to an anticorruption campaign to a governance reform–oriented party—my research evolved from a conventional study of groups at par with or below the anthropologist in terms of social standing to "studying up" (Nader 1974). Kejriwal, an activist colleague from my generational and class cohort, turned into a different public national figure and a top elected official in Delhi, becoming progressively more difficult and ultimately impossible to meet. Keenly focused on good governance as a power-laden field with complex outcomes, this book also comments on the equally power-laden dynamics of ethnography.

Like the shape-shifting politics it tracks, my book is a kaleidoscopic assemblage of stories, observations, theoretical insights, and documentary and media analysis. It offers a unique and wide-angled look at the elements, techniques, and actors that make up the field of governance—from transparency and corruption to swaraj, from legal reforms and moral injunctions to public protest, from citizens and activists to state actors. I have not used the real names of most of my interlocutors, except for Arvind Kejriwal, Aruna Roy, Shekhar Singh, Pushpa ji, and a few others, who asked me to use their names in the interest of transparency.

My style of writing and analysis can be described as "theoretical storytelling" (McGranahan 2015). Stories, as Daniella Gandolfo and Todd Ramon Ochóa (2017) remind us, are the "very lifeblood" (187) of ethnography, yet they tend to get overwhelmed by a will to theorize (Pandian and McLean 2017). Stemming from empirical observations on life as process that does not stand still for research, the stories people share with ethnographers often escape the rigid contours of dominant theoretical constructs. However, rather than using stories to shed light on and remold ideas, as academics, we feel compelled to straitjacket them to fit theoretical frameworks. These frameworks are of a distanced, totalizing sort, or what J. K. Gibson-Graham (2006), following Eve Sedgwick, describe as "strong" theory, which bears a "confident finality . . . an embracing reach and a reduced, clarified field of meaning" (4). As an alternative, they encourage a practice of "weak theory" that "welcomes surprise, entertains hope, makes connection" (8). Ethnographic storytelling, at once descriptive and analytically rich, is such a mode of theorization. Rather than foretelling givenness and finality, it "helps us to see openings" (7) that are partial and provocative.

In this book, ethnographic stories and vignettes do thinking work. They enable me to muse about, illuminate, and trouble big ideas about the state and governance, citizenship, bureaucracy, laws and rights, class and gender, and populism. Moreover, storytelling becomes a way to talk back to the bureaucratese, legalese, and other expert languages that I engage critically. These languages are laden and formal, presenting a challenge for ethnographers interested in crafting narratives that disrupt powerful enclosures. How can we write about bureaucratic reform or laws without mirroring the monotony, expertise, and inscrutability that these processes conjure? How can we write without overwhelming the narrative with strong theory, as if it could be separated from ethnography, like parenthetical citations? This book is my attempt at becoming comfortable with a differently expressed political voice. I go back and forth between subtle and explicit forms of analysis and between "story and theory" (Narayan 2012). I try to avoid letting efficient analysis overtake mellifluous details or provide reductive answers, because that is what my ethnography uncovered—not simplistic closure or consensus but contention, problematization, and contradiction.

This is also why I use juxtaposition as a methodological tactic, placing side by side conflicting takes on issues like transparency, corruption, democracy, and citizenship. Doing so allows me to convey and consider the unpredictable messiness of everyday political life as it unfolds without feeling the need to provide an ironed-out, precisely conclusive explanation that forms a perfect knot.

Even as I craft and tell ethnographic tales about governance reform efforts in twenty-first-century New Delhi, I am also a character in these stories, as are some of my family members. This book's subject matter—how good governance alters the landscape of statecraft, politics, and citizenship, and what that means for differently positioned subjects—involves us intimately. Connecting the personal with the structural, experiential, and political, I locate myself as a participant, volunteer, and researcher and my family as part of the differentiated publics implicated by the processes I write about. This book is reflexive and partly autoethnographic (Abu-Lughod 1986; Ulysse 2007; Walley 2013). It interweaves situated personal stories that are more than just mine, and that say something about the classed and gendered lives of the state, citizenship, and rights. I zoom into individual and place-based narratives and zoom out to explore the broader conjecture that specificity points toward.

There is another way that I am implicated in what I write about. This book is more than just an analysis of technomoral politics; it also speaks to my commitments as a moral agent and political critic. If the purpose of moral anthropology today is "not only an endeavor to analyze moral issues but also a moral engagement in the world with the ultimate intention to make it better" (Fassin 2012, 3), then this research is tied to my ethical and political orientation toward projects that seek to remake the world of democratic citizenship and statehood in just ways. If "cruel optimism"—the "condition of maintaining an attachment to a significantly problematic object" (Berlant 2011, 24)—describes the predicament of some of my colleagues and interlocutors who committed themselves to Kejriwal's good governance mission, as I suggest in chapter 6, perhaps it also captures my own engagement with the subject. Good governance is simultaneously an object of study and "an object of desire" that is hard to dismiss; it manifests as "a cluster of promises we want someone or something to make to us and make possible for us" (Berlant 2011, 23). It triggers optimism, or the feeling of "being drawn to return to the scene where the object hovers in its potentialities" (24). At the same time as it signals possibilities, good governance also raises red flags. Its self-proclaimed goodness and "it can be what you want it to be" quality is troubling, for it can be appropriated for various ends. Even as I discovered that the road to good governance is paved with tensions, tangents, betrayals, dangers, deferrals, limits, and even aporias, I continued on it; indeed, I kept returning to it as an object of study and desire. Perhaps the larger context of national politics in India over the past decade explains my own desperate draw toward Kejriwal's style of technomoral good governance, despite disappointments. The coordinated onslaught against democracy and the violent thinning of the field of political possibility under Modi's regime leaves few options but to hold on to cruel optimism for a less autocratic, more accountable and transparent good government; because the danger is that losing this "promising object," as trouble ridden as it may be, might well "defeat the capacity to have any hope about anything" at all (24).

1

The Indian Right to Information

An Exceptional Tale

I groaned at my watch. An RTI workshop was scheduled to start in twenty minutes, and I was jammed in traffic on Delhi's Ring Road. I had covered most of the twenty-two-kilometer journey from my mother's home in North Delhi to a venue in South Delhi where government functionaries from urban development and municipal services departments were about to learn about the RTI Act. On that freezing December morning in 2008, the city's infamous winter smog played havoc with visibility, slowing vehicles to a crawl and raising decibel levels as drivers tried to honk their way to their destinations. I took in this slow-motion din and swore under my breath. Why didn't I slot extra time for the commute?

I reached the venue frazzled and fifteen minutes late. My acquaintance, Omesh Sen, was waiting at the main gate. A lawyer by training and a history buff by choice, Sen was conducting the RTI workshop and had graciously allowed me to join—and now I had delayed everything. "I am so sorry, Omesh. The traffic . . ." I began. He shrugged. "It's Delhi."

Sen guided me to a well-appointed conference room where some twenty officials, both women and men, sat around an oblong table. After quick introductions and generous servings of tea and cookies, the workshop began. Our host, Mr. Jain, a senior civil servant, emphasized the salience of the RTI law, which he described as a "milestone" for overturning the "colonial mind-set" of secrecy legitimized by the Official Secrets Act of 1923.[1] It didn't matter whether the demand for the RTI arose out of "grassroots activism or pressure from the World Bank," he asserted; it was now the law of the land, and a "tool to empower citizens and to help improve governance." Jain turned the floor over to Omesh Sen, who clicked on his first PowerPoint slide.

Sen began by situating transparency historically and globally. "The thinking about the right to information goes back to the eighteenth century. Sweden's freedom of press law, the oldest RTI act, [was passed] in 1766," he said, adding that the French Revolution also had rumblings about transparency. By the mid-twentieth century, the RTI was "listed on the Universal Declaration for Human Rights as part of the freedom of speech and expression [and on] the International Covenant on Civil and Political Rights of 1966," which is a binding treaty.[2] Despite these historical precedents, sunshine laws did not gain global traction until liberalization took off. "Until 1990, only thirteen countries had transparency laws.... As foreign direct investment grew globally, there was a rising trend of disclosure laws across many countries." Securing investment inflows required a robust constitutional framework with transparency laws to promote market mechanisms. By 2008, eighty-eight countries had information freedom on the books. These were mostly countries with "strong democratic traditions and development indicators," declared Sen. Thus, "democracy and development go hand in hand with transparency," and transparency in turn curtails state corruption. "Take Finland, for example, which was rated the least corrupt country in the world by Transparency International in 2007. It has had a sunshine law since 1766, when it was part of Sweden."[3] Sen then described the "opening up" of Eastern European nations, which had different political-economic histories than democracies and "wrote constitutions" after the Cold War ended. "These were disciplinarian societies with [a history] of spying and a lot of information collected on people secretly. People declared that the data in secret files should be made open—in Romania, for example. Philanthropic NGOs, like the Soros Foundation, also played a role in supporting open access." In such countries, market and political reforms unfolded together, and rewriting laws was key to both.

India, however, was different: "In India, the RTI may have coincided with liberalization, but it was a *homegrown* movement," Sen declared, countering Mr. Jain's earlier suggestion that World Bank pressure may have played a role in the law's passage. India, he argued, had its own referents for open governance. The Supreme Court had ratified openness in the 1970s; grassroots and movement actors demanded it; and even the

Bhagavad Gita endorsed it as a moral principle. Sen recited a verse from chapter 4 of the *Bhagavad Gita:* "The truth about the action must be known. The truth of the inaction must be known. The truth about the prohibited action must be known." Thus, the idea of information freedom was as native, old, and morally profound as the *Bhagavad Gita.* But it was a contemporary people's movement that opened up the legal path to this truth.

"The campaign for RTI was started by poor peasants and workers in Rajasthan—by Mazdoor Kisan Shakti Sangathan [MKSS]," Sen explained. MKSS, a people's group in Rajasthan, undertook a fifteen-year-long struggle, organizing public hearings, rallies, and dharnas (sit-ins), meeting with local and national-level politicians, and enlisting sympathetic bureaucrats, civil society members, and activists to help draft the RTI law. Their campaign ultimately bore fruit in 2005, when the national-level RTI Act was enacted.

Mr. Jain nodded enthusiastically: "What Aruna Roy, Nikhil Dey, and other people from MKSS did in obscure villages of Rajasthan [established] loud and clear that transparency is a source of good governance." Sen nodded. "MKSS showed that the RTI is not just a civil and political right but also linked to water, housing, food, health, education, etc.," thus expanding its scope beyond conventional liberal freedoms.

I became familiar with the story of MKSS as I conducted fieldwork. Activists, newspapers, and journals all noted that India passed a transparency law because of a bottom-up, local effort (Sharma 2015): "The most important feature that distinguishes the movement for the people's right to information in India from that in most other countries, whether of the North or the South, is that it is deeply rooted in the struggles and concerns for survival and justice of [the] most disadvantaged rural people" (Mander and Joshi, n.d., 6; see also Baviskar 2007). Although many of my interlocutors readily acknowledged global influences on sunshine laws in other countries, they considered India an exception.

Why does the linkage between transparency laws and the neoliberal "freeing" of economies and governance, which Sen summarized at the aforementioned RTI workshop, matter less in India than in other countries? I do not mean to suggest that global trends look identical in different places, or that they overwhelm grassroots activism. Rather, I ask why the story of the Indian RTI Act is told as a distinctively rooted local tale. I take my cue from an interlocutor—Delhi-based journalist Ravi Kapoor—who questioned the RTI's singularly grassroots narrative (see also Sharma 2015). "The point is not that the MKSS movement played no part," he told me, but "how much role it played is a question mark." With a knowing half smile, Kapoor asked me to consider why "certain factors get more hearing space than others in the RTI [story]." Why indeed, I wondered, is it important for transparency activists to distance themselves from neoliberal development globalspeak?

Activism, Tsing (2005) suggests, "moves in 'charismatic packages' . . . that speak to the possibilities of making a cause heard" (227). The Indian RTI movement's localness contributes to its affective appeal and political potency across a variety of audiences, given the romance of the local and the grassroots as sites of resistance (cf. Abu-Lughod 1990). This is especially relevant in India, where a Gandhian legacy has shaped the rural as a locus of authenticity and a more recent, four-decade-long history of nonparty political movements has positioned the grassroots as a privileged site of ethical politics in contrast to both states and NGOs (Kothari 1984; Sheth and Sethi 1991).

An assertion of localness offers a refreshing antidote to narratives that position the global as a universal agent encompassing and determining everything "below" it in a top-down, one-way manner (Ferguson and Gupta 2002; Gregory 1998). But if disparaging the local as the parochial, nativized other of the global is problematic, so is privileging it as a pure space unsullied by the global. The latter approach may invert the global–local hierarchy, but it does not subvert the dualism at its heart; it also does not attend to the interconnections that produce these scalar differences (Goodale 2007; Gupta and Ferguson 1997).[4] The local is not a given container where politics takes place but a preferred site for movement building produced by activism. Steven Gregory's (1998) contention that "the political significance of place, far from being settled in the evolving global economy, is a hotly contested stake in contemporary struggles" (50) allows me to approach the local as a "problematic": a contentious claim performatively (re)made through mobilization. It is a mode of representation that confronts power and is also power laden: a space of resistance shaped in the cauldron of politics and activism.

This chapter considers the how and why of the RTI story. First, I examine how it is constructed as a tale of bottom-up triumph rooted in native soil and illuminate its charismatic political force. I then complicate this telling by highlighting translocal entanglements—that is, how the grassroots, regional, national, and global articulated to overdetermine the passage of the Indian RTI Act at a particular temporal conjuncture. I choose my words purposefully, calling on Althusserian insights (Althusser 2005; Hall 1985) to delineate the crisscrossing of forces across different scales whose effects cannot be known in advance. A "conjunctural" coming together is neither seamless nor predictable (Clarke 2010) but contentious. Second, I consider why the Indian RTI story is told as a local tale about marginalized people taking on a powerful state system and winning. Prashant Sharma (2015) describes it as a "*flattening* of the RTI narrative" (5), which downplays how the international context, sympathetic state actors, and the privileged status and networks of movement leadership enabled the Indian transparency law to pass. My purpose is slightly different. Rather than focusing on what a localized tale occludes, I am more interested in what it enables, as well as what it reveals about state-focused political activism articulated in moral, liberal terms. A grassroots framing, I argue, is a form of position taking (Gramsci 1971). It tactically uses "universal" liberal ideals of statehood and citizenship to demand that the Indian state protect the constitutional rights and freedoms of its citizens and ensure well-being and justice under conditions of neoliberal restructuring. Despite being liberal, this position taking is not pro-liberalization. It annexes the normative force of liberal universals while translating them into local terms (Merry 2006). This localized, tactical liberalism also serves as a charismatic package that makes RTI politics appear ideologically neutral and thus universally relevant.

In what follows, I briefly explore the global backdrop in defiance of which the exceptional Indian RTI narrative takes shape. I then thicken the Indian story, expanding its spatial and temporal scope to bring into focus the MKSS movement's antecedents. I jump between grassroots, national, and global scales to paint a translocally entangled picture of transparency politics in India. By juxtaposing different activist stories about the RTI law, I draw out the convergences across narratives and scales as well as the antinomies and friction involved in constructing a movement for transparency that at once forefronts liberal democratic desires and also keeps transnational neoliberal development discourse at bay.

Neoliberal Globalspeak: The Antipolitics of Transparency and Good Governance

The economic value of information freedom for late capitalist globalization was an established fact by the 1980s. In the context of space-time compression, as David Harvey (1989) put it, "privileged access to information of any sort (such as scientific and technical know-how, government policies, and political shifts) becomes an essential aspect of successful and profitable decision-making" (159). The political value of information came into the global limelight after the iron curtain lifted. Opening centralized economies and communist polities to the naturalized world of liberal capitalist democracy centered transparency as a desired public good and norm that was "nearly synonymous with *good governance*" (Sanders and West 2003, 1). By 1991, the World Bank established transparency as one of the "key ingredients" of its good governance bundle alongside "freedom, . . . participation, and accountability" (Landell-Mills and Serageldin 1992, 305), which simultaneously facilitated economic liberalization and democratization: "Efficient markets depend on good information—as does the exercise of 'voice'" (315). Indeed, for the handmaidens of global capitalist development, transparency and good governance became political prerequisites for development aid. For an agency like the World Bank, which is mandated to avoid politics, this meant carefully maneuvering and redefining what counted as political intervention.

The 1991 World Bank conference I mentioned in this book's introduction explored this issue at length. Experts agreed on the firmly political nature of governance and the necessity of democratic reforms for development success. However, they debated whether it was institutionally acceptable for the Bank to tie aid to such changes. Dictating governance reform to client states could challenge nation-state sovereignty, a fundamental structuring principle of international relations (Landell-Mills and Serageldin 1992). That said, however, analyzing and addressing governance failures was also necessary because donor agencies, like corporations, require a return on their investments, and lending to poorly managed states involves economic risk (Landell-Mills and Serageldin 1992, 307).

The question was not whether to push for political restructuring among debtor nations, but rather how to undertake this task without transgressing institutional and international legal norms.

On the advice of its general counsel, the Bank ultimately defined good governance as a technical, managerial, and administrative problem, focusing its interventions on the apparently neutral areas of policy advice and playing a supportive role in reform. The Bank marked four main areas of technical intervention: "public sector management, accountability, the legal framework for development, and information and transparency" (World Bank 1992, 6). Defining good governance in this manner defused its political charge and reduced it to a standardized, manipulable variable in the calculus of economic development. This "re-invention of the notion of '(good) governance' . . . [allowed] the launching of a new generation of political conditionalities" (Doornbos 2001, 98). Development lending would henceforth ride on nation-states freeing markets and trade; implementing privatization, deregulation, and fiscal discipline; and enacting legal and administrative reforms to make governance open, accountable, and noncorrupt. Political liberalization had to accompany economic liberalization (Abrahamsen 2000).

International actors began endorsing this transparency and good governance framework during the 1990s, instituting new programs and indexes to measure states' commitments to and performances of political reform. For example, Transparency International was established in 1993 with a mission to counter corruption; today, its annual Corruption Perceptions Index and Global Corruption Barometer are standardized governmental tools in the donor world, guiding aid activity.[5] George Soros's Open Society Institute (now Open Society Foundations) was also founded in 1993 to promote democratic governance, justice, and human rights efforts in and beyond East and Central Europe. By 1998, the IMF established financial transparency as a norm to which all its member states were beholden (Sanders and West 2003, 1). The United Nations jumped on this bandwagon as well, reconfiguring its sustainable development goals in 2015 to include goal 16: "Promote the rule of law. . . . Substantially reduce corruption and bribery in all their forms. . . . Develop effective, accountable and transparent institutions at all levels. . . . Ensure public access to information and protect fundamental freedoms."[6]

The law became the preferred site and technique of intervention when it came to transparency and good governance. Even though development experts acknowledged that in many postcolonial contexts, Western legal systems are not necessarily viewed as good, just, or even relevant (World Bank 1992, 8), they nonetheless positioned laws, such as those challenging state secrecy and corruption, as markers of state openness and democratic freedom. The flurry of activity around freedom of information laws across postcolonial and postsocialist worlds starting in the 1990s, therefore, is no coincidence. From a mere eight in 1989, the number of countries with RTI laws has now surpassed 125.[7]

This rapid multiplication of legalized transparency cannot be viewed at the nation-state level alone because it is impossible to isolate that level from global political-economic trends shaped by development actors. However, that disarticulation is effectively what the popular homegrown-activist story of the Indian RTI sought to achieve. I view this consciously distanced telling as a political act—a Gramscian position taking that challenges the reductive, apolitical, and instrumentalist rendering of good governance by unaccountable international organizations. These agencies promote democratic reforms in order to lend a veneer of representation and legitimacy to the austerity measures they purvey (Ferguson 2006). As Barry Hindess (2004) reminds us, "democracy ... is often thought to secure a degree of legitimacy for the activities of the state ... It is this, rather than the expansion of popular control itself, that particularly appeals to the development agencies and financial institutions which promote democracy as a fundamental component of good governance" (35). Neoliberal globalspeak also reduces transparency to formalized technocratic legalisms, which clashes with populist-activist imaginings of transparency as "engaged political activity" (Hetherington 2008, 61) aimed at meaningfully transforming the institutions and modes of governance. It is against neoliberal "doctrines of transparency, civility, governance ... and rationality ... [that] transcend the bounds of the nation-state" (James 2012, 57) that local stories of democratic mobilization must be situated. The activist telling of the Indian RTI tale is antiliberalization in that it contests dominant neoliberal discourse, but it also mobilizes and upholds liberal legal and state norms.

I now turn to the story of Mazdoor Kisan Shakti Sangathan.

The Charismatic Local: A Grassroots Tale

Aruna Roy, a founding member of MKSS, described the "pioneering role" that the people's movement played in the enactment of the RTI law.[8] Established in 1990 in the state of Rajasthan, MKSS popularized the slogan "Hum janenge, hum jeeyenge" (We will know, we will live), situating information as a human right necessary for survival. Interestingly, the movement did not begin with the goal of fighting for a transparency law, as Roy told me: "You see, we didn't decide that we were going to have a right to information act and then start working." Rather, the issue of wage labor led them toward demanding the RTI.

It was early morning on May 1, 2009, and Roy and I sat inside a hut on a small compound surrounded by bougainvillea bushes and desert vegetation. We were in Devdungri village in south-central Rajasthan, Roy's home and the nerve center of MKSS. A roughly ten-hour journey involving a train, a bus, and a jeep had brought me from Delhi to Devdungri, where I was one of several people from across India who had gathered to participate in MKSS's annual May Day festivities. After two days of attending meetings, organizing banners, observing conditions at local public works projects, and sharing cooking, stories, and laughter, we were ready for the big day. Roy and I hung back from the rest of the group for a conversation, during which she animatedly described how the demand for transparency arose.

"We began with a very, very intensely felt problem, which is universal among the rural poor. You work eight hours a day [on government projects], and you come back without your wage. It is a huge calamity for people who are very poor, because the minimum wage is the rock-bottom you can earn to just about have your staple diet. If you can't get that, then life is horrendous."

Rajasthan is a drought-prone zone where public works and famine relief projects offer a lifeline for the poor, allowing the possibility of breaking "the pernicious cycle of unemployment, debt, poverty, hunger and bondage" (Roy with the MKSS Collective 2018, 45). Roy became involved with wage justice struggles in the region after quitting the Indian Administrative Service in 1975. "No matter where I went in Rajasthan, there was no employment, no wages," she told me. "The first battle is that you can't even go to work [because your name is] not on the muster rolls"—

these are government records that list, among other things, the names of people who are eligible for public works projects, their labor hours, and the wages paid to them. "The second battle is to get a wage, and the third battle is to get the proper wage."

When Roy and her three compatriots—Shankar, Anshi, and Nikhil—established MKSS, they began by campaigning for minimum wages. "We went on two hunger strikes in 1990 and 1991 [that] created ripples in the government in Rajasthan . . . [and] up to Delhi," Roy recounted. The first strike demanded "rightful wages for a group of nineteen or twenty people—1,600 rupees! That's all!" she said, emphasizing the ludicrously small amount—approximately $75 at that time—for which they had to fight so bitterly.

They succeeded in getting the money but realized that hunger strikes were not viable. It would be impossible to organize such strikes at the hundreds of worksites in Rajasthan where people were not getting work and wages. Moreover, as Roy put it, "a hunger strike is a tortuous thing because you sit and you ask for redressal from the same system that is . . . illegal, unjust, and completely exploitative. They could care less! In fact, a member of the legislative assembly [reportedly] said, 'seventeen people [on hunger strike], seventeen less mouths to feed. Let them die!'"

Another lesson for the activists was that the lack of access to government records made their fight against work and wage injustice challenging. In the neighboring town of Bhim, for instance, MKSS members uncovered corruption by accident. They happened to be at the subdistrict magistrate's office as he reviewed records for a local development project. "We literally glanced over his shoulder," said Roy, "and saw a bill from a 'Bhairon Nath and Sons,' which had supplied materials worth 40 *lakh* [4 million] rupees for the project. But there was no entity [by that name] in Bhim. So we asked for an inquiry. . . . It turned out that three people from the local development office and a wife of one of the officials had formed Bhairon Nath and Sons, fabricated the muster rolls, and [stolen] the money." They similarly chanced on fraud in the village of Kot Kirana, where a government official "foolishly" let Roy's colleague, Shankar, examine the local muster rolls. "Shankar copied all the records by hand! We went to each household and each individual [noted on the rolls and found that] dead people's names were on the muster rolls and all kinds of things!" Examining and cross-checking government records allowed activists to trace corruption; these records could also help them demand accountability.

"I remember two or three people saying, right here on this *chabootra* [raised mud platform], that vo kagaz ko bahar nikalwana hi padega [those government papers will have to be accessed publicly]," recalled Roy. "That is what started it"—the demand for transparency.

MKSS organized a *jan sunvai* (public hearing) in Kot Kirana village to expose corruption. They collected testimonies of residents confirming inaccuracies in the muster rolls. "We had four demands: we wanted complete transparency of *panchayat* [village council] records; we wanted a 'social audit'—a public audit rather than a financial audit because we discovered all these [discrepancies] after a financial audit [had already taken place]; we wanted redressal—the money to come back to the village for the same activity; and we wanted accountability fixed." Predictably, MKSS faced backlash. After learning about the impending public hearing, some officials "went around to every person who had filed a *bayan* [testimony] or an affidavit and asked them to give another affidavit saying that [their] first affidavit was wrong. They plied [people] with liquor, money, threats, and tried to prevent the public hearing. The amazing thing was that the [people] of Kot Kirana said that the hearing would be held," come what may. The locals even protected MKSS activists— "They kept us in their homes."

On December 2, 1994, MKSS held its first hearing in Kot Kirana under a tent made out of an old parachute. "After that, it was history. News spread like wildfire. On December 7, we had a public hearing in Bhim; on December 17, in Vijaypura, and . . . it became a huge political battle."

The *jan sunvais* followed a pattern of what Lawrence Cohen (2010) calls ethical publicity, which relies on the public to scrutinize and discipline state representatives. MKSS hearings were attended by local residents, officials, and prominent and well-respected people acting as observers and rapporteurs. Muster rolls were read aloud. Those named were asked to verify their recorded labor and wage information. The hearings revealed many inconsistencies and errors: some names were fabricated while others referenced the dead; some people listed were never paid while others were paid less than minimum wage. State officials, public works contractors, and local bigwigs were clearly milking the system.[9] Activists and residents questioned the local administrators about these discrepancies. In some cases, intended beneficiaries of famine relief were paid retroactively. In other cases, fear of public shaming pushed officials to settle accounts with individuals before scheduled hearings (Mander and Joshi, n.d.).

These social audits also pulled the rural lower-middle classes into the struggle alongside the working poor because their names were falsely recorded on muster rolls as workers and their recorded wages were siphoned off. They were "completely insulted at being taken for a ride," Roy told me. "Yeh humein ulloo bana rahe hain [They are making a fool of us]! It united them in this battle [even though] their reasons were separate."

"That is how the real agenda of the right to information became apparent," stated Roy. "It was not merely a question of corruption [or] of workers' rights. We had two streams that were going out—the Right to Information Act and the National Rural Employment Guarantee Act. Our preoccupation with both these acts and processes was the same."

As a result of the MKSS-led mobilization, Bhairon Singh Shekhawat, then chief minister of Rajasthan, announced in the state assembly in 1995 that he would grant people access to photocopies of government documents; the local media reported on this. However, when MKSS representatives tried to obtain state records, they hit a wall. Some bureaucrats claimed they had "no written orders" from the chief minister's office to share documents; others allowed activists to inspect documents but not copy them.

After a year of refusals, MKSS decided to stage a dharna in the city of Beawar in 1996. "We marched into the middle of Beawar's marketplace and sat there for forty days," said Roy. "At that point, the demand was, of course, for government records, but it was also for accountability of a chief minister who made a promise in the assembly and didn't fulfill it. Our expanded agenda ... included political and bureaucratic accountability, broadly. And that attracted enormous numbers of people.... The Beawar dharna in 1996 ... began the right to information movement."

Roy beamed as she described the energy and euphoria of that protest. "It was a pitched battle and an amazingly interesting fight. Those forty days were great because they made us understand [our campaign's] strength, depth, and breadth.... Trade unions joined and political parties and many others [because] this was an important issue. Four hundred organizations signed up. And all sorts of people!"

Before publicly announcing the sit-in, MKSS had canvassed Beawar residents about the appropriateness of the planned action. After receiving the go-ahead, they requested that each local family spend four days at the sit-in and contribute a few kilograms of *anaaj* (cereals) to help feed the protestors. "There were at least 250 people every day, and sometimes more than a thousand. So much happened. Crazy things, you know! Vegetable vendors gave us *subzi* [vegetables] every day, twice a day, for free! We ate vegetables we [usually] never eat—tomatoes, cucumbers, *kakdi* [snake melon]! A *baniya* [shopkeeper] in the marketplace gave us space to cook. Water came free. Videography was free. The press picked up the battle. Middle-aged groups joined us, and flower vendors and rickshaw pullers. A male sweeper gave us 10 rupees every day. Police constables gave us money! 'Don't announce our names,' they told us, 'but take this money from us—yeh bahut vaajib larayee hai [this is a very valid fight].' We attracted all the eccentrics: the Communist Party of India and other party [workers]; poets would join in the evening. A young boy who worked to pay for his own education would give us 2 rupees every day." Roy smiled softly. "It was very touching! The whole thing was an extremely powerful emotional space."

A sit-in in a central space performatively conjured a political mass and a public sphere that was extraordinary yet woven into daily life. This was a politics of the ordinary, expressed as much through communal cooking and building new forms of sociality and mutuality as through slogans, poetry, and an assembly of people who otherwise may never have aggregated (Butler 2015).[10] Roy's narrative brought to mind a Durkheimian collective effervescence of a righteous rather than ideological fight to materialize the sacred ideals of democracy, which unified groups across differences. Freedom of information was such an ideal—a means to safeguard survival and other rights, and a democratic, constitutional end unto itself.

Roy described MKSS as "an instrumentality"—one agent among many—that catalyzed a broad campaign for information freedom as a universal right to which many causes could be attached. "What the MKSS did was come into the middle of a large area of concerns about lack of accountability, about governance. We said that this was a battle to keep constitutional rights secure, a battle to keep democracy alive. [Others] had their own interpretation [of the RTI agenda]. It was like water, you know; it takes the shape of any vessel you pour it into. It is a universal right!" she affirmed. "So, this is the story of RTI. And then there are the technical details." Before she could go further, her cell phone rang. "Just one sec," she said, excusing herself to take the call.

⁓

I would later glean the banal technicalities of drafting and institutionalizing the transparency law and other tellings of the RTI story from various people. Before moving on to those, I want to illuminate some elements of Aruna Roy's charismatic, embodied, place-based tale of struggle, for it was the affective friction and ethical force of this technomoral politics that "moved" and mobilized people across social and political divides (Tsing 2005), laying the ground for technical work.

It is important to remember that for MKSS, the need for a right to information was clarified over time and in tandem with the right to a livelihood, thus suturing political-economic issues of survival and justice with democratic governance. These issues and the resultant laws of 2005—the RTI Act and the National Rural Employment Guarantee Act (NREGA)—were coeval and inseparable. RTI guaranteed state transparency; NREGA ensured a hundred days of employment per year to one person per family who was able to work.[11] Together, these laws established that accessing government records was necessary for a democratic polity and for marginalized people's well-being. Unlike the rebellious subaltern subjects who resisted colonial exploitation and state power by destroying documents (Guha 1983; Scott 2009), MKSS members confronted state corruption by instead demanding government records, and positioning the information contained therein as a human right.

Roy likened information access to water—a malleable material that can take any form and be used for various ends. Indeed, RTI activists see information as a "national resource [and] the currency that every citizen requires to participate in the life and governance of society" (Mander and Joshi, n.d., 3). It is a medium of democratic exchange without which "people cannot adequately exercise their rights and responsibilities as citizens or make informed choices" (3). Thus, without information, political participation is impossible, and without participation, democracy is but a sham. Activists express a desire to uphold the promise of a liberal democratic state and to ensure that the Indian state lives up to that ideal.

As Aruna Roy put it, "The work of MKSS and the right to information movement have established . . . that we own the state. The state is part of our larger democratic structure. It is a mechanism which should be accountable and totally transparent to the people because the sovereign rights of free India rest in the people of India." I will return to this insistence on liberal statehood and citizenship later in this chapter.

The Local beyond the Grassroots: A National Coalescing

MKSS's Beawar dharna in 1996 served as the critical juncture at which a powerful local fight for wages, work, and state records in Rajasthan articulated with struggles over other issues in other places and grew into a nationwide campaign for state transparency. The National Campaign for People's Right to Information (NCPRI) was formed at this time; it undertook the task of drafting and promoting a transparency law. One of its prominent members—Delhi-based intellectual and environmentalist Shekhar Singh—spoke to me about the more-than-local spatial entanglements and temporal precedents of the grassroots RTI story.

Singh became involved in the struggle to obtain information from the government around the time of the Bhopal gas tragedy, when, as he put it, "there was no information 'movement.'" The leakage of toxic gas from a Union Carbide plant in Bhopal in December 1984 and its disastrous aftermath revealed a complete lack of accountability at the level of both the Indian state and transnational capital (Fortun 2001). Despite activist efforts, the government refused to share details about its settlement with Union Carbide; it also invoked the Official Secrets Act to arrest people participating in a workshop on the medical problems of victims (Mander and Joshi, n.d.). After Bhopal, Singh and his compatriots "filed a case in the Supreme Court asking the government to provide information about hazardous industries in Delhi and across the country. And for some years, we kept fighting for environment-related information access." Other development-linked disasters also become battlegrounds for information. In the case of the Narmada River Valley dam project, for instance, activists were denied access to dam- and resettlement-related documents that would have exposed the project's devastating human and environmental consequences (Khagram 2002; Mander and Joshi, n.d.).

Singh dubbed the 1980s the "first phase of the information movement" that preceded the MKSS campaign, adding that "in many countries across the world, it seems like transparency movements started with environmental concerns." The 1986 Chernobyl disaster corroborated his assertion in that it galvanized demands for information and accountability from the Soviet and later Ukrainian states regarding the radiation leak's containment, spread, and exposure-related illnesses (Petryna 2003).[12]

Environment-led transparency advocacy in 1980s India, however, did not gain traction with conventional political players, including the Congress Party (then in power) and oppositional forces like the mainstream left. As Singh explained, "There was a certain antienvironmentalism among the left parties at that point—because the left was focused on industrialization and environmental concerns came in the way of that. Environmental concerns were [also] seen as Western concerns [with] a certain sort of capitalist tag. And they were projected as concerns of the elite in the country, who [worried] about tigers and trees, and not as concerns of the poor." MKSS's call for transparency garnered the support of the traditional left and other groups because it connected information freedom to labor and economic justice issues.

NCPRI's formation in 1996 ignited the national RTI movement's next phase. Singh described it as "a coming together of people from diverse interests who had been struggling for access to information. You had groups, like MKSS, which were working on rural development issues; groups working on information in relation to human rights, especially in Jammu and Kashmir and other areas with conflict; groups working on the environment; and so on." The RTI campaign also "didn't lend itself to a left-right divide." Although disagreements would emerge—with pro-business groups arguing to keep private sector institutions outside the purview of transparency and right-wing groups declaring that transparency and democracy "*se bahut* time waste *hota hai* [they waste too much time]"—ideological differences did not matter in the early phase of the national campaign. "When people from different walks of life get caught up in the initial flush, there is a certain blanking out of individual ideologies and perspectives. That is what happened in the RTI movement initially. People from all shades of ideology, who had very [contradictory] standpoints on matters relating to communalism or something else, seemed to be on board vis-à-vis RTI," said Singh, echoing Roy on the affective force—the first flush—of mobilization in addition to the postideological significance of transparency that enabled collaboration.

NCPRI members, alongside activists, lawyers, and sympathetic bureaucrats, drafted a national RTI law in 1996, which was circulated by the Press Council of India and widely debated. Meanwhile, the government convened the Shourie Committee to prepare an alternative transparency bill for the country, undermining some of the provisions included in the Press Council draft (Mander and Joshi, n.d.); this alternative government bill ultimately sat in limbo. At the level of individual states, however, transparency laws fared much better, with Tamil Nadu enacting the first RTI law in the country in 1997, followed by Goa.[13]

The NCPRI kept the pressure on at the federal level, where, in 1998, the right-wing BJP-led National Democratic Alliance gained power. In 2002, the NDA government passed a weak freedom of information law, which activists opposed. Luckily for them, this law never came into force because the government failed to "notify" its date of operationalization in the *Gazette of India*, a requirement for any act to become law.

As the 2004 elections approached, the NCPRI redoubled its lobbying efforts with parties and state actors (Kirmani 2007). Shekhar Singh recounted how Sonia Gandhi, the Congress Party leader, invited activists to draft a statement for her party's manifesto.[14] Once elected, her party formed a coalition United Progressive Alliance (UPA) government. The UPA included the RTI in its minimum common program, appointing some key members of the information campaign, including Aruna Roy, to the newly established National Advisory Council. Being part of this prestigious top-level body set up to advise the UPA government on policy matters provided activists with strategic space for their advocacy efforts. The National Advisory Council declared that the RTI draft bill would be its first official agenda, causing antitransparency bureaucrats to "wake up in [a] panic," Singh remarked. They threw many wrenches in the RTI's path, attempting to revive the inactive and toothless 2002 freedom of information law and proposing amendments.[15] However, activists pressed forward, using the support of the media and the former Indian prime minister V. P. Singh (known for his Mr. Clean image and tough stance against corruption). An amended bill was passed in May 2005. By October, the RTI Act was in force.[16]

Like Singh, several activists I spoke with acknowledged Sonia Gandhi's role in the passage of the RTI Act (Roy with the MKSS Collective 2018; Sharma 2015). In the words of Sunil Gupta, "the political class was against the RTI, including members of the Congress Party. The bureaucratic class was against it. Sonia Gandhi believed in the RTI to some extent, and it passed primarily because of her."[17] Singh agreed that movement activists would have faced a tougher battle without assistance from sympathetic political figures like Gandhi. However, he cautioned against personalizing success. "People think that getting the Indian state to pass the RTI law is a remarkable achievement of a few individuals [like Sonia Gandhi]. No! Power structures don't unravel on their own, even when there are individuals [inside] who want that. Power structures only unpack when they are forced. . . . I think the nature of power in this country was evolving to a point where the people who control power realized that they had to progressively share more and more of this power with the people [or] get zapped out. The Congress [Party] realized this. And it realized that the RTI would get [them] goodwill."

Singh offered a conjunctural analysis of the law's passage: certain forces converged to produce this result at a particular moment. In his telling, timing was critical: by the 1990s, the Indian public desired more open and participatory democratic governance. The postindependence state model, which combined an inherited colonial bureaucratic structure with highly centralized rule established by Nehru to hold together a partitioned nation, was no longer adequate. Colonial-era state secrecy did not serve the interests of a free and sovereign public. Governance had to be more accountable.

The RTI, thus, was "a law whose time had come," as Renu Kumar, a member of a Delhi-based civil society organization, described it to me. Kumar looked a bit harried when we met at her office one afternoon in March 2009. She rubbed her eyes, apologizing for asking me to wait while she put the final touches on a talk she had to deliver the next day. "No worries," I shrugged, taking a chair in her large, high-ceilinged office and listening in on a conversation with her assistant. After relaying instructions on the sequence and layout of her PowerPoint slides to him, Kumar turned to me and spoke about the RTI.

She viewed the law as "a mixed blessing. It is an enabling law . . . long overdue. I mean, you can't run a democratic government with an Official Secrets Act!" Although recognizing MKSS's critical role in the fight for information, Kumar contended that "there were many other [groups] in that struggle for many years." Grassroots pressure alone could not have succeeded in forcing the government's hand to pass the RTI Act. "Much bigger movements have been ignored in India: movements where they could get two hundred thousand people demanding this or that, but the government would just ignore [them] and yield only near election times. . . . MKSS had a moral voice [and] ran a high-profile campaign, at the right time. It looked like it came from [below], which is not to underestimate or to belittle its significance" (see also Sharma 2015).

Naveen Rai, a retired civil servant and an ardent backer of state transparency, concurred with Kumar that the RTI did not result from grassroots efforts alone and that the push for governance reform also came from within state structures when the time was ripe. "In the late 1990s, the government of India was already trying to . . . share information," he explained. "Ministries were asked to set up counters outside their offices where their [records] would be on display. At the same time, a number of states came up with their own RTI laws. Although these were highly restrictive, it showed that the need was being felt [inside the government]. I wouldn't say the RTI happened only because of the grassroots."

⁓

The national narrative thickens and broadens the popular local story about the RTI law. Calls for transparency and robust democratic state accountability had been made in India before MKSS came on the scene, and many of these calls unfolded on the terrain of the law. Indeed, ever since nationalist leaders established the law as an instrument of democratic and socioeconomic transformation at the time of India's independence (Chatterjee 2014; De 2014, 2018), it has served as a critical arena for judicialized politics and activism in the country (Bornstein and Sharma 2016).

As I explained in the introduction to this book, the 1970s initiated a particularly intense phase in state-directed judicialized activism following Indira Gandhi's declaration of the Emergency in 1975. After she lost the election in 1977, many watchdog and social action groups coalesced in reaction to state repression of democratic freedoms. Refusing both party and NGO affiliation—hence their "nonparty political" label—they expanded the agenda and tactics of activist politics, mobilizing around issues like gender, the environment, and human rights, which were ignored by the mainstream left (Menon 2013). Law was one of the key tactics of resistance used by these "new social movements" (Menon 2013). The PIL tool established by the Supreme Court in the late 1970s was essential in this regard, mobilized by watchdog groups and activist campaigns, including survivors of the Bhopal Union Carbide disaster and the Narmada dam movement, to challenge the state and seek justice (Bhuwania 2016). These new social movements also galvanized calls for state transparency using the legal antecedents available to them.

The Indian Supreme Court had endorsed freedom of information as the norm of democratic governance in some trend-setting judgments since the 1970s (Jaipuriar and Satpute 2009; Mander and Joshi, n.d.). Many activists I spoke with considered the 1981 case of *S. P. Gupta v. The Union of India* especially significant in this regard. Building on a 1975 case—*State of Uttar Pradesh v. Raj Narain*[18]—where the Court had ruled that government documents must be disclosed and that public interest overrides state secrecy, the Gupta judgment declared:

> In a government of responsibility like ours . . . there can be but few secrets. The people of this country have a right to know every public act, everything . . . done in a public way, by their public functionaries. . . . To cover with veil of secrecy the common routine business, is not in the interest of the public. . . . The concept of an open government is the direct emanation from the right to know which seems to be implicit in the right of free speech and expression guaranteed under Article 19(1)(a). Therefore, disclosure of information in regard to the functioning of Government must be the rule and secrecy an exception justified only where the strictest requirement of public interest so demands.[19]

Despite the Supreme Court's recognition of the principle of state transparency, the government continued to invoke the colonial-era Official Secrets Act during the 1980s, which posed serious challenges for environmental and human rights campaigns (Singh 2010; Mander and Joshi, n.d.; Sharma 2015). However, by the 1990s, the Indian state could no longer ignore ongoing activist and public calls to dismantle colonialist state secrecy and establish democratic accountability. MKSS played a pivotal role in igniting this cause, becoming one among several instrumentalities, as Aruna Roy described it, that made India's RTI Act possible. MKSS's pioneering ground-level work in Rajasthan revealed the connection between state secrecy, corruption, and wage labor injustice, invigorating a national platform to demand legalized transparency for the country.

The national transparency campaign created an inclusive meeting ground for several state and nonstate political actors from various corners of the country and ideological affiliations struggling to obtain information from the government in their disparate fights: social movement actors, media representatives, lawyers, ordinary citizens, political party functionaries, and some senior civil servants and judges. Those questioning the state from the outside were as integral to the RTI story as insiders—and some outsiders, like Aruna Roy, were former insiders. Alongside timing, the water-like nature of information freedom facilitated this conjunctural assemblage of local political forces to produce a particular result.

But what about translocal factors? For something else was happening in the 1990s, something coeval with state transparency discussions and activism in India: liberalization, afoot in the country and elsewhere. Expanding the local frame to include liberalization shines light on how transnational forces articulated with the homegrown Indian struggle for information freedom.

Presencing an Absence: The Global

That liberalization positively influenced state transparency around the world was generally acknowledged by the activists I interacted with. Indeed, this was one of Omesh Sen's key points during the RTI workshop with which I began this chapter. Yet Sen and many others I spoke with disconnected India from this broader trend of the convergence between neoliberal restructuring and transparency.

I probed Sen on this point during one of our follow-up conversations. "Didn't international development agencies actively push economic and political opening up everywhere?" I asked, quoting his example of post-1989 Eastern Europe, where development aid was targeted at countries liberalizing their markets and establishing "good governance." Sen nodded, agreeing that "transnational influences" were part of the many streams that "added up into a big river" of information transparency. He also agreed that donor pressure was real: "The Asian Development Bank and the World Bank [use] loan conditionalities and have much more impact [on RTI laws] than local advocacy efforts in different countries. I have seen it with my own eyes!" Sen described the case of a country where "the first installment of an international development loan came with fifty-four conditionalities and the second installment came with seventeen. One of those seventeen was RTI. And [the lender specified that] the installment would not be released until all those conditionalities, including RTI, were met." Having transparency laws in place also enabled donor agencies to "check if their money was being well spent." That said, Sen asserted that in the case of the RTI law in India, such transnational arm-twisting was minimal. The RTI Act passed because "the right people, at the right time, had the ear of the right people, like Sonia Gandhi." Thus, the temporal overlap between the struggle for the Indian RTI and the consolidation of neoliberal restructuring and good governance globally was dismissed as a mere coincidence.

Naveen Rai, whom I introduced previously, also disavowed transnational influences. A former civil servant, Rai averred that although organizations like the United Nations Development Progamme and the Department for International Development supported and funded RTI efforts globally, the Indian government enacted this law solely because of "internal pressure.... International pressure on India on policy issues is minimal. The Indian government has never been very keen to get more money from international agencies. India has always believed in self-reliance. In 2003, the BJP ... was attacked internationally on the issue of nuclear testing; as retaliation, they said, 'OK, we will not take any money from any donor with the exception of four or five [agencies].'[20] The total amount of funding that we get from all multilateral and bilateral aid comes to only 0.3 percent of the GDP. In practice, the reach of the World Bank [in India] is almost zero." Rai went as far as to argue that the Bank "saw RTI's potential only after India's success"; until then, it had been "talking about good governance and decentralization but [not] information sharing." In this inverted, nationalist narrative of influence, India, once again, was exceptional.

Rai's representation of India's relationship with the international development industry was curious. India is one of the Bank's largest borrowers. In 2009, when I met Rai, India's cumulative borrowing from the various agencies of the World Bank group stood at $74 billion (Kirk 2011, xv). The Bank's annual lending portfolio in India has stayed between $3 billion and $4 billion for many years, and it is involved in all kinds of projects, including infrastructure, agriculture, education, women's empowerment, health care, and rural livelihoods.[21] Although this funding comprises less than 1 percent of the country's national income, it is not insignificant in absolute terms.[22] Moreover, the influence of neoliberal policies backed by powerful global development institutions cannot be measured solely in terms of loan amounts. Rather, it is by normalizing a particular worldview and political-economic benchmarks that global development discourse exerts power (Escobar 1995; Ferguson 1994). India cannot disavow these development measures.

Demonstrating concrete adherence to these normative standards (including Western-style political and market freedom) admits countries onto the world stage as legitimate members of a liberal family of nations (Gupta 1992; Hindess 2004). Such legibility and recognition, measured by development indexes (Merry 2011), has material and symbolic benefits for states transnationally in terms of soft power, democratic capital, and credibility. Indeed, when Omesh Sen asserted that transparency laws are most prevalent in democratic and more developed countries, he was doing more than iterating developmentalist common sense. His statement, repeated by several government officials I interviewed, confirms India's rightful inclusion in a politically and economically evolved group of nations.

This international positioning in turn solidifies the image of a responsive and responsible state locally. Shekhar Singh alluded to this when he described the Congress Party's savvy in realizing that passing the RTI Act would accrue them public "goodwill" at a moment when people were clamoring for more political accountability. Renu Kumar also referenced symbolic returns for the Indian state in a bottom-up framing of the RTI story: "It is nice to say that we [the government] responded to pressure from below. . . . It is good that people believe that," she stated, underscoring the narrative's charismatic force with the public. However, she also cautioned that "we can't build a whole mythology around it. The pressure from below was much smaller. . . . MKSS raised the issue at the right time and rode the wave that was coming."

That wave was liberalization. "RTI would not have happened in a pre-1991 scenario, no matter what," Kumar stated categorically. "Because if you are liberalizing and the rules of the game are not clear, then you won't get foreign investment. . . . So no doubt the corporate sector and, of course, the World Bank . . . were exercising pressure points. Absolutely."

India's infamous "license raj"—an opaque, labyrinthian web of formal rules and informal rule-bending practices—carried a legacy of centralized planning and overblown bureaucratic proceduralism. This maze had to be downsized and rationalized to ensure investment, profit, and growth. For Kumar, there was an unquestionable link between neoliberal currents and the passage of the RTI Act. Although various groups had previously challenged the Official Secrets Act, translocal currents ripened the time and space in which the MKSS-led campaign succeeded.

It is important to note here that the global context did not determine the course of transparency in India in any one-sided manner. Rather, it overdetermined the passage of this law at a particular conjuncture. As the conversations above reveal, the place of the global and its articulation with the local was contentious and not agreed on by my interlocutors. Although most of the time this articulation was disavowed, as in the case of Sen and Rai, it was occasionally recognized, as in the case of Kumar. Those who acknowledged the global context, moreover, did not necessarily consider it an enabling factor for state transparency in India but instead a disabling one. (Conjunctures are nothing if not messy.)

Shekhar Singh, for instance, described how the global discourse and practices of securitization in the wake of the 9/11 bombings were counterproductive for transparency activism everywhere. His argument reminded me of Naomi Klein's (2007) idea of "shock doctrine"—that is, how crises are created and used as opportunities by state and corporate actors to enhance their power and push through regressive economic and political changes without much resistance from a shocked and suffering people. "Governments by their very nature are bloodsuckers," said Singh. "They grow fat every time there is a tragedy: 'Oh, there is an international crisis, and we have to take some drastic measures, and for that, people have to make some sacrifices—some human rights, some social welfare measures, the environment.' Governments then get away with . . . things that they would never be allowed to get away with. They are constantly going to try and turn any out-of-the-ordinary event into a justification for taking away our—I shouldn't say taking away—but for consolidating their own power. The perceived security threat [after 9/11] has strengthened the hand of fascist elements of [all Indian parties] who feel that we need a strong state. These threats [make it] harder to retain, let alone to progress, the RTI." Here was a global trend that worked against information freedom.

Where Singh explained how the instrumentalization of terrorism and security were shrinking the space for state transparency, others criticized the hypocrisy of international capital and development institutions. Corporate capital desires easy global access and compliant, open-for-business governments everywhere, but it wants its own deals and profit making to remain sealed. Development institutions facilitate and model this behavior; they promote worldwide transparency even as their free-market liberalization policies subvert it, and even as their inside workings remain opaque. According to Renu Kumar, "If you want to have the kind of economic policies that [India] has, transparency doesn't make sense. All these public–private partnerships, the manner in which privatization is going on, the manner in which all kinds of dubious deals are taking place—the RTI is the last thing that the government and businesses would like. Foreign companies are much worse than Indian companies, and international bodies are even worse [in this regard]."

Arvind Kejriwal echoed this perspective on the duplicity of global actors during one of our early conversations in 2008. "International organizations want a very weak . . . um, they don't want a strong RTI because then even the World Bank will be exposed." He recounted a water privatization scandal involving the World Bank. In 2001, PricewaterhouseCoopers (PwC) was awarded a $2 million contract to develop water privatization plans for Delhi. In 2005, Kejriwal used Delhi state's RTI law to uncover how the World Bank helped subvert competitive bidding norms and rig the playing field to grant this contract. Representatives of the Delhi Jal Board (water authority) rated PwC's proposal lower than other bids, but the city government, under pressure from the World Bank, chose PwC's proposal. Documents obtained by Arvind and others showed that the Bank had modified the evaluation criteria to favor PwC's proposal and pushed to exclude an expert assessment that had given PwC's proposal a low score. Kejriwal demanded that "in the interests of being a 'transparent public institution,' [the World Bank] should change its global disclosure policies to enable public access to such information by the citizens of any of the countries concerned."[23] Once confronted, the Bank denied any corruption, claiming that the events outlined by the Delhi activists "were broadly correct but the interpretation put on them is not."[24] It cited its global norms as evidence of its good ethics: "In order to ensure that the development outcomes for which its money is borrowed are achieved, the Bank has developed . . . a high set of standards in areas such as procurement, financial management, and environmental and social safeguards to which its borrowers commit. These are accepted as global benchmarks by its supporters and critics alike. . . . The insinuation that the Bank attempted to favour PwC is completely unfounded."[25]

Arvind called the World Bank's move for what it was: a charade. "International organizations talk about transparency," he told me bluntly. "They don't believe in transparency. This is just a public relations exercise for these international bodies [that] make loans conditional on transparency. They want transparency to a limited extent, not beyond." Global capital was no different. "Foreign companies do not want the license raj, but they also do not want transparency—not just about their own workings, but also about their dealings with the government. Would PricewaterhouseCoopers be happy if their entire contract [negotiation] with the Jal Board was open? Because if [things] become transparent then public pressure comes up, and then the political class stands up against [the company]. It is much easier to work with governments that deal with you within four walls."

Given this fraught relationship between the global neoliberal policies, institutions, and capital, it was unsurprising that many of my interlocutors denied any relationship between the Indian RTI story and the transnational context. On the one hand, liberalization brings top-down pressure from large development agencies and donors; on the other, it represents a further entrenchment of corporate power and a rearticulation of state power antithetical to democratic politics (Brown 2015). As much as it opens up nations, economies, and states (as if they were ever closed) to capital, legalization, and scrutiny, neoliberal restructuring also narrows the scope of welfare rights, justice, and survival for many. This is why many activists I interacted with distanced themselves from the dominant notion of good governance mainstreamed by international institutions, offering alternative visions of what goodness might entail and how to get there. Aruna Roy put it to me thus: "'Good Governance' is jargon [that emerged] after the break-up of the USSR. We talk about governance, not 'good' governance to avoid co-optation. . . . We talk about sangharsh, seva, nirman: struggle, welfare, development." MKSS's fight for wage justice and information freedom, in other words, couldn't be more unlike World Bank–style good governance.

Tactical Liberalism as (Translocal) Politics

In this chapter, I took seriously Ravi Kapoor's provocation to consider why the popular Indian RTI story is told as a tale of a good local fight for justice. The local here is imagined as a congeries of the grassroots, the national, and everything in between, but it remains within a nation-state framing. In this predominant telling, the global context is either absent or enters after the triumphant local story ends, and usually as a negative force. My impetus in presencing the global coevally, even as a negation, and juxtaposing it against varied local scales was to paint a complex translocal picture of state transparency in India. In so doing, my point was not to represent the global as encompassing a given local (Ferguson and Gupta 2002) but to illuminate conjunctural and frictional articulation that not only overdetermined the successful enactment of the Indian RTI law but also produced different spatial scales. The grassroots, in this story, was the ultimate local—an affectively charged locus of political authenticity and ethical purity that enabled a national (local) movement to take shape and compelled a recalcitrant state's response. Telling the RTI tale from this location, as a triumph of a bottom-up people's movement, matters politically, at home and abroad. It interrupts other narratives about the RTI as a top-down act of state generosity or one entirely shaped by broader neoliberal flows.

Indeed, Indian information activists fiercely contest neoliberal ideas and policy mandates antithetical to their pro-poor, pro-justice demands. This is a strategic positioning, a political stance that curiously disavows neoliberal global entanglements even as it invokes liberal universals to hold the Indian state accountable for securing livelihood and welfare rights and ensuring democratic accountability. For liberalism, despite its mystified provincial origins (Chakrabarty 2000) and imperialist history, cannot be easily dismissed. This language of power doubles as a powerful language of protest in postcolonial contexts, especially when adapted by movement actors to further their justice-based goals (Merry 2006).

Mobilizing liberal rights, freedoms, and constitutionalism offers activists and dispossessed groups a critical form of technomoral opposition to the "cold, technocratic, economistic justification . . . and literally '*demoralizing*' logic" (Ferguson 2006) of neoliberal restructuring. This is one reason why human rights discourses and lawfare proceed apace with neoliberalism (Moyn 2014; Sieder, Schjolden, and Angell 2005). The uptick in judicialized activism in India, directed at passing new laws to protect citizens' rights, welfare, and livelihoods, participates in this broader trend of expanding liberal lawfare (Bornstein and Sharma 2016). Anna Tsing (2005) contends that the "use of [transnational] liberalism to disturb the assurance of what was supposed to be a liberal state [is] especially apparent in movement encounters with the legal system . . . to vitalize the legal system . . . [and] to push the state to live up to its laws" (219). The RTI movement is squarely part of this state- and law-directed liberal politics, which "promises a much more benign method [compared to the Indian Maoist movement] of making governments answerable" (Singh 2010, 6).

This is why some radical left groups in India have called out transparency activism as "bourgeois" liberalism. According to Omesh Sen, these groups "accuse the RTI movement of undermining popular movements for social justice, which would prefer a direct course of action rather than a bourgeois method of asking for information, then trying to get a response, and then finding a solution. The ultraleft groups see this as a bourgeois way of trying to bring about change—a constitutional way—that will only lead to change in incremental degrees. It will not bring about radical change. 'Why are you being so accommodating with the state? Why are you being so gentle?' they ask." Sen's sentiment was confirmed by a far-left activist I met, who criticized RTI advocates' view of the state as a "neutral" entity for progressive change rather than an entity that embodies and entrenches social hierarchies and injustice. This "liberal view has no critique of the state!"

When I queried Aruna Roy about this charge of liberal statism, she historicized MKSS's strategic positioning. "There has been a tradition among Indians, whether on the far left or from the movements, to stay away from government. There has been a high moral ground occupied by people who are not part of . . . the state machinery. [The belief that] fighting against the state will give you credibility is . . . a legacy of the nationalist movement, I think. We fought against a state which was then the British raj. . . . It has some validation because Mahatma Gandhi and people with great credibility did not assume office. And those who [did] were pushed into the gray area [of ethics] either because of the predicament of governance or because of their own actions. So we have tended to see the state as the enemy . . . [to not] have anything to do with it. . . .

We did not own the state." Although this political strategy made sense in the aftermath of independence, Roy argued that the present situation demanded something different.

"I think the state is ours! MKSS coined a slogan: yeh sarkar hamare aap ki, nahin kisi ke baap ki; yeh desh hamare aap ka, nahin kisike baap ka [this state is ours and not anyone's private property; this nation is ours and not anyone's private property[26]]. . . . The state has a relationship with the people not as an oppressor but as a servant . . . deputed to carry out the mandate of the constitution. We've had to face a lot of criticism within our own political groupings [for taking this stance]. We have also had to labor to make people understand that saying that the state is ours is not being co-opted by the state but actually to own . . . the largest decision-making system in this country. If it is not claimed as ours and influenced, it ends up doing consistently antipeople activities. And we are then pitched into a position where we have to confront the state, and then we get indicted as antinational, and then we have to establish credibility. It gets us into cases and litigation. And half the time that we should have [spent] fighting for people's rights is spent in getting ourselves extricated from the web that the state lays for us."

The irony of avoiding that exhausting trap of legal confrontation with the state through fighting for new laws notwithstanding, Roy's formulation cannot be easily collapsed into universal, bourgeois liberalism writ large. Rather than rehearsing liberal abstractions, she offered a specific understanding of these norms, grounded in a particular political history and her experiences working with disenfranchised rural groups. Roy defended liberal citizenship, which locates sovereignty in "the people." However, "the people" she invoked was not a generic moniker. It referenced those inhabiting the social and economic margins of a postcolonial and postliberalized India; both these "posts" are symbolically and materially important. How this public exerts sovereign mastery and ownership over what kind of state makes a difference. Roy's idea of ownership did not follow the logic of private property, where the state is a protected enclosure of special interests, whether caste, class, or gender. Rather, she imagined it as a "public commons" over which people must exert collective control to make it function as a postcolonial liberal democratic state—that is, to uphold universal rights and freedoms, and to ensure survival and welfare under conditions of disenfranchisement and precarity.

Tsing (2005) proposes that "protest mobilizations . . . [relying] on universalizing rhetorics of rights and justice . . . are shaped by liberal logics. Yet they must make these rhetorics work within the compromises and collaborations of their particular situations. In the process, new meanings and genealogies are added to liberalism" (5). Liberal universals, in other words, travel neither evenly nor as is; their time- and place-based settling in is also an unsettling of their origins.

The RTI movement instantiates a translocal and tactical liberal politics that provincializes liberalism differently. As a language of protest, it constructs the local as the privileged site from where stories about universal ideals must be told because that is where these ideals are worked on and fought for. When RTI activists call on liberal norms, they translate them (Merry 2006) and then reroot them in a local soil rife with other moral, political, and historical strains. Alongside the languages of constitutionalism, law, and policymaking lie stories of traumatic hunger strikes and euphoric dharnas that recall Gandhi. We learn about antagonistic state representatives and supportive insiders. And we hear echoes of a left-leaning discourse on labor rights and a critique of globalization. These local tales enunciate "structures of feeling that bind space, time, and memory in the production of location" (Gupta 1992, 76). As charismatic packages, such stories produce the local as a space of foment and challenge while invigorating abstract ideals with affective force and substance. "Sangharsh, seva, nirman," which Roy invoked alongside the rights to livelihood and information, does something more than simplistically reference liberal freedoms. It illustrates tactical liberalism as an overdetermined assemblage that takes shape in and through local political practice. In the following chapters, I expand on the forms and dilemmas of this practice, examining the effects, promises, and limits of state-focused judicialized activism.

2

Rightfully Worded

A Law, a Petition, and a Few Stories

> The art of storytelling is coming to an end. . . . It is as if something that seemed inalienable to us . . . were taken from us: the ability to exchange experiences.
>
> —WALTER BENJAMIN, *The Storyteller*

August 2008. I took a bus to the metro to an auto-rickshaw to a cycle-rickshaw. Ninety minutes later, I arrived in Kaushambi, just past the eastern edge of Delhi, to meet Arvind Kejriwal for the first time. I had written to him expressing my wish to volunteer with his NGO, Parivartan, as part of my ethnographic research on the social, political, and activist life of the RTI law and to understand how it was reshaping citizenship, bureaucratic practices, and democratic statehood in urban India. He had agreed.

I was on edge, as anyone embarking on a new research project would be. I was also soaked. The monsoon rain had given me a serious licking during the last leg of my commute, despite my attempts to wield my ratty green umbrella against the downpour. Kejriwal's flat was in a Kaushambi high-rise that housed civil servants. The guard checked me in and pointed to the elevator. I took the stairs instead, giving myself time to squeeze the rainwater out of my clothes, shake out my hair, and wipe my glasses. I wanted to look presentable.

I rang the doorbell. A dark-haired, bespectacled man with a thick mustache opened the door. I recognized Arvind instantly from media coverage. "Aradhana?" he asked, smiling easily. I nodded, dropping my umbrella by the door and holding out my hand; "Please call me Anu." We shook hands, and he directed me to a sofa in the living-cum-dining area. His apartment reminded me of the middle-class government residences I had grown up in: whitewashed walls, fluorescent lighting, ceiling fans, and two, maybe three bedrooms, decently furnished, nothing too flashy. I noticed a laptop and some papers strewn across the dining table and guessed that this area doubled as a workspace. An older woman—Arvind's mother—soon brought in tea and a plate of cookies. I said namaste, grateful for the steaming chai after my battle with the rain.

Arvind, as Kejriwal preferred being called then, was energetic and engaging. He began by asking questions about my research proposal and shared the names of other RTI activists to contact. Because I had offered to assist him and his coworkers at Parivartan with their daily work, Arvind described a "right to food" case they had recently initiated.[1] They were using the RTI Act to expose corruption in the government's Public Distribution System, which provides subsidized food rations to people living below the poverty line through designated ration shops. Parivartan activists filed information petitions with the food and supplies department to retrieve monthly sales and stock records of local ration vendors, which listed who received rations, in what quantity, and when. They were simultaneously conducting surveys in East Delhi camps or slums,[2] asking recipients if they received their full quota of monthly rations promptly; most had not. Arvind planned to use the survey data to initiate legal action in support of the food-related public interest litigation underway at the Supreme Court since 2001. This PIL sought to establish freedom from hunger as a fundamental, state-protected human right.[3] Arvind's legal strategy dovetailed with the PIL but did not rely on the latter's human and welfare rights-based arguments. Instead, he sought to invoke the Consumer Protection Act. "We have tried everything [to improve the food ration system]—mobilizing people, public hearings, PIL, RTI. Our coworker Santosh's throat was slashed right outside the government's food and supplies office! Nothing has worked. So we are going to try the consumer court."

Arvind asked me to help complete the surveys, translate them into English, and produce depositions for the lawsuit that Parivartan was planning to file on behalf of a group of people alleging that they had been wronged as consumers of subsidized food rations and deserved compensation from specific shopkeepers who would be named as defendants. Working on this project, he stated, would allow me to observe firsthand the highs, lows, and frustrations of RTI activism. He also directed me to get a copy of the RTI law pamphlet from Parivartan's office, mentioning that it would be a quick read: the people who had drafted the law had taken care to use simple language so ordinary folks could understand easily.

On my metro ride home, I leafed through the twenty-three-page-long pamphlet originally published in the *Gazette of India* in June 2005. "WHEREAS the Constitution of India has established democratic Republic," it began, "AND WHEREAS democracy requires an informed citizenry and transparency of information which are vital to its functioning and also to contain corruption and to hold Governments . . . accountable to the governed; AND WHEREAS revelation of information in actual practice is likely to conflict with other public interests including efficient operations of the Governments . . . ; AND WHEREAS it is necessary to harmonise these conflicting interests while preserving the paramountcy of the democratic ideal; NOW, THEREFORE, it is expedient to provide for furnishing certain information to citizens who desire to have it."[4] My eyes were already glazing over.

There is a staccato quality to legal texts—a "boom, boom, boom" rhythm, a pithy curtness that appears to convey fact and clarity through its list-like style and utilitarian yet grave language. I found its apparent simplicity confusing, not to mention tedious. The whereases and therefores, the sections with subsections and subsubsections—2(h)(d)(ii), 4(1)(b)(iv), etc.—overwhelmed me. How would a novice or someone unfamiliar with legalese fare? I plodded along.

Here is the gist of what I understood after reading that pamphlet: Any citizen acting in the public interest could submit a written application for disclosure of any information held by public authorities, as long as it did not pose a national security risk. Every government department had to designate public information officers (PIOs) who constituted the first tier of the information bureaucracy. The PIOs had thirty days to process an RTI query. If they delayed or refused disclosure without providing written justification, or if they released wrong or partial information, applicants could appeal to the first appellate authorities (FAAs) within the same department. If an FAA agreed with a PIO's denial of information, applicants could turn to the next tier of the information bureaucracy, state-level information commissions. New Delhi's Central Information Commission was the highest decision-making body in the RTI universe. Information commissions had the power to adjudicate appeals—that is, to decide whether PIOs and FAAs acted lawfully and to impose a fine on PIOs of 250 rupees (roughly $3) per day up to a maximum of 25,000 rupees (just over $300) for wrongfully withholding or destroying information, or giving incomplete or incorrect information. This penalty clause, which affected only the PIOs, was meant to give teeth to the transparency law.

Here is what confused me. The law defined information as "any material in any form" that is either held or can be accessed by public authorities (Government of India 2005, 2). How would the law work in instances where there was no physical record or traceable evidence of decisions? What if a decision was not documented in writing, or records were missing? The directive that all public authorities must divulge information in the public interest was straightforward enough. But what counted as public interest was less obvious. Which public? Whose interest? I found the definition of "public authorities" equally ambiguous. This category included not only government departments but also agencies that were "owned, controlled or substantially financed . . . directly or indirectly" by the government (2). Did this include private institutions that receive land and tax concessions from the state? What about semigovernment bodies and NGOs that are registered with the state but may not receive government funding? Political parties?

The law's imperative was to share information, not hide it. Section 4 sought to make transparency routine by requiring public authorities to provide information voluntarily or *"suo motu* to the public at regular intervals" (Government of India 2005, 5) rather than waiting for citizens to file RTI petitions. However, there were exemptions to the transparency rule. Section 8 of the law detailed instances where information could be withheld: if its public release would "prejudicially affect the sovereignty and integrity of India, the security, strategic, scientific or economic interests of the State, relation with foreign State or lead to incitement of an offence" (7). The document's second schedule listed several intelligence and security organizations—which were technically "public authorities"— as lying outside the purview of mandated transparency.[5] These exceptions made me uneasy. Terms like national "sovereignty," "integrity," and "state interest" are hardly self-evident and can be manipulated to obstruct the sharing of information as much as to facilitate it. Couldn't any information be potentially labeled as sensitive and be withheld? Who gets to decide the limits of national interest or when it should outweigh public interest?[6] Section 8 contained an important proviso that public authorities may allow access to sensitive information "notwithstanding anything in the Official Secrets Act, 1923 nor any of the exemptions permissible [in the RTI Act] . . . if public interest in disclosure outweighs the harm to the protected interests" (8). Who decides when public interest supersedes state interest, and how?

The language of the RTI Act did not convey stable or clear meaning; interpretations could diverge. Equally, its filing and appeal procedures left me with lots of questions. I sought clarification from Arvind when we next met. "Just file an RTI application, Anu!" he encouraged smilingly, stating that the best way to learn how the law works and what its various clauses mean is to submit an information query. "What would I file an RTI petition about?" I wondered aloud. "Oh, about anything. MTNL [government-owned] telephone service,[7] potholes in roads in your neighborhood, anything at all!" Arvind retorted, implying that signs of poor governance were ubiquitous; all I had to do was pick one, write a petition, and file it.

～

Choosing a suitable topic for an RTI query was on my mind as I took a walk in a park near my mother's home that evening. Arvind's suggestion to focus on bad roads or erratic landlines seemed appropriate enough; they were common signs of infrastructure failure and government inefficiency in Delhi's middle-class colonies. The streets in our area needed repair, and sidewalks were essentially nonexistent—where built low, they were taken over by two-wheeled traffic quite like a road shoulder, and where built high, they deterred everyone but the most athletic from attempting to climb them. Maybe I could use the RTI to ask about the stipulated height and width of sidewalks so these "footpaths" could actually accommodate *foot* traffic. Sharing the road with vehicles made walking anywhere frenetic and treacherous. Perhaps that is why neighborhood parks were important but embattled spaces. While some residents fought to keep parks amenable for walking and socializing, others wanted to convert them into parking lots. A few parks in our neighborhood had already turned into de facto car parks, inciting acrimony. The walkers pointed fingers at the parkers, alleging that the latter lacked civic sense and morality because they bribed local municipal officials to turn a blind eye to such misuse of public spaces. Could an RTI petition improve the municipal maintenance and oversight of parks in this area?

I mulled over these issues as I rapidly walked the trapezoid path inside one of the few green, well-tended parks left in the neighborhood. The park was bustling with its usual evening activity. I saw the regular walkers greeting each other with nods, smiles, and hollers; groups of grandmothers sharing snacks and chatter; children playing soccer and cricket; a few older yogis doing asanas on the grass; and the usual group of older men sitting in their designated spot, newspapers in hand. These uncles—as everyone called them—showed up at the same time every day, reading news stories aloud, exchanging personal experiences and complaints, and conversing about local and world politics. It was impossible not to overhear them grumble about state corruption and the many ways in which the government routinely failed senior citizens: telephone workers and government clerks who took bribes simply to fulfill their responsibilities; problems with pension payments; lack of proper care at government-run health dispensaries; bureaucratic red tape and mistreatment; and so on. This group of uncles constituted a microcosm of the class-differentiated public sphere in India that is alive with criticism about governance and government.

Any of the uncles' middle-class concerns would have been suitable for an RTI petition, but I found a problem closer to home. My grandfather, then ninety-one years old and a retired civil servant, had made a substantial out-of-pocket payment for an emergency surgery. He was covered by the government's health plan and was entitled to reimbursement, but the health department had taken no action on his reimbursement application for nearly a year. Following the case on my grandfather's behalf, my mother called the Central Government Health Scheme's reimbursement desk every Monday afternoon between 3 PM and 5 PM, per department instructions. The staff had become so familiar with Amma's voice that she didn't even need to introduce herself. "Yes, Mrs. Sharma," they answered as soon as she said hello. While this persistence brought aural recognition for my mother, it did not resolve my grandfather's case. Amma was given some version of a standard response each week:

"The case is still under consideration."

"The file is under review by the officers at level x or y of the health bureaucracy." (No names were ever divulged.)

"Madam, all approvals and authorization oopar se ayenge [will come from above]. There is nothing we can do."

A retired government schoolteacher herself, Amma was well acquainted with vague bureaucratic sound bites: "usual responses," she called them, which redirected responsibility and conveyed nothing. "The government is dragging its feet because they know he is old. They are just waiting for him to die," she surmised ominously, echoing the popular public image of a callous, crafty, and deliberately inept state.

Amma and I decided that this issue was ripe for an RTI intervention. However, I had some misgivings about spinning this personal problem as a matter of public interest. When I consulted Nisha Bedi, an activist colleague, she reassured me that my grandfather's story was not singular but a symptom of a wider malaise. Resolving his case would benefit other people facing similar problems and improve the overall responsiveness of the health bureaucracy. I needed no further confirmation: this effort was in the public interest after all.

I sat down with Papa, my grandfather, the very next evening and asked him to tell me what he wanted me to say in his RTI query. Papa straightened his wiry and fragile frame, took a deep breath, and settled into what I recognized as his storytelling mode. This was going to be a long session of listening, translating, and inscribing Papa's story into an information petition. I opened my laptop screen to a blank document, crossed my legs on the sofa, and settled in.

Information and Documents, Stories and Subjects

What would it take for me to turn Papa from a richly textured being who chose to narrate his life as an ever-evolving compendium of stories into simply Tulsi Das Dhawan, a flattened citizen with a complaint and a rights claim printed on A4 sheets of paper? How would his signature at the bottom of the petition, meant to authenticate him as an individual, fit with the "signature of the state" (Das 2004) inscribed in the words and style of the petition itself, meant to truncate personhood and render it generic (Cody 2013)?

In this chapter, I offer a thick description of my experience filing an RTI petition. Petitioning as a mode of address to those in power has a long history in colonial and postcolonial India, with people using oral and written means to complain or appeal to the state, or to request something from it (De and Travers 2019). The RTI petition is a newer entrant in this rich field. Part grievance and part rightful and moral demand for information, it asserts a claim as opposed to making a deferential appeal (Cody 2013). It is a written document with a specific aesthetic form "that involves a set of framing techniques establishing a standardized and more legible text" (Cody 2013, 178) for state eyes. A petition, furthermore, "is not just a thing—the petitionary message via a specific medium—it is also a process" (Mathur 2019, 282), which involves learning the format and language of appeal, calling and visiting offices, submitting and resubmitting paperwork, and waiting. I track this process, moving between my grandfather's oral life stories and my written account of his RTI petition, and juxtaposing both against ethnographic snapshots of activist routines and official interactions. This superimposition illuminates the social and stylistic translations that RTI petitions require and the political and aesthetic work they do to normalize (classed) citizenship, inscribe state langue and power, and shape transparency activism. Whereas chapter 1 juxtaposed different scalar stories about how the RTI law was demanded and enacted, this one focuses on how the law is used by middle-class citizens and by activists.

I use a deliberate autoethnographic mode to craft this chapter, telling personal stories that are at once mine and "also about the social worlds in which we live" (Walley 2013, 5; see Hurston 1969). I locate myself and my family in the very grid of class, citizenship, and bureaucratic state power that I analyze. This allows me to hold together the informal and the formal, the intimate and the impersonal, the vernacular and the authoritative in ethnographic tension while parsing the social effects of statist modes of documentation and legally enforced transparency.

In tracking the life cycle of my grandfather's RTI petition, I attend to the forms of communication and subjectification that this specific genre of legalistic paperwork—the written exercise of rights—generates and restricts. My musings are framed by insights drawn from the work of Benjamin (2007) and Foucault (1991, 1995) as well as from ethnographic scholarship on the aesthetics and productivity of records (Reed 2006; Riles 1998, 2006). I situate these insights in the broader interdisciplinary scholarship on the symbolism and impact of bureaucratic documentation.

That documents are "paradigmatic artifacts of modern knowledge practices" (Riles 2006, 2), rationality, and power is widely agreed on; but whether they merely compile or also distort and create realities, and how they do this, has long been a matter of debate. In the Weberian worldview, documents are instruments and markers of bureaucratized capitalist modernity (Weber 2006), which aligns with an evolutionary perspective that views written communication as an advancement over oral cultures (Morgan [1877] 1985).[8] The presumptive assumption is that orality marks traditional cultures of memory, community, and affect, whereas writing references the abstract, individualistic, rational, and record-based modern ethos (Goody 1986; Havelock 1986). Less settled is whether the movement from the former to the latter is a triumphant narrative of human civilization from primitivity to modernity or one of downfall. Taking the latter view, Claude Lévi-Strauss (1961) argued that the "primary function of writing . . . is to facilitate the enslavement of other human beings" (291–92).

Leftist critics take this thinking further, positioning writing and documents as symbols of state power and capitalist exploitation. James Scott (2009) argues that certain Southeast Asian hill people chose orality over writing as a way to escape from social hierarchies, settled agriculture, centralized state authority, and servitude. They burned records, much like peasant groups in colonial India, who destroyed rent rolls, deeds, files, bond and debt registers, and decrees because they saw writing as "the sign of [their] enemy" (Guha 1983, 52).[9] Documents, then, are not a means of rational advancement, as Weber would have it, but instead are fetishized objects enabling state and capitalist domination and wealth accumulation while mystifying the material conditions of inequality and dehumanization (Graeber 2015).

Benjamin (2007) argues that these reproducible and verifiable artifacts imperiled the artisanal craft of oral storytelling in modern, information-logged Europe. The rise of individually authored and read novels, capitalist industrialization, and the information age of printed facts and news threatened oral archives of experiential wisdom from distant times and places, endangering the aura of storytelling and shared aural communities. Benjamin writes that "with the full control of the middle class, which has the press as one of its most important instruments in fully developed capitalism, there emerges a form of communication which . . . confronts storytelling as no less of a stranger than did the novel, but in a more menacing way. . . . This new form of communication is information" (88).

Harvey (1989, 2005) also offers a Marxist reading of the centrality of documented information to political-economic and cultural change, linking it with late capitalism and neoliberalism. He argues that under post-Fordist globalization, "accurate and up-to-date information is . . . a very highly valued commodity" (Harvey 1989, 159). The normalization and spread of the market values of competition, efficiency, and productivity under neoliberalism—what Wendy Brown (2015) describes as the "ubiquitous economization of all features of life" (31)—relies on "technologies of information creation and capacities to accumulate, store, transfer, analyse, and use massive databases to guide decisions in the global marketplace" (Harvey 2005, 3). This widespread dispersal of utilitarian technologies, knowledges, and "audit cultures" (Strathern 2000) across social domains and down to the level of the normative neoliberal individual, has given rise to "a new kind of 'information society'" (Harvey 2005, 4), which has in turn led to a "creative destruction" of "social relations . . . ways of life and thought, reproductive activities . . . and habits of the heart" (3).

Harvey's scenario of the creative destruction wrought by information society under neoliberal capitalism resonates with Benjamin's view of information as a mechanized menace to experiential exchange and affective communities; both focus on what bureaucratized capitalist modernity ruins. Foucault's (1991, 1995) work, in contrast, is more attuned to what modern institutions and documentary practices produce. It reveals the power-laden generativity of governmental regimes and disciplinary knowledges, discourse, and artifacts—how they conjure truths, norms, social relations, and governable as well as resistant subjects. For Foucault the "questioning of the *document*" (1972, 6) is central to interrogating the workings and effects of modern knowledge/power. A document is never merely a record, disinterested and alienating. Rather, it is a key element in governmental networks that create individuals and populations as subjects of administration, directing their conduct toward specific ends. Records and documentation are ineluctably entangled with bureaucratic power most commonly associated with the state (Gupta 2008; Hull 2003).[10] For example, censuses and statistics do more than compile information; these instruments of enumeration also operate as technologies of governance and subject formation (Cohn 1987; Hacking 1982). Official artifacts, such as passports, seals, and stamps, are not just products of bureaucratic state practices; they also do the active and daily work of constructing the state by graphically manifesting its authority and truths on the one hand, and animating legible citizens on the other (Hansen and Stepputat 2001; Sharma and Gupta 2006).

Provoked by Benjamin's (2007) claim that the artisanal craft of oral storytelling atrophied in industrial, information-saturated Europe, in this chapter, I analyze the fraught relationship between storytelling and a written information petition to demand a right in neoliberal, late capitalist times. I tell the story of my grandfather's petition as a way to track the social and activist life of the RTI law in India. The petition here is not merely an individualized record. It is a process and it symbolizes a "pattern" (Riles 1998, 379) of a particular bureaucratic kind that is more than just an artifact of control; it is an actant (Latour 2005) in its own right that does things in excess of Foucauldian normalization. In what follows, I tease out the creative destruction—the potentiality and danger—of the information petition as an actant in the universe of state transparency. Thinking in both Benjaminian and Foucauldian veins, I describe the translation of spoken, biographical, and socially dense parole into a formatted, thinly inscribed, disembodied appeal that addresses the state in its own langue (Cody 2013), and consider its effects.

Through Thick and Thin: A Storyteller and A Supplicant

"So, tell me what you want me to write in your RTI application," I asked Papa, my fingers paused over the laptop keyboard. "Write that I am ninety-one years old and a retired government servant." Every story needs context. Papa's tale had to narrate the failure of the health bureaucracy to furnish his reimbursement and to compel it to do so, but he couldn't possibly begin there. So, he began by emphasizing his social legitimacy and claim on state services—the reason why his application carried moral weight and urgency.

Prone to digressions, Papa described his three-and-a-half-decade-long career as a state functionary. The colonial state hired him as a stenographer because of his knowledge of the English language and his typing and shorthand skills. "I was fast!" he declared, sucking in his breath audibly through his nose with pride, and emphasized how much his English bosses appreciated his work ethic. "Good work, Dhawan!" they would say, referring to him by last name only. Papa described these Englishmen as upstanding people from whom he learned a lot. "The English colonized us for nearly 200 years, Papa!" I reacted irritably. Papa raised his palm slowly, signaling me to slow down and, with his eyes closed, he let out a sigh—his way of gently admonishing me for my naiveté. Indeed, I was surprised at my own knee-jerk righteous indignation. Papa had lived in colonial India and understood its violence firsthand. Yet his *tajarba* or experience as an underling in the colonial state machinery was a decent one. It taught him important, lasting lessons about dedication, hard work, discipline, and honesty. He recounted that after independence, he passed up key chances for promotions within the civil-aviation ministry that would have put him in charge of departments like "procurement," where opportunities for bribes were ripe. His rise through the ranks was slower but admirable. After serving for many years as Section Officer—"Grade One," he specified, emphasizing the inverted vertical prowess of "one" over other levels in the bureaucracy—he retired at the mandated age of fifty-eight as "Under-Secretary, Civil Aviation."

This was no small achievement for someone who was, for a long time, the only member of his family of petty traders with a college degree, who moved away from his hometown Bahawalpur (now in Pakistan) to Delhi at the urging of his "friend and old class-fellow," Satpal, in search of a job, and who got a break as a low-level government clerk. Papa's initiative and resourcefulness helped his extended family survive the displacement and trauma of India's partition in 1947. His family members were among the many millions of Hindus, Muslims, and Sikhs rendered "refugees" in the only home/land they had ever known, forced to move across newly made-up borders to escape bitter violence and to negotiate their belonging to redrawn nations. Papa worked his connections within the colonial government and with powerful Muslim friends in Bahawalpur to ensure a safe passage for his family across unfamiliar and bloodied boundaries. His tiny flat in Delhi became a temporary shelter for his father, six brothers, and their families as they struggled to find their feet and refuge in a remade India.

Papa beamed and gave me "the look." He was proud of how far he had come—professionally, personally, and socially. His life story, his service to his family and nation, and his age demanded respectful listening and reciprocity—in this case, from the very state he had worked for.

I smiled back. Papa was in his signature storytelling mode, which I knew intimately since childhood—the gestures, the posture, the eyes, the use of breath, the changes in tone, the deliberate slowness. And, of course, the digressions. I found myself drifting away, reminiscing about the hours upon hours of summertime joy and thrill my brother and I derived from hearing Papa's ever-unfolding stories about goddesses and gods, queens and kings, demons and benevolent beings.

Papa's gift as a spinner of enrapturing tales wasn't just happenstance; or so I believed. He had a legacy to live up to. His namesake, Tulsidas, was a sixteenth-century North Indian Hindu poet-saint known for translating the Hindu epic *Ramayana* from formal Sanskrit to vernacular Awadhi.[11] Tulsidas was a key figure of the *bhakti* movement of his time, which challenged religious orthodoxy dominated by Brahmin pundits and their tight, caste-based control over scriptural knowledge. The movement propagated a religiosity based in developing personal, affective ties with deities—devotional love, friendship, and loyalty—rather than in formal, ceremonial ritual (Hess 1988; Lutgendorf 1991). The *bhakti* tradition relied on translating and rewriting religious texts into colloquial dialects—like Tulsidas's rendition of the *Ramayana*—and on oral and embodied expressive forms to disseminate devotional messages: songs, verses, aphorisms, and public performances of epics for largely nonliterate, mass audiences. Unlike what Benjamin observed in interwar Europe, epic tales in India, like Tulsidas's *Ramayana*, are still sung, recited from memory, and experienced collectively—whether on television or on local stages across north India—more often than read by isolated individuals. As Linda Hess (1988) writes,

One does not have to be literate to know Tulsidas. Grandmothers tell Ram's stories; neighborhoods may have an annual Ramlila; and public discourses on [Tulsidas's *Ramayana*] are delivered by specialists who lecture with gusto, chanting verses and pouring forth commentary with a . . . popular preacher's sense of the dramatic. . . . Singers perform Tulsi-*bhajans*—lyric verses by the poet set to music. (238)

Tulsi Das, my grandfather, was well versed in these bhajans, verses, and tales. When he was a fifth grader, Papa's Hindi teacher would call on him to recite *chaupais*—four-line stanzas—from his namesake's *Ramayana* on his school's stage. He had learned so many chaupais "by heart" that he could go on for hours, nonstop. If "memory is the epic faculty *par excellence*" (Benjamin 2007, 97), Papa had honed his at a young age. "You have been named appropriately, Tulsi Das!" his delighted teacher—*master ji*—would exclaim, giving an approving thump on his back and a small *inaam* (reward) for his recitations.

It was easy to get drawn into Papa's stories and memories, to get lost in the details and detours, savoring them unhurriedly, at his pace. There would be no shortcuts, for his stories were never summaries. Unanticipated tangents along the way were to be expected even when we knew the endings. His were "legendary tales whose focus is a righteous [being]" (Benjamin 2007, 85) and where "good"—whether embodied in acts (karma), people, animals, or mythological characters—always triumphs. Papa's stories conveyed important lessons gleaned from religious and other traditional sources or from his life experience, his tajarba. "Every real story contains . . . something useful," wrote Benjamin, such as "a moral . . . some practical advice . . . [or] a proverb or maxim. In every case the storyteller is a man who has counsel for [others]" (86). I had already gleaned a few moral lessons from Papa's opening of his reimbursement parable. However, in that moment I was not simply a listener absorbing his wise counsel but also a trained field note-taker and a scribe who had to produce something more mundane and thin—an RTI petition—before the day was out. Storytime and bureaucratic time could not proceed apace, and I let the utilitarian impulse overtake more interesting, contemplative reveries.

"Tell me about what took you to the hospital last year, Papa," I nudged gently, trying to steer both of us back to the task at hand. "Last summer,

I was in Bombay," he began, catching a new thread of his tale. He was visiting my aunt when he collapsed one afternoon after lunch. "I think it was *bud-hazmi* [indigestion]. I had eaten *rajmaa-chawal* [red kidney beans and rice]. This food doesn't suit me. Every time I eat *rajmaa* . . ." I interrupted with laughter. "I don't think the government is interested in what you ate, Papa. Tell me what happened after you collapsed."

Papa obliged, explaining that my cousin had administered CPR and then had taken him to the nearest hospital in the Santa Cruz neighborhood. The doctors said that he had a "missing pulse." I nodded: "You've always had arrhythmia." "Yes, *that*," replied Papa, pleased that his condition had a legitimate, technical name. Amma, who had joined us by this time, added that after the doctors stabilized him, the cardiologist suggested surgically inserting an Implantable Cardioverter Defibrillator (ICD)—a fancy pacemaker. "The doctor said that an ICD would reduce the possibility of sudden heart failure as a result of abnormal rhythm," my mother explained, "and would be good for five years." My family agreed, and the doctors went ahead with the device implantation. Nobody had the time to consider whether the hospital was part of the government's health network or what this surgery's financial consequences might be.

"The doctor told me that the ICD runs on batteries," Papa mused. "Umm-hmm," I nodded. "I think they should have an on/off switch for the device," he continued. "Why?" I asked, baffled. "Because then I can turn it off if I am feeling good, and the batteries will last longer!" Always the one to turn off lights and fans before leaving a room and to never let faucets run longer than necessary, Papa now wanted to conserve his life beyond the five-year promise of technology. "This is not that kind of on/off battery-run device, Papa," I chuckled, picking up a thick blue folder that my mother had placed on the coffee table. "Let's look at your medical reimbursement application." I leafed through Papa's hospital bills, reimbursement documents, health card, and state-issued IDs and drew the following timeline:

September 25, 2007: Hospitalization and surgery.
December 14, 2007: Original reimbursement filed.
Five-month wait.
May 28, 2008: Health department sent a letter stating that the reimbursement application had a totaling error.

June 1, 2008: Revised application with corrected total sent by Amma. *Two-month wait.*

August 18, 2008: Health department sent another letter saying that "justification for an ICD implantation and report of electrophysiological studies are required." These reports were already attached to the original application.

September 8, 2008: Letter sent to health department notifying them of their error and resubmitted copies of requested documents.

Insufferable foot-dragging! The mind-numbing "stupidity" (Graeber 2015) of bureaucracy, which is nevertheless so consequential for the "evil" (Arendt 2000) it can produce, was all too apparent for me in that one blue folder.

I translated and streamlined Papa's story into a petition suitable for official eyes, molding the document to serve a specific purpose—to inform the government of the validity of Papa's case, to demonstrate the health bureaucracy's egregious inefficiency and lack of compassion, and to prompt a quick response and action. This required excising everything but the facts regarding Papa's hospitalization and medical claim. His digressions and parentheses, his trajectory with colonial and postcolonial governments, his self-diagnosed indigestion—in other words, his stories—had no place in an information petition. Michael Jackson (2017, 64) distinguishes between academic and ethnographic writing that seeks to "impress" rather than "express," critiquing the former as self-interested and antisocial as opposed to relational and convivial. Practiced in both these forms, I found myself tasked with straightjacketing and condensing Papa's narrative into something that was even further removed from the impressive and expressive imperatives of communication. If academic jargon was confining and abstract, bureaucratese, I felt, was even more alienating.[12]

As I translated Papa's stories into a litany of typed dates and facts, I intentionally kept one thing intact: his opening sentence. "I am ninety-one years old and a retired government servant." Why not frame the technical facts of his case in moral terms, as Papa had, to ethically tilt the reading of summary details that were to follow? My technomoral tweaking of bureaucratese was intended to make "them"—whoever they might be, in whatever state office—pay attention and feel sorry for how they had treated an elderly man, to the extent that this was possible for functionaries practiced in the skill of "indifference" (Herzfeld 1992). Quite pleased with my work, I showed the letter to my grandfather the next morning. He silently mouthed the words as he scanned the sentences. The document ended by reiterating that the original reimbursement request was filed nearly a year ago and asking why it hadn't been processed. "*Shabash!*" said Papa. Well done.

Still awash in my sense of accomplishment, I showed the petition to Nisha, my colleague at Parivartan. I wanted to make sure I had crossed my t's and dotted my i's on the petition before sending it away. Nisha took one look at the two-plus-page, single-spaced document and told me to cut it down. She then deleted the first sentence—the very one I had kept for its moral heft—and substituted it with, "On December 14, 2007, I filed an application for reimbursement of medical claims, which has not been processed till date." She also deleted the question with which I ended Papa's query—"Why has no action been taken?" Nisha dictated to me exactly what I needed to write instead:

1. Please give me the daily progress made on my application so far: on which date my medical claim application reached which officer and what did this officer do.
2. Please give me the names of the officers who were supposed to take action on my medical claim reimbursement and have not done so.
3. What action will be taken against these officers and by when?
4. By when will I get my reimbursement of medical claim?

I was curious why Nisha instructed me to replace what I thought was one simple question with four new ones. Moreover, I did not quite understand why I should shorten the petition. The RTI Act did not dictate a word limit. I thought I had already trimmed Papa's story into an appropriately "factual" narrative of the kind I imagined officials wanted to read. Ironically, neither Papa's skill at administration and shorthand (which got him hired as an employee of the colonial state) nor my experience gathering information from various sources and condensing complex arguments prepared us to solicit information from the state. Neither Papa's experience in a government bureaucracy nor mine in academia sufficed for this emergent and unfamiliar genre of a rightful bureaucratic demand. If "the dissemination of information . . . had a decisive share in [threatening] . . . the art of storytelling" (Benjamin 2007, 89) in interwar Europe, information petitions in India in 2008 also had a complicated relationship to the art.

Nisha alerted me to the bureaucratic-legalistic rubrics for RTI queries, but didn't have time to explain the reasons for the changes she suggested. I followed her advice to a "t." She gave the newly edited, single-page document a thumbs up. It apparently met the broad aesthetic and substantive criteria of written petitions: it was functional, abbreviated, banal, and mimicked the staccato of the RTI Act itself, substituting the clauses and whereases with a series of who, when, and what questions and facts. I mailed the document and the required 10-rupee fee to the relevant health department PIO. With fingers crossed, Papa, Amma, and I awaited the magic that RTI queries were supposed to produce.

An Ideal Information Query

I soon found out that Nisha's edits for Papa's petition reflected a standardized set of rules followed by RTI activists in Delhi to systematize the use of the law and maximize the possibility of state responsiveness. On a crisp November morning in 2008, I accompanied Arvind and two other Parivartan colleagues to Delhi Public School for an RTI workshop with high schoolers. One of the teachers had invited us because she believed that learning about the transparency law was a "worthwhile exercise" in civic citizenship, even though it had not been easy for her to justify to her administration why high-achieving, academically pressured students should be excused for a two-hour, extra-curricular workshop. This teacher met us at the main entrance of the school's impressive red brick building and led us to a well-appointed lecture hall where thirty-four eleventh graders awaited us. She introduced Arvind to the students, who already seemed to know him because of his TV appearances. Arvind shared our names with the students and dived right in.

"The RTI law [allows us] to ask [for] information from the government. The Supreme Court has said that the RTI is a fundamental right . . . embedded in the right to speech. We can't speak unless we know!" Arvind added that "People pay taxes and they have a right to know how that money is spent by the government. [Because] government officials are servants and people the masters." He then asked the students to name some problems for which the RTI could be used. Hands went up immediately, and a few students voiced "poverty" and "corruption." "These are good but huge issues," said Arvind, urging them to consider more specific problems in break-out groups. We stood around the room as the students brainstormed excitedly and came up with an impressive list of RTI-ripe problems: no traffic cops at intersections; awful sewage systems; poor road conditions and street lighting; routine power cuts; opaque admissions' procedures in schools and colleges; huge backlog of cases in courts; better protection of heritage monuments; airlines losing luggage; lack of care for stray animals; poor implementation of the NREGA law guaranteeing basic employment; unsafe drinking water; disorganization in railways; lack of information on World Bank loan usage; lack of accountability of bad politicians ("They should be arrested!"); no security around shopping centers; corruption in Delhi government's expenditure on commonwealth games, and so on.

My colleagues and I were happily surprised, having expected sixteen-year-olds from largely privileged backgrounds to struggle to think of any examples. We had come prepared with a backup list of issues, just in case they faltered. Arvind lauded the students' efforts and asked them to draft RTI petitions for the problems they had identified. They would have to figure out the department from which to seek information and write an application to the concerned PIO. He cautioned them: "The questions you ask have to be very specific, or you will get vague answers." To illustrate an ideal RTI request, he gave the example of a person whose passport processing had been delayed. How might this individual use the RTI law?

"Begin with the date on the top," instructed Arvind. Then "the subject line, 'Application under Right to Information Act 2005.' The body [of the petition] should ask four questions:

1. Please give me daily progress made on my passport application so far, i.e., on which date my application reached which officer and what did he do with my application.
2. Please give me the names of the officers who were supposed to take action on my application and who have not done so.
3. What action will be taken against these officers and by when for not processing my passport in time?
4. By when will I get my passport?"

I was struck by this prescribed format: Nisha had instructed me in the exact same wording and sequence on Papa's petition. Even though Arvind's sample petition was meant to find out *why* a person's passport had been delayed, none of the questions posed asked "why." Time and time again, at activist-led RTI workshops, I encountered this standard list of what, who, and when queries, but no whys.

I discovered the reason behind this omission while attending a meeting organized by representatives from the Department of Personnel and Training (the agency that implements the RTI law) and the Information Commission (which hears appeals against denial or withholding of information and assesses penalties against errant PIOs). The officials had invited members of local "Resident Welfare Associations" (RWAs) in Delhi to air opinions and grievances about the RTI law. RWAs are independent, generally elected bodies present in almost every middle- and upper-class neighborhood in the city. Run largely by retired men, RWAs organize community events and oversee infrastructure, security, and other collective needs of area residents for which they frequently liaise with government agencies (Srivastava 2015). This meeting was part of that "networking" activity where RWA members who were avid users of the RTI Act had gathered to share their experiences of information retrieval with concerned officials.

The venue was one of many nondescript "complexes" in Delhi, which house a mix of government, commercial, and even educational institutions. The building was scaffolded in bamboo—it was undergoing renovation and looked fairly deserted. I took the stairs up to the appointed floor and made my way to the only room from which sounds emanated. Sixteen men and two women—well-dressed people, middle-aged and older—were seated on neatly arranged chairs, facing a desk for the yet-to-arrive officials. They seemed well-acquainted, chatting animatedly. Some nodded at me as I took a chair near the open windows.

Everyone stood up when three male officials walked in—a formality, I guessed. Just as people had settled into their seats and things were about to begin, a pigeon flew in through a window and unsettled everything. The room rose in uproar. Some men tried to shoo the little creature. Others covered their heads with their hands. "Aa-aa-aa," said one man, beckoning the pigeon toward the window. "Pankhe band karo! [Turn off the ceiling fans!]"—shouted another, worried that the whirling blades would hurt the bird. A third flapped his large handkerchief at the bird to steer it in the direction of the window. The petrified bird flapped its wings, trying vigorously to find an exit. And, after some coaxing, it did. So much for official formality, I chuckled inwardly, as the feathery reminders of the wayward bird floated to the floor.

Windows shut and order restored, the proceedings finally began with a quick round of introductions and a conversation about the issues the attendees used the RTI law for. Only men spoke. They brought up a variety of class-specific "RWA-type" problems, quite like the ones the uncles in my neighborhood discussed every evening: unauthorized building in residential areas, including shanties and commercial establishments; property and income taxes; corrupt real estate deals where much of the transaction happens in black money; municipal agencies not notifying residents about infrastructural work and disruptions; lack of parking space and misuse of public areas for parking, etc.

The conversation then turned to the problems the attendees had experienced with the RTI law. One man complained that government agencies did not follow the legal directive of proactive disclosure, and refused to share of information through websites and other mechanisms. Others were frustrated with the "devil may care" attitude of officialdom, which resulted in inconsistent responses and even willful flouting of the law. "The bureaucracy is . . . playing a guessing game," opined one man, "where they have the upper hand." He gave examples of PIOs who either ignored RTI requests or refused to share information because they knew that most petitioners would not file an appeal. Some PIOs responded with classic bureaucratic excuses: "The file is untraceable." Others directed applicants to check the department website for the information they sought. "Not every person is so hi-fi," grumbled an older gentleman, pointing to access and skill issues. Another suggested that PIOs were not afraid of the RTI law's penalty clause because Information Commissioners were inconsistent in levying fines. "The penalty is needed to keep the PIOs alert," he stressed, "or they will lose all fear of the law."

The officials nodded sympathetically and acknowledged these obstacles. "The word 'untraceable' is not in my dictionary," stated a representative from the information commission, adding that he refused to accept it as a justification during appeal hearings. "If a file is lost, I ask [the PIO] to file an FIR [First Information Report] with the police." The men in the audience hummed appreciatively. But he also cautioned that the penalty clause must be used carefully, or the bureaucracy would push back. He encouraged the petitioners to do what he did instead: "We can all exercise a moral authority. Unpe hasna shuru kar dijiye (start making fun of [the recalcitrant PIOs])!"

A chorus of skeptical hums and snickers filled the room. The audience seemed to question the value of social shaming over legal penalty. One man offered a different solution for official insouciance: flood PIOs with petitions for every issue under the sun. "The RTI law is my boss," he declared proudly, saying that he filed several petitions per day.[13] His tactic was to overwhelm the PIOs with so many applications that they were forced to take notice and change their ways. "Unke naak mein dum kar do [harass them till they can't breathe]," he advised, adding that he had recently sent thirty-five RTI petitions to the same department in a single day. Inundation had nuisance value and could help routinize transparency and information disclosure.

An official behind the desk cringed visibly at this maverick approach. "You have to remember that this *sarkar* [government or state] is yours," he said gently, "and if you pressurize it too much, then it will be less effective." He advised filing short, pithy applications. "A good application should be 150 words to be effective. If it is longer, then you burden the system. Stick to one topic. Don't ask twenty-five questions [in one petition] because it will put you at a disadvantage." He also counseled those gathered to pay close attention to how the RTI law defines information and word their petitions accordingly. "The law says that information is what exists in government records. PIOs can copy and share records in their existing form, but they should not have to generate information." The official advised against posing vague questions like, "when will *x* or *y* work get done," or "when will you end corruption" because they were difficult to answer. And "as a general rule of thumb [you] should not ask 'why' questions. 'Why did I not get my passport' is not an informational question." Posing a "why" question could invalidate an RTI petition, he warned.

I was intrigued by this advice. Nowhere did the text of the RTI law state anything about the invalidity of petitions based on the nature of their questions. "What does 'why' have to do with anything!" I probed Sunil, a Parivartan colleague, a few days later. Sunil gave me a knowing smile and explained that the law defines information as anything that exists in government records in any form, including documents, files, images, and computer data. Officials tend to interpret this narrowly. Sunil offered an example. Suppose you file an RTI application asking why your passport was denied, but the reasons for that denial have not been recorded anywhere. In this case, your request can be refused because the information you demanded is nonexistent. You cannot exert your right to information because you asked an unanswerable "why" question. But if a comment or "noting" in your passport file specifies the reasons for rejection, then accessible "information" exists. However, because state representatives lean toward not documenting the reasoning behind their decisions, as I explain in the chapter 3, "why" questions run aground in the RTI world.

Sunil's explanation clarified why activists avoided "whys" in their "best-practice" four-question formula that I repeatedly observed and replicated on my grandfather's petition. Nisha's strategic advice to delete the "why" question on his application and reword it in terms of "what, who, and when," made sense now—there was likely no note in his health department file indicating why his payment had stalled. She anticipated that Papa would not be able to exercise his right unless he posed properly worded "informational" questions whose answers lived in the pages of a government file. A "why" question was not transparent or factual enough for official eyes. The requirement that information must "sound plausible" (Benjamin 2007, 89) seemed to hold true for informational questions as well. Questions had to mirror the answers they sought: that is, information compressed into "digestible and verifiable facts" (Reed 2006, 175) and readily available for quick access in state records. Because answers to "whys" and other vague queries were not available for "prompt verifiability" (Benjamin 2007, 89) or retrievability, the petitions posing them were illegible in the bureaucratic world of information freedom.

Sunil shook his head in frustration. "The reasons why . . . should be recorded! We have been fighting to have such information included in files." I intervened: "Well, maybe you could pose the informational query in a more creative manner without using 'why.'" I mused about the possible ways to phrase an RTI petition beyond the four-question template that he and other activists routinely used. "But that just says that if you can use words and the English language better, then your petition will be heard," interjected Sunil irritably. "The [RTI] law is not about the creative use of language, Anu!" Even as he chastised me, Sunil admitted that this was indeed happening. State functionaries were compromising the spirit of the law by narrowly interpreting the letter of the law and miring it in technicalities. If individuals desired information from the government, they had to appeal to it primarily in a formalized and abbreviated writing style that mimics statist langue. Indeed, RTI activists were playing a key role in the "socialization [of people] to state linguistic practice" (Cody 2013, 179).

Vineet Kumar, one such activist, ran an RTI helpline. He told me that crafting an appropriate information petition was anything but simple. In addition to using "key phrases [and] the right language," people needed to follow procedural norms. Vineet claimed that 60 percent of the RTI appeals in Delhi get rejected because they are not typed, are not written in English, or lack an index of the attached papers and a list of dates. He mentioned innovative experiments, like an RTI call center in Bihar where people could call in with their queries and these recorded calls were treated as valid information petitions. He also recalled a "touching story" about a villager in Gujarat who filed a petition for information but did not receive a reply. He had heard of an information commissioner in his state who was a good and helpful man. So, the villager wrote his plea on a 3 × 5–inch postcard and mailed it to the commissioner, who accepted it as a valid appeal. "He didn't ask for a properly worded complaint, typed on proper-sized paper!" Vineet exclaimed, suggesting that this commissioner's act was exemplary of the spirit of the RTI law. However, other state representatives were stifling this spirit by insisting on following the letter of the law and reducing it to its technicalities. "Delhi lawyers have found a new life" because of RTI, scoffed Vineet. They often called his hotline, seeking advice on how to word and format petitions and appeals on behalf of people who could afford their services. The ones without such means—like people on the margins in whose name the information campaign arose in rural Rajasthan—sought out NGOs to help draft their applications.

Success?

I received an initial reply to Papa's petition within two weeks. Impressed, I quickly opened the letter, only to discover that the petition had reached the wrong PIO, who had forwarded it to the right one. Two weeks later, I received another letter from the correct PIO requesting some case-related details, which I had already included in the original document. The inefficiency and unaccountability of rules and procedures! The health department staff was performing foot dragging to perfection without obviously flouting the RTI law. Lips pursed in frustration, I typed a curt response restating the facts and my four questions.

A few weeks went by and we heard nothing, so my mother and I decided to visit the zonal health office in Rajinder Nagar to inquire about Papa's case; this *chakkar marna,* or making the rounds of a government department, is a common part of the petitioning process, as Mathur (2019) contends. We knew Rajinder Nagar well because most of Papa's family members had been resettled in that area as refugees from Pakistan. As a child, I often visited their humble, single-level "dollhouses" packed with people, metal trunks, canvas holdalls, and other things. I played with cousins in tiny rooms with even tinier, barred windows. Getting free candy from one of my great uncles, who ran a small grocery store in one of the rooms in his house, was the highlight of my visits. This beloved store had long since shuttered; upward mobility had led most of our family members out of Rajinder Nagar. The dollhouses had given way to shiny, multilevel apartment buildings with stone and glass exteriors and granite interiors. Returning there after decades felt disorienting.

As I reminisced while waiting to meet the chief of the zonal health office, Amma began conversing with one of his assistants. She let on that we had filed an RTI inquiry about Papa's reimbursement delay. The assistant's eyes widened instantly. "RTI?" he repeated. "Oh, ab to aapka kaam ho jayega [now your work will get done]." I wasn't sure if I detected frustration, resignation, or matter-of-factness in his voice, but I got the message that we need not wait for the big boss. The RTI petition was about to work its magic.

Eight more weeks passed. We were well past the thirty-day deadline for PIOs to respond to RTI queries. February rolled around, and just as I began preparing to file an appeal, it happened. Amma received a phone call from the health department. The representative informed her that Papa's reimbursement had been approved, and the money would be disbursed after the new federal budget was announced at the end of February.

Papa was delighted. "*Wah* (Bravo)!" he said, applauding the power of the new RTI law. "Chalo, mooh meetha karte hain"—let's sweeten our mouths to celebrate this auspicious occasion, he suggested, and I was game. I dashed over to our neighborhood *halwaai* or sweet maker, and picked up a half kilogram of *jalebis*. These otherworldly, crispy fried dough spirals dipped in thick, cardamom-laced sugar syrup were a family favorite, made fresh daily at 4 PM. I got the first hot, drippy batch that afternoon. Amma had chai ready when I returned. We settled around our wooden dining table, slurping tea, licking our fingers, and congratulating ourselves on successfully working the health bureaucracy.

However, there was an interesting caveat. While the RTI law helped my grandfather obtain his health entitlement, it failed to deliver on his right to information. Papa received approval for his medical reimbursement after filing an RTI petition, but he never got answers to his informational questions. We did not find out the names of the health department officials who processed Papa's file, when they did so, or if they would face disciplinary action for the delay. The magic conjured by Nisha's petition template with its four standard questions took the shape of monetary payment in May 2009; it came without explanations or accountability per se. This, as I would learn, was a common experience, and a point of activist contention.

I interacted with many users of the law who shared our experience. "RTI se kaam ho jata hai [RTI gets work done]" was a frequent activist refrain. They appreciated the law's success as a "grievance redress" mechanism. "The RTI works better than bribes! If you ask the four magical questions, your work gets done within fifteen to twenty days," Nisha claimed. Others felt that this did not necessarily address the larger aim of information disclosure. Limited improvement in governmental efficiency through individual RTI petitions—as in Papa's case—could not stand in for widespread state transparency, which many activists saw as the law's main goal. For instance, Ashish Patel, an activist involved in a national RTI impact study undertaken by the RTI Assessment and Advocacy Group in 2008-9, expressed optimism about the reported increase in RTI petitions across the country. He saw this as a sign of rising public consciousness and empowerment, but he asserted that the ultimate measure of the law's success would be a decline in RTI queries. The law would triumph when it obviated its own need. That is, when the government shared information of its own accord, citizens wouldn't need to use the RTI at all. By that measure, the law was falling short. Not only was the lack of proactive disclosure on the part of state agencies a matter of constant activist frustration, but disclosure of information sought through formal petitions was also not a given. Although its success as a mechanism of citizen complaint and redress was praiseworthy, the RTI was less successful in rendering transparent behind-the-scenes state work—the whos, whens, and hows, but most importantly the whys.

And the Technomoral of the Story Is . . .

Even though my grandfather's legal petition failed to furnish the information he sought from the government, it brought him his refund. What else did it do? What forms of communication, personhood, and activist practices did it inhibit, produce, and normalize?

Appeals to the state for rightful information and the process of putting these appeals together are significant "for the stories they will recall" (Reed 2006, 174). Papa's tales leading up to the petition are a case in point. However, these stories disappeared in the final document, which came with a different set of normative constraints that I, as scribe, had to follow. The logic of information, and the translations required to frame everyday life in legal terms, got in the way of storytelling.

Petitioning entails narrativizing experience and wrongdoing while replicating the legalese of law and the officialese of procedure (Cody 2013).[14] RTI petitions, like the law itself, mirror bureaucratic rationalization and simplification (Weber 1968); miniaturization, as James Scott (1998) reminds us, is an exercise in legibility and discipline. As activists and petitioners follow official rules and formulaic writing, they become normalized as certain kinds of citizen-subjects and also help normalize statist communication styles as modes of protest and claims making. This reproduction of official langue bureaucratizes everyday life. The transparency law in that sense functions as a governmental mechanism that disperses "modalities and spaces of rule" (Chalfin 2010, 91). It helps to replicate and spread officialese while overwhelming more enchanting forms of experience sharing, agitating, and complaining about governance.

The uncles I overheard in my neighborhood park every evening and the RTI petitioners I encountered over the course of my fieldwork narrated their complaints in rich detail. Their stories, like my grandfather's, partook in broader politicomoral criticisms of governmental failure and corruption that suffuse the Indian public sphere (Gupta 1995, 2012). RTI queries constitute a recent form these criticisms take through which people can lodge formal complaints, demand an official hearing, and seek redress. Bureaucratic-legal demands, however, tend to reduce these claims and protests to banal and concise appeals made by supplicants to a higher power; they are not a creative condemnation of that very power. My grandfather expressed his frustration with the state as a thick, moralizing tale about his career in the government, displacement, retirement, old age, ill health, and social standing. His meandering narration, displaying a storyteller's "counsel . . . [and] incomparable aura" (Benjamin 2007, 108–9), was nothing like the records my mother had collected about his case—a blue folder of paperwork that cataloged, factually and chronologically, Papa's emergency hospitalization, out-of-pocket payments, and application and appeals for reimbursement. The blue folder represented exactly what statist proceduralism called for: paper, paper trails, and pared-down information, all in a reasoned mode, disinterested and disengaged from dense social context. It prioritized the "aesthetics of [bureaucratic] logic and language" (Riles 1998, 386) over sensual meaning, textured life histories, and affective charge (Cody 2013).

RTI activists undertake the pedagogic project of mimicking and disseminating statist words and ways as a form of countertrickery. Their simulation anticipates official subterfuge of rules and norms, outmaneuvering "bureaucraft" (James 2012) with craftiness. The standardized petition template attempts to preempt official trickery by design. What one activist described to me as the "four magical questions" must appear exactly so in order to do something—to beget results. The rational and utilitarian aesthetic of the petition is understood to have the generative capacity "to act upon the beholder" (Reed 2006, 172). It is a key actant in the RTI network, which helps produce official responses, and much more.

The petition template has "strict criteria for correct form" (Reed 2006, 171). This skeletal pattern (Riles 1998, 385), with its mathematical function-like structure and its input–output, solution-oriented logic, is endlessly reproducible. Following it "enables a continuous, real-time critique of the state," as Sunil put it to me, albeit in statist terms. This pattern reifies official langue, procedure, and style. This makes it risky, because, as Audre Lorde (2007) warned, "the master's tools will never dismantle the master's house. They may allow us temporarily to beat [the master] at his own game, but they will never enable us to bring about genuine change" (112). Contesting opacity and outwitting a "cunning state" (Randeria 2003) with statist langue achieves momentary successes—refunds, grievance redress, and even information—but it keeps intact the mode and structures of mastery—in other words, the expertise-based, hierarchical, disciplinary logic and force of liberal, bureaucratic state power (Brown 1995; Foucault 1995).

Indeed, simulating statist ways helps reproduce faith in the promise of democracy and idealized bureaucracy. David Graeber (2015) reminds us that "all bureaucracies are to a certain degree utopian, in the sense that they propose an abstract ideal that real human beings can never live up to" (26-27). We know this and yet we perpetuate this powerful fiction, for bureaucratic systems "create a culture of complicity . . . [and] all of us start playing along" (26). The RTI template perhaps represents that complicity in a fiction: it expresses activists' aspiration to manifest an elusive Weberian utopia by holding up a procedural, rule-bound mirror to officials in an attempt to make them follow bureaucratic norms. Petitioning for information also renews a belief in the law as an ideal corrective and in an idealized democratic state that is subject to the law and responsive to its citizens. While full of promise, such fetishization of the RTI law as a deus ex machina that can rectify everything also carries dangers.

Activists are aware of these dangers. Shekhar Singh, whom I introduced in chapter 1, was cautious about "overselling" the prowess of the law. "It is a very difficult task. How does one sell [the RTI] to the public and yet be able to get across that [it has] pitfalls and problems? . . . I am uncomfortable with the people who paint a very rosy picture [and] sing about all the wonderful things that the [RTI Act] is achieving," said Singh. "Because if you start making people believe that all they have to do is file this little application and suddenly all their problems will disappear, I mean that it is better than going to a temple and giving some money there, then I am afraid you are going to create a situation where there is going to be a fair amount of disillusionment. That's the danger—that we oversell it [and] build up people's expectations a lot." Like a ritually ordered offering to God, a properly composed RTI petition promises desired change. This near-religious faith in the power of law as an agent of democratic transformation is risky because it might fail to realize liberal democratic state norms—indeed, these are the very norms that conceal liberalism's constitutive illiberality (Hindess 2004), given its checkered bourgeois and colonial legacies.

Beyond generating such idealizations and faith, a standard RTI petition also constructs a normative author—the legible citizen-petitioner. This author, however, is not a unique person who, like a turtle, carries a biography on its back, but a copycat, disembodied citizen produced by the logic of repetition inscribed into tightly formatted RTI petitions (Cody 2013). These "lifeless statements of fact" (Reed 2006, 175) about what are often matters of life and death, as in my grandfather's case, materialize bureaucratic "impersonality": generic citizenship cemented by formulaic words and patterns. Their mechanical codes thin out and bracket off (Riles 1998) the vernacular density and sludge of personhood—situated in space, time, and social relations—because it is irrelevant for the official time being. Conformity and bureaucracy overwhelm particularity and individual life stories, producing a cloned and substitutable citizen who could be anyone.

The design of the RTI petition "makes individual response conform to an abstract pattern" and hails a subject who is "unable to . . . go beyond format coordinates" (Reed 2006, 168). This is an allegory for normative liberal citizenship itself: generically equal and formal. The stylized RTI petition template anticipates cloned, "authorless" citizenship stripped of flesh, blood, and peculiarity. If followed faithfully and in the proper sequence, this pattern also portends success in making oneself legible to official eyes and eligible to question the state. Does this fill-in-the-blank, formulaic pattern render petitioners "passive actors" (Reed 2006, 168)? Adam Reed (2006) contends that it does, that those who fill standardized prison forms in Papua New Guinea—both prisoners and wardens—sense that "agency lies not with them but with the document technology" (168). Unlike Reed, I argue that the subjectification and subjection of petitioners as normalized citizens, as Foucault would describe it, does not equate to a lack of agency. Indeed, conformity and even passivity are enactments of agency under conditions of constraint (Mahmood 2001). Acting out a normative script is as agentive as resisting or exceeding it;

it is not necessarily experienced as robotic control. Papa certainly did not feel passive in the process of petitioning. I experienced the strain of conformity as Papa's scribe, as I tried to copy faithfully the expected bureaucratic patterns and produce a "good specimen of a particular genre" (Riles 1998, 381), in this case the RTI petition. This was important for me and my activist colleagues because this document would be a coagent in Papa's exercise of rightful citizenship, an actant that would shape material outcomes (Latour 1992, 2010).

I end with a caveat. I am aware that my analysis of Papa's RTI story goes against that which has been so vital in shaping this chapter: Walter Benjamin's spirited defense of storytelling in the age of modern facts and information. A story, he argued, has "chaste compactness which precludes . . . analysis" (Benjamin 2007, 91); it doesn't "come to us . . . already shot through with explanation" (89). Even as I tried to avoid replicating the stiltedness of the bureaucratic documents I focus on here, I realize that my rendition is burdened with explanation. If "it is half the art of storytelling to keep a story free from explanation as one reproduces it" (89), then perhaps I have let the nature of the object of my study, not to mention academic imperatives, get the better of my storytelling impulse—a normative straitjacketing of communication of a different sort, perhaps.

～

I now pivot away from the social life of RTI petitions to focus on their bureaucratic life. Even as petitioners are compelled to address the state in its own authoritative langue, how has the legal requirement of transparency reshaped bureaucratic inscriptions and modes of communication? If information is that which is stored in government records, then how do these routine bureaucratic scripts become enlivened and morph in the world of state transparency?

3

Where the State Goes to Hide

Bureaucracy, Bureaucraft, and the Limits of Transparency

> Researching Anonymous felt like following a thread through a dark and twisty path strewn with rumors, lies, secrets. . . . Beyond the consequences of its actions, Anonymous's organizational structure itself felt similarly convoluted and bewildering. . . . This was no static labyrinth. . . . It was an infinite machine operating a tight recursive loop wherein mazes generated maze-generating mazes.
>
> —GABRIELLA COLEMAN, *Hacker, Hoaxer, Whistleblower, Spy: The Many Faces of Anonymous*

There is a strange resonance between Gabriella Coleman's description of the hacktivist group Anonymous and my own encounters with state bureaucracies. At first glance, an avowedly antibureaucratic group of trolls and tricksters couldn't be more unlike a hierarchical, rule-bound, top-down state machine. Yet if you substitute Anonymous with "bureaucracy" in the epigraph above—or better yet, just switch the proper noun "Anonymous" with "anonymous"—you have an intriguing proximity between Coleman's interest and my own: bureaucracy as an infinitely convoluted machine that is, by its very (Weberian) definition, and, in the Indian case, its colonial British antecedents, secretive. What happens when this rationalized apparatus meant to preserve insiderness and opacity is legally mandated to accommodate transparency?

In this chapter I ethnographically enliven the apparently lifeless object called bureaucracy—often referred to as a machine, iron cage, or steel frame—that ironically administers life. I take my cue from Laura Bear and

Nayanika Mathur (2015), who make a case for an anthropology of bureaucracy that sees it as more than a mind-dumbing governance apparatus. State bureaucracy is also an "expression of a social contract between citizens and officials" (18), organized to achieve public good. Under neoliberalism, "fiscal austerity, marketization . . . [and] transparency" (28) become desired public goods. Bear and Mathur ask us to attend to the "ethical and affective conflicts" (31) that these rational-technical neoliberal public goods engender in bureaucratic institutions. Yael Navaro-Yashin (2012), in a similarly counter-Weberian stance, makes a case for a "sensorial," affective rendering of governance (33).

I use the Indian transparency law as a prism to refract bureaucracy as a technomoral ensemble of ideals and practices, formalities and informalities, material calculations and embodied affect, and ethical dilemmas. This is my attempt to "enchant" (Bennet 2001) an objectified and purportedly unimaginative realm, "to see it as animated, as having its own charge" (Navaro-Yashin 2012, 33), and to explore ethnographically the dangerous entanglement between the disinterested techniques of bureaucratic administration on the one hand and the exertion of state power on the other; between the craft and craftiness of rules and procedures that may well be "stupid" (Graeber 2015) but that also produce violent effects (Gupta 2012); between rational indifference (Herzfeld 1992) and affective structures of feeling (Williams 1977); and between visible and invisible flows of power (Ballestero 2012; Sanders and West 2003) that work in tandem to hide things in plain sight. This messy push and pull sheds light on why even "in the laws promulgated by the most benign democracies lurks the possibility of bureaucratic repression" (Herzfeld 1992, 6). This is as true for activist-demanded laws, like the RTI Act, as for top-down legislative dictates. Even as the RTI ostensibly meets the activist demand for public information, information guarantees neither state accountability nor legibility (Valverde and Moore 2019). In practice, the RTI materializes more hiding places for the state. There is an irresolvable tension between bureaucratic state power and transparency, I argue, that is fortified by ordinary state work and that a sunshine law cannot overcome (see also Sharma 2013).

I almost wasn't allowed to enter the venue where a workshop for PIOs—government employees who process RTI requests—was about to begin. It was a December morning in 2008. After a painfully sluggish twenty-five-kilometer drive, I found myself at the auditorium entrance, frustrated and pleading with a man to let me in.

"What is your name and government affiliation?" he asked me, his lanyard identifying him as a state functionary. I explained that I was an academic researcher interested in learning about the RTI law. He shook his head. The training was strictly for PIOs. I persisted, explaining that I had obtained permission to observe. Now he eyed me warily. Why did I need to observe? Who gave me permission? Before I could answer, the high-ranking Indian Administrative Services (IAS) official who had invited me to attend the workshop happened to walk by. He gave me a nod of recognition, likely judging my predicament by the look on my face. "Inhe aane do [Let her enter]," he instructed his junior colleague. The gentleman blocking the door stepped aside deferentially. The bureaucratic hierarchy had worked out in my favor, but only momentarily; the same staffer refused to share workshop materials with me once inside the auditorium. These packets were limited in number, he explained, and PIOs would get priority. This was understandable, enough even though I wondered if I was being put in my place; and never mind the irony of not having access to documents about a state transparency law at a government-organized RTI workshop! I pleaded some more, and the gentleman relented; he would give me a packet if there were any left over.

The plush auditorium was at capacity with nearly two hundred PIOs; of these, barely 10 percent were women. Some attendees flipped through workshop materials while others conversed among themselves, complaining about the obscure location and how difficult it was to reach. The ambient buzz quieted as the room was called to order and the chief guest, a top-tier male civil servant, was invited to make opening remarks.

"The RTI law has the potential to transform the nature of governance and the nature of the relation between those who rule and those who are ruled," he began. "It makes government accountable to the governed. *This is democracy.* The RTI has a huge mission. Firstly, good, noncorrupt, and responsive government and secondly, empowerment of the common man.... For sixty years, [officials] were told not to give out any information—a continuation of the colonial mind-set. Accountability in [this] setup was only to one's superior officer.... But now you are accountable to the people, [who] can question your decisions.... Every government employee . . . even a [lower level] Group D employee . . . is an elite citizen. The RTI Act asks you to use your knowledge and resources as elite citizens to empower other citizens. There is a lack of awareness among PIOs [about the RTI Act].... Their attitude seems to be, find some exemption provision to deny information. This attitude must change. The law is very clear. Everything *has* to be disclosed." He ended by underscoring, once again, the monumentality of the RTI law as he exhorted the PIOs to do their part in undoing colonial secrecy and normalizing transparency.

The unambiguous message of the chief guest—that the RTI signified a fundamental reorganization of democratic rule and administrative practice—set a somber tone that was echoed by the two workshop facilitators. Mr. Dev and Mr. Goyal, both government employees, opened their PowerPoint presentation with a world map of countries colored red and green. The taller, leaner Dev identified the green shapes as protransparency nations: "All countries that have comprehensive RTIs in place are democratic." He explained that sunshine laws had expanded worldwide since the late 1980s, when the Cold War ended and economic liberalization looked off. The first dealt a blow to authoritarian state secrecy in the Soviet bloc, and the second opened nations like India to deregulated economic flows. To attract foreign investment and combat corruption, governments had to ease up license regimes and enact disclosure laws. Thus, implementing information freedom signaled a country's progrowth commitment and democratic credentials. In India, Dev elaborated further, this was enabled by a grassroots struggle that demanded state transparency from below. He proceeded to describe in glowing terms MKSS's campaign to establish information as a right.

Then Dev and Goyal turned to the nitty-gritty of the Indian RTI Act. "The principle behind RTI is maximum disclosure, *suo moto* disclosure," began Goyal, conveying the importance of sharing information when so petitioned as well as proactively, before veering into a clause-by-clause overview of the law.

The questions the PIOs raised during this presentation reminded me of the questions I had when I first read the law pamphlet, revealing confusion about some fundamental terms. Does "public authority" include private institutions that are partially funded by the state? What precisely counts as "information"? Are all government records, including notes of internal discussions, seen as information? How can PIOs determine whether petitioners desire information for public interest or for private or commercial gain, given that they are not required to reveal the reason why they are seeking information? Coming from PIOs, who constitute the front line of information sharing, these queries were not surprising. Clarity is critical. If they fail to share information promptly and appropriately, they are personally liable and may be fined up to 25,000 rupees.

The facilitators answered these questions by iterating the same overall message: err on the side of disclosure. "Information sharing must be complete, accurate, and timely," Dev stated. "All information that a public authority holds is in the public interest. But is the disclosure of all information in the public interest? No. The RTI Act allows exemptions." He and Goyal spent a considerable amount of time discussing section 8 of the law, which specifies when information may be legally withheld for reasons related to national security and sovereignty. PIOs bombarded them with anxious queries regarding lawful exemptions and denial of information. Could they reject petitions that were "voluminous" or "frivolous and vexatious," or that constituted a national security risk, or ones that posed "noninformational" questions? There were instances when information could be legitimately withheld, replied the facilitators, but they also urged the PIOs to exert caution when invoking section 8. "You can take cover of the exemption clause only if you give a 'reasonable' reason," warned Goyal. "Don't apply two or three clauses [randomly]—8(1)(g) or 8(1)(h) or 8(1)(j)—and think *ki kuch to ho hi jayega* [something or the other will work out]. As officials, think of yourselves not as owners of the information but as custodians or trustees." Dev nodded and smiled encouragingly. "Please don't look at this as us versus them; that you have to give information to outside citizens. You are citizens too. This is your right too. When you receive an application, ask yourself a question: What is the harm in giving information? If there is no harm, then give it."

I use this PIO workshop to enter into the bureaucratic lifeworld of the RTI Act: how it has affected routine state work and elicited varied reactions from officials at different tiers. I do so to draw out the tensions between the logics and ideals of bureaucracy and transparency that limit the latter's reach. State transparency, "as it is used in contemporary globalspeak, presumes a surface to power that can be seen through and an interior that can, as a result, be seen" (Sanders and West 2003, 16). Sunshine laws position government documents as the locus of this hidden interior that must be revealed. Yet as Latour (2010) asks, "Who has said that the central institutions on which contemporary civilization are based should be simple and fully opened to the gaze of the ordinary citizen?" (vii). This chapter illuminates the constitutive antagonism between transparency and bureaucracy by focusing on the everyday fortifications of bureaucratic life or what Ilana Feldman (2008) calls its "form, shape, and habits" (14)—administrative hierarchy, records, formal procedures, and informal customary practices—that stand in the way of transparency.

While at odds with each other, transparency and bureaucracy are both firmly entwined with the worldviews of enlightenment and modernity (Ballestero 2012; Sanders and West 2003). Transparency references the modernist connection between visibility, truth, and objectivity. Bureaucracy, as a rationalized and calculable form par excellence, manifests modernity like no other prior structural principle or form. In Weber's (2006) words, the "fully developed bureaucratic apparatus compares with other organizations exactly as does the machine with non-mechanical modes of production. Precision, speed, unambiguity, knowledge of files, continuity . . . unity [and] strict subordination . . . are raised to the optimum point" (57). When working as it should, this hierarchical, rule-bound, rational, "dehumanized" (58), and predictable mode of organizing social and state institutions is not only necessary and ideal but also enduring. As Weber famously put it, "Where administration has been completely bureaucratized, the resulting system of domination is practically indestructible" (62).

The Weberian tale about bureaucracy as streamlined perfection is an evolutionary and functionalist one. Bureaucracy signifies progress, advancement, efficiency, and "technical superiority" (Weber 2006, 57). Given this dominant lore, a critical examination of state organization, operation, and breakdown in the Global South can be read as a narrative of lag and lack that typifies Third Worldness—the condition of "not quite" modernity, of imperfect and corrupted mimicry (Bhabha 1997). To prevent such a misreading of my argument about the bureaucratic subterfuge of governmental transparency in India, I want to stress at the outset that my purpose is not to single out India as an example of a particularly dysfunctional or even a malintentioned state; rather, I use ethnographic evidence from India to trouble the Weberian universal ideal of bureaucracy. I signal the impossibility of a perfectly transparent bureaucratic machine and show that what appears as rational and calculated administration is also calculating; machinations are integral to the machine.

Here I reference Erica James's (2012) idea of "bureaucraft." Focusing on the humanitarian aid apparatus in Haiti, and making a linguistic connection with witchcraft, James coins this term to explain how opacity and public corruption allegations are connected. Like witchcraft and sorcery, the obscurity of the aid bureaucracy is interpreted by people as malevolent and self-interested; it is used to explain why relief projects fail, or why aid regimes benefit some and harm others. "The ambiguity, secrecy, and opacity of [bureaucrats'] mandates and practices generate accusations characteristic of bureaucraft, alongside the covert acts that may underlie their work" (James 2012, 70). I invoke bureaucraft to describe ordinary state work: daily techniques, normally hidden from public view, that allow administrative institutions to function. Formal hierarchical protocol, rules, procedures, and unwritten but widely shared customary expectations that shape insider culture comprise the routine stuff of bureaucraft. This craft is already crafty. Fitting complex, lived, and unpredictable realities into objective frameworks and ensuring predictable results while maintaining the administrative machine requires more than a mechanistic, dehumanized application of legal rules and rational calculation. It requires creative interpretation, affective performativity, and craftiness as much as secretive, malicious actions.

In the next section, I draw out the fundamental tension between bureaucratic hierarchy and transparency by focusing on the practices and positioning of PIOs at the forefront of information disclosure battles. I then spotlight state records to reveal how ordinary bureaucraft techniques produce secrecy, including who records what, how they record it, and what they leave out. In the concluding section, I consider why the idea of a bureaucratically organized transparent state is a contradiction in terms.

Between Bosses and Masses, or How Hierarchy Heckles Transparency

November 2008: Mr. B, PIO, department P, agreed. December 2008: Mr. H, PIO, department R, refused. January 2009: Ms. R, PIO, department H, refused; Mr. G, PIO, department M, refused. March 2009: Mr. D, PIO, department E, agreed; Mr. Y, PIO, department F, refused.

Organizing one-on-one meetings with PIOs outside of training workshops proved harder than I had imagined, as the excerpt from my cold-call records show. Most PIOs seemed wary or taciturn at first. Take the case of just one section of Delhi's municipal department, whose PIOs I called randomly from an online list to request a meeting. A few turned me down outright. Others were suspicious. Who was I? Why did I want to talk to them? Did I represent an NGO registered with the government? Was I a lawyer seeking information to implicate them in a case? Did I represent the media, looking to spin a scandal? Some PIOs explained that their bosses had forbidden them to talk to the media, which, as one put it, "has a vested interest . . . in sensationalist breaking news."

I tried to allay their distrust, clarifying my position as an academic and independent researcher, an Indian based in the United States, and a volunteer with RTI organizations in Delhi. For some, that sufficed. "If this is for your own project," said one PIO graciously, "then you are most welcome." Others asked for my business card at workshops to authenticate my institutional bearings. Still others made me follow a tight protocol before we could meet.

Mr. Bajaj was one such PIO. After verifying that I was a legitimate interlocutor over the phone, he said he would talk to me if his boss allowed it. He told me to seek permission from his department's deputy secretary, or D.S., an elite IAS officer. The D.S. in turn referred me to his own superior: "As a government officer, I am bound by a certain code of conduct. Please talk to my joint secretary." The J.S. agreed.

Even with these approvals, reaching Bajaj was convoluted. We were to meet at 2:30 PM on a Tuesday at his office: North Block, Raisina Hill. Raisina Hill is perhaps the most iconic symbol of (post)colonial governance, power, and stateliness in India. It consists of Rashtrapati Bhawan, the Indian president's residence that formerly housed the British Viceroy, and North and South Blocks, two secretariat buildings that now house important ministries. In all my years in Delhi, I had only gazed at these Lutyens-designed sandstone buildings—in a hybrid colonial-European and Mughal architectural style—from afar and on television. I had no reason to want to be inside one of these grand structures—until that Tuesday.

It was just after 2 PM when I trudged up Raisina Hill from the Central Secretariat metro stop. Taking in the spectacular geometry of power—the huge center dome of the Rashtrapati Bhawan flanked by the North and South Blocks—felt at once familiar and intimidating. I veered right, climbing the stairs toward North Block and passing armed guards. Once inside, I stepped through metal detectors to reach the reception desk, where I was asked to provide the name of the person I had come to see. The receptionist checked his directory and dialed Bajaj's extension—no answer. He motioned me toward the chairs. "Bajaj sir is not at his desk."

I sat down and took in the reception area. A long, spacious hall with sandstone walls and beautiful arches was randomly interrupted by frosted glass partitions; a bowl of marigold petals here, a tangle of cables there; and a metal detector at the far end that looked out of place. The interior was an uninspired pastiche, a palimpsest of functional renovations conjuring none of the awe or cohesiveness of the exterior. Yet I knew that what took place routinely within these utilitarian, even haphazard spaces produced the idea of the state as an organized, centralized, and singular authority. As an imposing colossus, the imagined state was greater than the sum of these banal, everyday parts (Fuller and Bénéï 2000; Hansen and Stepputat 2001; Sharma and Gupta 2006).

Fifteen minutes later, I returned to the receptionist's desk. He dialed again and got a response this time. "Achha, to aap interview ke liye aayi hain [oh, so you are here for an interview]," he remarked nonchalantly. I presumed Bajaj had to state a reason to allow me entry. The receptionist handed me a pass and directed me upstairs. I looked at the pass, which listed the joint secretary's name. Why would Bajaj not want to put his name on record as having met with me? Perhaps he was being especially guarded. I took one flight of stairs to a wide and long hallway. It was scrubbed clean and lined with potted plants and flowers floating in shallow, brass bowls. I walked past a series of closed doors with brass nameplates. These rooms housed high-ranking civil servants, secretaries and joint secretaries of various ministries. A big sign on the home secretary's office door read, "Entry Strictly Prohibited Except for Official Business." It was at once daunting and ironic to see this brazen declaration of inaccessibility in the age of state transparency, participation, and public accountability. A telling sign of the times?

When I reached the room listed on my pass, its door was closed. A sign noted the location of the official's personal assistant (P.A.). Loathe to knock, and figuring that I already had the J.S.'s approval to meet with Bajaj, I chose to seek out the P.A. instead. I took the elevator up to another floor. This hallway was different from the last, with no planters, brass bowls, or grand doors with ornate plaques. Down the hall, a sign directed me to the RTI section. Ah! I might find Bajaj there. Abandoning my search for the P.A., I followed the arrow toward the RTI office but couldn't locate it. I finally asked someone for help. She instructed me to go back around the corner to the fourth door on the left. I had walked right past the RTI section, apparently.

I retraced my steps and found a bland door bearing many signs, one of which indicated, in small type, that an RTI cell was located there. I knocked and entered a standard shared office space: white walls, five desks, and tall metal storage cabinets. The person at the desk nearest to the door directed me to Mr. Bajaj, who was tucked away behind a partition and some cabinets. He looked up as I approached his desk. "Anu Sharma," I offered. "I am Bajaj," he responded, motioning me to sit. I had finally managed to reach him.

Bajaj and I spoke for about forty-five minutes, during which we were interrupted twice when his superiors summoned him. I found him to be a pleasant but cautious man who gave measured responses to my questions. Bajaj viewed the RTI law as a positive force. "Globalization," he began, "has changed the world. People have access to all kinds of information on the net. Information is power and is necessary for development. And it is a known fact that corruption has gone down in the government in the last two to three years." He added that the RTI law had helped "increase the efficiency [of government offices] somewhat." For PIOs, it also brought stress. They had to process information petitions within thirty days or face a penalty. "Is the penalty clause necessary?" I queried. "Do you think it is unfair to the PIOs?" He shrugged. "The penalty is a deterrent for those who are not working, who are lackadaisical. Aise logo'n mein thoda sa dar baitha hai [Such people have become a little afraid]." "Do your PIO colleagues support the RTI law?" I persisted. "Fifty-fifty," he answered. "Fifty percent oppose it.... They are forced to give information now." He added that PIOs are also frustrated because RTI work "is a drain on their time. They get the same salary for doing two jobs." As PIO, he processed about fifty RTI applications and five appeals monthly, which took up about half of his regular work time.

When I asked Bajaj if the RTI was good for citizens, he replied, "RTI is a potent *purza* [tool] in the hands of citizens. Voh kisi bhi file ko dekh sakte hain [they can look at any file], which was not possible earlier. But people also misuse the RTI." Bajaj named RTI petitioners who were infamous among PIOs. "Goyal, Agarwal, Sahni.... They are in the habit of making repeated applications to all departments. They have made it their daily *dhandha* [business] to pester officials. They follow a set format for their petitions and ask the same fifty questions each time." Then there are those who request "voluminous information." Bajaj told me about a petition for which he had to compile a three-hundred-page cabinet note. "These are frivolous and vexatious people," he declared, who accounted for 20 percent of RTI applicants. Some "unaware" people also ask unanswerable questions. "'Why have you not done *x*?' or 'When will you do *x*?' These are noninformational questions! The [law says] that [we] can't create information [but give] what is existing. We are only responders, not creators of information." Bajaj repeated what I had heard time and time again at PIO workshops. Although he could reject applications posing unanswerable questions or requesting information that no longer existed, "my motto is not to deny information," he iterated, as long as the petitions fit the parameters of the law.

When I asked how the RTI could be improved, Bajaj mentioned two things. First, "more awareness generation among the public" about the proper use of the law; and second, "capacity building of public authorities," including infrastructural support for PIOs beyond training workshops. Bajaj gestured toward the decrepit file cabinets, old computers, and piles of paperwork in his office. "Do you see what I have to work with?" he said frustratedly; poor record organization made it difficult to find requested materials. I nodded sympathetically, recalling my experience with the district office of births and deaths, which had lost my mother's birth certificate application. When she and I visited the office to inquire about this loss, we saw stacks of papers and files lying in a partially covered veranda, getting splattered with rainwater; no one had bothered to bring them inside. Small wonder they couldn't find Mom's application. Bajaj smiled ruefully. "We need better file and computer storage facilities and electronic record management so that retrieving information is easier. Section 4 of the RTI law mandates that all state records must be computerized and all departments must be networked. India has made tremendous progress in software," he remarked, but somehow the digital revolution had not touched state work as much as it should have.

⁓

PIO Shah echoed the sentiments of Bajaj, even using the same phrases to express his frustrations. It was as if all PIOs shared an insider vocabulary learned through workshops. Like Bajaj, Shah was not easy to reach. I had to prove to him beforehand, on the phone, that I was not a whistleblower or a journalist with suspicious intentions. His trailer-like office was tucked away at one edge of a large recreational-cum-institutional complex in Delhi. After circling the complex several times and asking around, I finally found him holed up in a dim, poorly ventilated shed, hidden behind stacks of dusty files. The shabby metal and plywood furniture signaled that this space housed lower-end government employees. Indeed, Shah bore no markers of rank or class privilege. Dressed in a simple checkered shirt, pants, and open-toed sandals, he spoke primarily in Hindi with a few English phrases (rendered in italic below) thrown in. He also kept looking at the door during our conversation, as if expecting eavesdroppers; as if he were doing something he wasn't supposed to; as if he did not want to be seen talking to me.

"RTI is a very good thing," Shah began, "but 70 to 80 percent of the RTI applicants use the law as a weapon. People misuse the RTI for *vested interest, not public interest.*" He complained about "*serial petitioners*": "Yesterday, I received thirty-five applications from the same person asking questions about *unauthorized construction* in different neighborhoods. . . . Why does this person want information about neighborhoods where he doesn't live!" Shah threw his hands up in disbelief. "Habitual complainers should be shamed and punished! Some people ask for ten-year records. Or they ask fifty questions about the entire administration of the government of India! And some people don't know the difference between *asking questions and asking for information,* [sending] silly applications [that] have *no meaning*. They waste time, and our work suffers. There is a need to create awareness among the masses about *voluminous information* and *noninformational questions*" so that PIOs' workloads can be lightened. Shah suggested amending the RTI law as follows: allow only one question per petition, increase the filing fee from 10 to 500 rupees, and require a clear statement of the reasons for seeking information. "Petitions must explain what public purpose will be served by this information and what [the petitioner] will do with it. Otherwise, all these *odd, frivolous, malicious* applications by *unreasonable* people will weaken the goal of the RTI."

The English words that Shah used marked a pattern much like the activist template for RTI petitions I described in chapter 2. These stock phrases comprised an archive of bureaucratese and red flags that allowed PIOs to establish ground rules for processing RTI applications—and, dare I say, for rationalizing rejection. If an application asks a "why" question, then label it "noninformational" and reject it; if it asks too many questions, then mark it "frivolous and vexatious" and reject it; and so on. "Calculable rules," observed Weber (2006), allow for the efficient and "'objective' discharge of business" in modern bureaucracies (59). Deploying a predictable if–then calculus not only functioned to standardize the processing of RTI applications but also helped protect PIOs from taking actions that might get them into trouble with their superiors or the public, making them liable to personal fines.

Shah admitted that he was scared in his role as a PIO. "I am afraid of getting sued by *blackmailers* and *sansani-khez* [sensationalist] media," who use the transparency law as a threat. He was also afraid of his boss, who considered the RTI a nuisance and was loathe to share information. "He says, 'Yaar yeh RTI, bas museebat laadee humare liye [Dude, this RTI has only created problems for us].... When we receive an RTI petition, he tells me to figure out some compromise or a way out. So I have to settle with the applicant. Some people demand money [for withdrawing petitions]. The bigger the fish, the more money they ask for." The RTI was thus being used as a mechanism for extortion. Shah lowered his voice and glanced at the door for the umpteenth time. "Hum thoda dar ke kaam karte hain kyunki hum phus sakte hain [I work with fear because I can be framed]. A PIO is a *'lone soldier.'* As a government employee, the scrutiny over me has increased. I feel like I am a culprit in a court, and I am being questioned."

~

"Our administrative system is totally feudal! I like to be ruled by my boss, and I like to rule my underling—that mind-set." This outburst came from Vish Anand as he sat across from me at a Barista café near the hallowed Indian Institute of Technology campus in Delhi and complained about how the provincial hierarchy and subservience bred by the bureaucracy interfered with the RTI law. Vish, an employee of one of India's public sector undertakings—essentially state-owned corporations[1]—was neither a PIO nor an elite officer but a midranker and a self-described transparency advocate. At his agency, like in other government departments, employees were the main users of RTI. "Government servants seek information with regard to their annual confidential reports and ratings. Because if you don't get to grow in your rank and salary, or your juniors supersede you, then it is humiliating. *Theek hai?* [OK?] RTI helps them to access performance reviews, but it takes a lot of courage to question your superior's review. It can have a serious backlash. We still haven't gone outside the concept of the ruler and the ruled." I nodded, sharing my observations about how the bureaucratic hierarchy impeded information disclosure: PIOs felt caught between their fealty to the office and chain of command, and their legal duty to share records. "They seem a little afraid," I remarked.

"By and large, yes," affirmed Vish. "I told you, the feudal mind-set, the monarchy. Top down. There are some officers who have placed their weakest fellows as PIOs, or the most thick-skinned ones, or the ones who are not very smart or savvy"—essentially those who "feel they need their bosses' approval" to share information. I had encountered this myself, having met a senior officer designated FAA, who openly acknowledged consulting with his PIO on what information to release and withhold. This was a clear subversion of the law; as FAA, this officer was responsible for deciding impartially on appeals filed against his PIO for unfairly delaying or rejecting information requests. But he collaborated with his PIO from the get-go, effectively deciding the fate of RTI petitions. Vish continued. "See, you put a weak man as PIO because he'll have trouble retrieving information independently. When he approaches you [the boss] for records, you tell him, 'aaj time nahin hai' [I don't have time to meet today]. Or you put a person who is good at compromising [with petitioners], who will settle things and ensure that no information is provided. I told you: 'meri sultanat, mera darbar' [my kingdom, my court]." Vish sighed. "Any information in the public sector is never provided willingly. Trust me on this. Nobody gives information willingly."

～

The elite officers I encountered at various workshops and those whom I interviewed expressed broad formal support for state transparency. The high-ranking chief guest at the training session I began this chapter with, for instance, positioned RTI as the harbinger of a powerful shift in governance. It marked an end of colonial-style rule where "accountability . . . was only to one's superior officer" and signaled a new era where "you are accountable to the people." Similarly, a senior officer from the Department of Commerce told me that the RTI was a "golden opportunity to help [the public]" and "absolutely a priority with my department. Heavens would have to fall for our PIOs to not attend trainings." Yet another, who worked for the comptroller and auditor general's office, called the law "a historic legislation. For so many years, we—the government—were working in a veil of secrecy. Openness is a hallmark of the new regime. The change from a secret to an open regime . . . is painful. There is a lot of resistance to it among the PIOs. But we have to implement the RTI Act effectively." Interestingly, elite cadres used a pro-transparency disposition to mark their distinction from the presumably less enlightened, resistant PIOs who needed coaxing to break the colonial tradition of state secrecy.

My activist colleagues contended that the notion that senior officials were more supportive of transparency than lower-level PIOs was simplistic and misleading. Shekhar Singh described officialdom as harboring "varying levels of resentment [*viz.* RTI]. I have spoken to a large number of high-level civil servants [who] theoretically conceive that RTI is a good thing. Now, they might do this because they think that is what we want to hear. But they are free to take a liberal, positive attitude because they don't have to respond to RTI petitions." Omesh Sen concurred, stating that "senior bureaucrats in New Delhi generally show a high level of consciousness about RTI, but they are usually the ones who haven't encountered it directly." Meanwhile, PIOs involved with the daily nitty-gritty of legalized transparency, were, in his words, "a scared group, a harassed lot. They ask higher-ups for permission [to disclose information] even when they have been given the power [to do so]. It's very unfortunate."

Some former state insiders were also critical of RTI-related grandstanding among the elite cadres. An ex-officer described this outward ratification of the law as "lip service" that should not be taken at face value. Mr. Handa, whom I met at an RTI forum in Delhi, told me that "the bureaucracy is not geared toward meeting the demands of the citizens or to modify their systems and activities to meet that demand." He believed that the spirit of change, participation, accountability, and openness that the RTI law represented was fundamentally at odds with the bureaucratic mentality. As a trainee at the civil services academy nestled in the Himalayan town of Mussoorie, Uttarakhand, Handa was taught that "a bureaucrat should not upset the apple cart . . . [but] be a part of the system. If a system has stood the test of time, don't dislodge it. I remember these exact phrases. . . . So by and large, the training of a bureaucrat is oriented toward preservation of status quo, isn't it? The obduracy of the state apparatus is at the root of the reluctance of the bureaucracy toward any measure which leads to effective public accountability. A bureaucrat regards himself as a sahib, not a servant of the people. I don't think that . . . colonial-era mentality has undergone a major shift."

Arvind Kejriwal, himself a product of an elite officer training institute, also criticized this superior sahib mentality as an obstacle to changing governance. "Where does a bureaucrat draw his power from? From keeping the information to himself. That is what his power is—what he will *not* do for the people. There is more negativity to his power than positivity. If he has to start sharing information and becoming answerable even to his peon, he doesn't like that. He doesn't want people to question him; he wants them to salute him. . . . Even honest bureaucrats don't part with information. It is a cultural problem."

If bureaucratic culture nurtured and naturalized opacity as a hegemonic value across rungs, then resistance against RTI was not just a reflection of PIO ineptitude, ignorance, or malicious mind-set—itself a classist view—but a sign of a pervasive, system-wide malaise. Vish's comment that "nobody gives information willingly" referenced this as well—the active subversion of transparency by a feudal bureaucracy en masse. His assertion that public office operates as a private fiefdom where rational hierarchy fuses with arbitrary power and patronage (Herzfeld 1992, 55) unravels the ideal of bureaucracy as a streamlined machine that "eliminat[es] . . . the completely arbitrary disposition of the superior over the subordinate officials" (Weber 2006, 68). This fiefdom, moreover, maintains its "overtowering . . . power position" (Weber 2006, 63) over the governed by "keeping secret its knowledge and intentions" (64).

Common criticisms of the RTI law that I heard from PIOs and surmised as something fed to them during workshops—people misuse the law for "vested interests," people are asking "noninformational, vexatious, and frivolous" questions, time and money are being wasted—were not limited to PIOs. Omesh Sen described these as the typical "clichés that all government officials always fall back on." Indeed, in 2012, former prime minister Manmohan Singh used these same words when he spoke about ongoing "concerns about frivolous and vexatious use of the [RTI] Act in demanding information the disclosure of which cannot possibly serve any public purpose. Sometimes information covering a long time-span or a large number of cases is sought in an omnibus manner. . . . Such queries, besides serving little productive social purpose, are also a drain on the resources of the public authorities, diverting precious man-hours that could be put to better use."[2] The Supreme Court struck a similar tone: "The Act should not be allowed to be misused. . . . Nor should it be converted into a tool of oppression or intimidation of honest officials striving to do their duty. The nation does not want a scenario where 75% of the staff of public authorities spends 75% of their time in collecting and furnishing information to applicants instead of discharging their regular duties."[3]

These stock phrases express a shared sentiment and an emergent "structure of feeling" (Williams 1977, 132) among state actors in a context where a new legal norm of transparency sits in tension with the bureaucratic values of secrecy and hierarchy. Raymond Williams (1977) describes a structure of feeling as a "living . . . [and] widely experienced" (133) sensibility that emerges from a "disturbance of older forms" (134) of hegemonic worldviews and practices. The RTI law deems transparency an ideal of state work and secrecy an undemocratic, immoral tradition in and of the past. Secrecy, however, proves sticky. As a legal mandate guiding colonial and postcolonial state work since the late nineteenth century, official secrecy is rooted as bureaucratic common sense. Changing this dominant culture provokes a whole gamut of reactions from officialdom: discomfort, strain, fear, resentment, grudging compliance, and "this is a good law but . . ." kind of lip service, which Williams terms "formal assent with private dissent" (132).

The burden of change is also differently experienced by state officials. Where elite cadres can dodge transparency by pulling rank and invoking procedural protocol, PIOs are limited in their capacity to do so. Beholden to both the bosses and the masses, PIOs must navigate the contradictions between emergent state openness and long-honed practices of opacity, between following the mandate of the RTI law and deferring to bureaucratic hierarchy and fealty. PIO Shah's words, "Hum phanste hain beech main [We get caught in the middle]," capture the dis-ease of inhabiting a tight spot. Unlike their bosses, who have privileged resort to bureaucratic anonymity and "buckpassing" (Herzfeld 1992, 143)—they can frame their underlings—PIOs have less wiggle room. They face a curious conundrum. They are at once the depersonalized face of state bureaucracy and named individuals held personally liable for erroneously privileging the raison d'état over public interest. Their salaries can be docked for mistakes and decisions that are not theirs alone. Ironically, the PIOs' individualized exposure as designated fall guys and penalty bearers preserves the anonymity and opacity of the machine as a whole; it fails to address the fundamental conflict between bureaucracy and transparency.

Idealized bureaucratic values of hierarchy, complicity, and loyalty to a machine that is greater than the sum of its parts, and in which each "small cog . . . [is] above all, forged to the common interest of all the functionaries in the perpetuation of the apparatus and the persistence of its rationally organized domination" (Weber 2006, 62), work to preserve opacity. These values also shape bureaucratic practices of recordkeeping, which have direct relevance for a sunshine law focused on government documents. I now turn to these ordinary bureaucraft techniques and explore how they shift under a transparency regime to protect secrecy.

On Files, Codes, and Trickery:
The Craft of Transparent Illegibility

"Have you seen a government file?" an information commissioner asked me as I sat in one of the many chairs near his expansive desk and surveyed its contents: a computer screen, a landline, a cell phone, a buzzer to ring for assistance, and neatly stacked files. Before I could answer, the commissioner picked a sample. "This is what a government file looks like." It was a green folder with a red paper band in the middle—the infamous red tape—secured with cotton twine. The commissioner untied the twine, folded back the red paper band, opened the file, flipped through the pages inside (which were secured with another white tie), and pointed to the notes section on the left. He then shut the file, refolded the red band, and retied the white twine. How tedious, I thought. Indeed, that was precisely his point. "I am bad at tying strings," he said scornfully. "If I look at fifty files in a day, I spend twenty to thirty minutes opening and closing files. It sounds ridiculous, but this is what happens [in government], and we all do it."

The Indian state's paper rule, or *kaghazi raj* (Hull 2003), which was put in place by the British, relies on an elaborate system of files for orderly recordkeeping. There is something so banal about a government file that one forgets that "every file is a sovereign domain" (Visvanathan 2008, 54)— an artifact, quite like state letterhead, a signature, or a seal, that actualizes rule in people's lives.[4] Administrative tools are not merely instruments of bureaucratic rationalization (Weber 2006, 62) and end products of state practices, they also actively work to materialize an authoritative state (Sharma and Gupta 2006).[5]

The occult-like force of these "paper shrines" (Hull 2003, 295) and "wily little 'actant[s]'" (Mathur 2012, 79; Latour 2010) is widely acknowledged. "Almost all of India, even the illiterate . . . knows the diabolical significance and power the file holds to control the destiny of many people."[6] Like other official credentials and artifacts, files appear as "magical objects conveying power in their own right, entirely apart from the real knowledge . . . they are supposed to represent" (Graeber 2015, 22). Indeed, whether state records accurately reflect the real is beside the point, for these political artifacts do not compile truths as much as conjure them. Their religico-magical aura is sustained by the "paperealities" (Dery 1998) they construct, which are hidden and beyond ordinary reach. As chronicles of bureaucratic work and stand-ins for the behind-the-scenes workings of state power, files operate as fetishized facsimiles.[7]

The RTI law centers this statist "economy of appearances" (Tsing 2005) as the key to making power legible. It redefines the privatized bureaucratic archive as a "public commons" of precious "information" directly linked to the knowability and accountability of the state.

> Government information is a national resource. Neither the particular government of the day nor public officials create information for their own benefit. This information is generated for purposes related to the legitimate discharge of their duties of office, and for the service of the public for whose benefit the institutions of government exist, and who ultimately ... fund the institutions of government and the salaries of officials. It follows that government and officials are "trustees" of this information for the people. (Mander and Joshi, n.d., 3)

By unlocking this national treasure, the RTI law promises to take the magic out of government files. In effect, though, it iterates their fetishistic power in the public sphere. It is no surprise, therefore, that government files have been the site of bitter struggles between officialdom and activists since the law's drafting. These struggles shed light on how transparency can be thwarted as a matter of routine. Ordinary bureaucraft, as I explain below, makes room for craftiness, cunning, and subterfuge.

Every government file has two sections: the substantive papers relating to a particular project on the right, and official notes, known as notings, on the left. File notings are a form of official writing created during colonial rule to chart the flow of work between different levels of a departmental bureaucracy regarding specific issues—who saw the documents and when; what the opinions and oral deliberations were of these functionaries; and how the final decision was reached and how it will be implemented. In Weberian terms, notings are material evidence that "a system of rationally debatable 'reasons' stands behind every act of bureaucratic administration" (Weber 2006, 59). The British fashioned notings for "internal transparency and oversight" (Baviskar 2007, 18), not public accountability. The Official Secrets Act protected colonial administrators' identities, opinions, and acts from scrutiny.

However, signed or initialed bureaucratic notes carry different symbolic and material significance under transparent democratic rule. File notings become a dangerous and unsecured paper trail for bureaucrats—a potentially enduring record of past communications and actions that reveal the who, how, and why of state acts. They can expose the individuals who comprise the bureaucratic behemoth, threatening the depersonalized "rule of Nobody" (Arendt 2000, 381). Notings can reveal the how of decision-making—procedural bureaucraft—and challenge strongly guarded "administrative secrecy" (Weber 2006, 64). Finally, they can uncover the why behind governmental acts and decisions—that revered raison d'état—and endanger the very heart of state sovereignty. The same official note in a file that enacts state verticality, sovereignty, and mystique when hidden can threaten to unravel state reason and the arbitrariness of power when exposed.

Predictably, the status of file notings as information has been at the center of disputes among state actors and activists since before the enactment of the RTI Act. The bureaucratic establishment opposed the activist inclusion of notings in the definition of information in the law's draft. Although their phrasing was deleted in the final version of the bill passed by the parliament, activists maintained that these internal scripts were unquestionably covered under the law (Singh 2010). After the law's passage in 2005, the state agency that implemented RTI legislation declared that notings do not count as public information because they record in-house discussions on issues before final decisions (Singh 2010). Citizens challenged this reading in their appeals to information commissioners, who upheld the activist interpretation that notings constitute a "paper trail, vital to establish a chain of transparency and accountability," and excluding them was tantamount to "taking the life out of the RTI Act."[8] Officialdom failed to amend the RTI law to exclude notings in 2006, but it reorganized for the same fight in 2009.

During the first phase of my fieldwork from August 2008 to June 2009, the issue of file notings cropped up at every PIO workshop I attended. At the training session with which I began this chapter, a PIO claimed that notings were "for internal purposes only" and were irrelevant to the public. RTI entitled people to access a government decision, but "why share how we arrived at it?" another PIO questioned. In response, the workshop facilitator, Mr. Dev, said, "See, this is the wrong attitude! Who owns public institutions? The people. The law says that internal mechanisms must be shared with the public." He picked up an RTI booklet and quoted from it: "Any material in any form including records, documents, memos, e-mails, opinions, advices [etc.]" counts as information (Government of India 2005, 2). "Opinions," Dev asserted, were nothing but internal discussions noted in files. They had to be revealed.

This struggle over file notings reveals accepted truisms behind India's RTI law. There is, first, the "ideology that believes that transparent governance emerges from control over and access to state documents and records" (Mathur 2012, 170). Second is the faith in the veracity of documents. The logic of transparency, as Hetherington (2008) argues, relies on a straightforward relationship between "the signifier and the signified, or between representation and reality" (47). Files are meant to chronicle, through meticulous bureaucraft, backstage realities of state work; they constitute a permanent archive of "real" administrative facts and decisions. Official notes, moreover, are sanctified as written facsimiles of state officials and their deliberations that give power a face, or at least a name inscribed therein. If people can access files and noting, they can rein in arbitrary state power—that, at least, is the presumed ideal.

In practice, however, bureaucratic documents rarely function as unchanging, legible, and readily available stores of administrative work. Consider this quote from a 1989 memo from the vice chairman of the Delhi Development Authority's slum department: "Not much care is being taken for proper up-keep of files and papers. Many times files become so bulky that corners of pages are torn and previous notings become totally illegible. In the majority of files, the correspondence and noting portions are not page numbered, leading to a situation where any paper can be taken out if somebody had malafide intentions" (Tarlo 2003, 120). Papers and files are malleable; they can fall apart or go missing. In the world of bureaucraft, however,

> a file is never acknowledged as missing. It is aptly reported as "not traceable" or better still, "not readily traceable": for, after all, on the one hand we know it couldn't have slithered away on its own and, on the other, the Indian Evidence Act 1872 says it is valid to presume that a government

servant has carried out his normal duties unless proof to the contrary is presented. (Mukhopadhyay 2007)

The "file is untraceable" phrase takes on a particularly charged connotation in the age of transparency. Activists allege that officials use it as an excuse to prevent or stall disclosure. "How can a file be untraceable!" Omesh exclaimed during one of our conversations. "If a file is lost or missing, then [officials] should file a police report and show us proof." I shared his frustration, having encountered the same words of (un)reason when requesting colonial-era material about the Official Secrets Act at the national archives in Delhi. Some of my requests came back with the "file is untraceable" response. There was nothing I could do about it except laugh at the irony of secrecy surrounding the Official Secrets Act.

Even when files are available and their notings accessible, it does not necessarily guarantee transparency; notings can obfuscate as much as illuminate decision-making and decision makers. Consider this example of "a typical government note sheet" that Vish provided: "In my department, somebody writes a note about a proposal. Note 1 has the original proposal. In Note 14 I differ and give some tangential [reason]: 'The estimate is high. This may please be reviewed.' And then somebody else writes, 'This cannot be reviewed,' etc. And eventually my boss calls me and says that 'I am marking the file back to you. This is what you need to [write], and then will I approve the file.' So in Note 26 I change my opinion. These kinds of stupid things keep happening on a note sheet. And when I get verbal instructions to put up a proposal [from my boss], which I think is likely to be questioned, I word it in a manner that specifies that my intention is bona fide, that I am doing it because I was told to do it."

Vish's description sheds light on everyday bureaucraft of a different kind than the witchy craftiness that James elaborates. It reveals the extent to which administrative rule involves an interplay between particular forms of writing and orality (Goody 1986; Gupta 2012). Although writing is privileged as the script of the state because of its apparent certitude in conveying meaning and permanence as "record" (Weber 2006; cf. Lévi-Strauss 1961; Scott 2009), orality's "jellyfish like" (Scott 2009, 230) fleeting quality makes it an equally important mode of state work.[9] Indeed, written notes may never appear if official conversations are not inscribed.

Unrecorded oral discussions can combine with cryptic officialese to produce state-authored truths that are empty and fading signifiers.

File notings convey abbreviated snapshots of state work that obscure the tracks of bureaucratic power. They conjure an appearance of a wheel where cogs at different levels work together to produce certain outcomes, but individual agency, intentionality, and originality are muddled. Vish alluded to some of the techniques that effectively produce authorless texts, such as using passive voice and vague language—"this may please be reviewed"—to confuse the who and how behind decisions (Hull 2003).[10] This passive, thin writing style avoids explanations of why something needs reviewing, by whom, and through what mechanisms, shielding the people who give orders as well as those who carry them out.[11] Even when particular officials initial or sign notes in files, their signature is less a mark of a unique person and decision maker and more an "icon . . . [that] reproduces a generalized form" (Herzfeld 1992, 82)—that of a generic official. Notings construct a reified image of the state as an abstract "competent authority" (Chowdhury 2013) and a chain of command that becomes increasingly fuzzy and faceless the higher one ascends.

File notings are pared-down administrative scripts that follow their own discursive codes and documentary expectations. Amitabh Mukhopadhyay (2007) gives examples of some of these codes:

> *Angrezi likhna,* literally "to write English" . . . means officialese that crafts a proposal/decision/communication by weaving the rules and procedure . . . to justify a crafty decision arrived at by . . . discussion in the vernacular. *Doli sajana,* literally "decorating the bride's palanquin," refers to flagging the referenced papers, tying the final knot of . . . the file, and launching its journey up the hierarchy.

Performing proceduralism by "dressing up" and "veiling" official paperwork—as the reference to a bride's palanquin indicates—and inscribing notes in "English"—the language of rule and formality—privatizes state knowledge and amplifies bureaucratic power. These are ordinary mechanisms and customs by which officialdom "tends to exclude the public, to hide its knowledge and action . . . wherever power interests of the given structure of domination *toward the outside* are at stake" (Weber 2006, 64).

Routine bureaucraft not only helps maintain the superiority of state actors over nonstate ones but also reinforces internal distinctions within bureaucracies. When underlings construct records according to verbal orders from above, they demonstrate their allegiance to the institution over the public while simultaneously protecting themselves from being upbraided for bad decisions. Bureaucratic proceduralism secures hierarchy, and both work together to ensure state opacity.

―

Because the RTI Act threatens to breach the statist enclosure of insider knowledge and techniques, a writing-wary officialdom has become even more vigilant about paper trails, making already coded scripts even less intelligible. I quote Vish once again: "We have become cautious about making questionable decisions. We still make a note sheet. But if I have something [a question, a contrary view], I use a notepad." I interjected: "So you don't make a noting in the file?" "Yes," answered Vish, "you don't make a file noting. You write on a separate notepad, 'please discuss.' A notepad can be removed, you know." Yet another strategy officials use to mystify legibility, authorship, and accountability is writing on removable sticky notes. Neel, a researcher for an NCPRI-sponsored study of the impact of the RTI law (RAAG 2009), termed this the new "Post-it culture" of bureaucracy during an activist meeting in spring 2009. He reported that even when officials inscribe and initial a note, they often write "see me" or "discuss with me." Discussions largely happen in person or over the phone; what gets recorded in the file is the phrase "seen, discussed, deliberated" alongside the final decision. Aruna Roy, who was present at this meeting, disparaged such meaningless bureaucratese and deliberate opacity: "If seen, what was seen! If discussed, what was discussed! Whenever there is a difficult decision to take, bureaucrats choose a scapegoat and make this person write and sign the final note." Elite officials can thus frame their junior colleagues by forcing them to inscribe notes and take the blame for poor decisions. They are also practiced in the art of "empty language," which Herzfeld (1992) defines as the "ultimate defensive wall" for bureaucracy (81).

When thinned-out language doesn't work, officials avoid writing entirely. "What I was taught was, don't make public anything you write, or it might land you in trouble," stated Priya Bhagat, an IAS officer with whom I shared a lunch table at a workshop. She believed that activist criticisms about the bureaucratic drag in implementing transparency and their demands for rapid results were flawed. "See, we make discretionary judgment calls all the time. You never write reasons for decisions in a file. You just record the decision, or you write 'for discussion'. . . . When you are taught to keep everything secret, then changing . . . quickly is not possible. This is not magic!" Indeed, the magic of disappearing, temporary, and vacuous writing would be difficult to counter because it isn't magic at all but ingrained common sense and learned customary bureaucraft geared to ensure secrecy. Preserving it requires no illicit, malevolent craftiness; transparency can be "thwarted so simply by bureaucratic finesse" (Mukhopadhyay 2007).

Cryptic bureaucratic scripts raise issues of inscrutability for activists because their meaning remains obscure even when disclosed. Writing about Canadian public–private infrastructure projects, Valverde and Moore (2019) contend that even when documents are made publicly available, their "content, assessments and language . . . do little to empower citizens or serve to hold the agencies accountable" (690–91). Amrita, who worked for the Delhi-based RTI advocacy group Satark Nagrik Sangathan (Society for Citizens Vigilance Initiatives), gave me an example of a "coded" reply she received. She had filed a petition inquiring about development projects undertaken by a member of the legislative assembly (MLA) in Delhi. In response, she was given information about a road project in the form of a string of letters and numbers that was totally opaque. "P/L of C.C. . . . or something," Amrita said, half laughing and half apologizing for forgetting the precise combination of characters. She had to seek the help of a civil engineer to understand what it meant. "How many people have the resources or expertise to decode officialese!" she exclaimed. Indeed, Shekhar Singh viewed this as among the key "challenges of the RTI movement. How does one ensure that in a world which is growing more and more specialized, where people use a sort of scientific language that lesser and lesser people understand, how does one make sure that [information] is put across in a way that it is understandable by the people? That is where the state is going to go and hide. It's going to say, right, if you are forcing us to make everything public, then we'll make it public in a way so that people don't understand what the hell it is all about."

Even when made transparent, however, the surfaces of state power can never be "completely stripped away . . . [but] only be transformed/replaced/covered over" (Sanders and West 2003, 16). Ordinary bureaucraft sustains obscurity. Accessible state records ensure neither legibility nor democratic accountability (Bear and Mathur 2015; John 2015). Government representatives can maintain state verticality and impenetrability in the age of transparency by altering how they communicate and what they record. Thin bureaucratic writing atrophies further and remains only partly legible. Passive phrases like "seen, discussed, deliberated" and alphanumeric codes become symbols that refuse to signify anything to outsiders. They guarantee neither intelligibility nor the traceability of power (Derrida 1997; Morris 2004). Ephemeral Post-it notes disappear, oral deliberations go unrecorded, and files become untraceable, keeping official records as partial and evanescent as ever.[12]

Vanishing and atrophied bureaucratic scripts and records, rendered more powerful for what they fail to say than for what they do, ensure that the state continues to be spoken and written under erasure (Derrida 1997) despite the legal push for transparency. Accessing a file in this context becomes akin to making one's way through puzzles and fictions (Tarlo 2003, 70)—"maze-generating mazes" (Coleman 2014, 9)—rather than following a certain path to truths about state authority and reason. This perpetual deferral complicates the work of citizens and activists. The RTI law governmentalizes social life and fosters bureaucratized activism and procedural, simulated citizenship, as I showed in chapter 2. As citizens learn to mimic officialese and formal proceduralism to exercise their rights, state actors shift their documentation practices to alter the very substance of information. Rather than solely fighting over the status of file notings as information, they inscribe them differently. Even when shared, these remade state scripts hide in plain sight. This is achieved by following institutional protocol and without overtly breaking the RTI law. Indeed, creative compliance with the law, formal procedures, and customary bureaucratic directives can secure opacity. RTI activists recognize such loopholes and demand faithful documentation that makes bureaucratic decision-making and authors unambiguous and the state decipherable. However, this may be difficult to achieve—not only because "lawfully" shared documents might themselves be incomprehensible (Valverde and Moore 2019), given routine bureaucraft, but also because of the very nature of bureaucracy and sovereign state power, as I discuss next.

Where the State Goes to Hide: Bureaucracy against Transparency

The belief that government records constitute a repository of information and truths about power, and that the ability to access these documents will make governance more transparent, accountable, and participatory, has an "allure of simplicity" (Redfield 2013, 32), much like the idealized Weberian bureaucratic machine. Such a belief lends technomoral elegance and political force to activist work even though the relationship between records and state power is rarely straightforward. While documents are iconic of state work, they are neither containers of stable facts nor privileged keys to unlocking "the state." Legally opening the bureaucratic archive to public scrutiny, then, reveals a checkered and uncertain terrain that condenses contradictions.

As I stated at the outset, by highlighting the obstacles in the working of the RTI law, I do not wish to mark the exceptionalism of the Indian bureaucracy as a sign of typical Third World problems. Rather, the Indian case has broader theoretical relevance for understanding the convoluted relationship between transparency, bureaucracy, democracy, and state power; it is typical in that regard.

Weber alludes to the uneasy fit between bureaucracy and democracy. While democratic rule needs bureaucratic organization, the hierarchical and secretive organization of the latter also contradicts a democratic ethos. This assumes that secrecy and democracy are antithetical, which, as I have elaborated, is not the case. Secrecy is not a distortion of a liberal democratic state but inherent to it. Moreover, transparency and democracy are not an ineluctable pair, as is commonly understood in global good governance discourse and conveyed in RTI trainings, for sunshine laws are not unique to democratic states. Shekhar Singh told me that "a lot of totalitarian states are getting into the field of RTI. One could argue that transparency regimes can be seen by totalitarian governments as less challenging alternatives to a democratic system. In fact, when China was entering this field, there was talk among activists that if China does not want to move rapidly into becoming a democracy, it must provide the right to information!" Neither democracy and transparency, nor bureaucracy and transparency is a seamless pairing. As Sanders and West

(2003) write, "In a world where varied institutions claim to give structure to the 'rational' and 'transparent' operation of power, power continues in reality to work in . . . capricious ways" (7). Indeed, there is a constitutive tension between bureaucratic and sovereign modes of state power (Brown 1995) on the one hand, and the ideal of transparent government on the other, where the former subvert the latter from within.

Bureaucracy is premised on structures and procedures—bureaucraft— that are supposed to keep the governmental machine working predictably. Conjuring a dehumanized Weberian ideal type[13]—where rules rule, not people; where bureaucrats are defined by their function and personal ties and histories are irrelevant; and where administration is hierarchical, streamlined, and calculable—requires tremendous effort. This onstage appearance of order, rationality, visibility, and liberality of modern democratic states is constructed by concealing backstage arbitrariness, opacity, illiberality, and machinations. "On the one hand, bureaucratic institutions accentuate their rational side . . . in the form of transparent criteria. . . . The flip side of the transparency of bureaucratic institutions . . . is the public erasure of irrational actions and decisions. . . . This is done by hiding what goes on inside . . . through a whole range of naturalized and logical strategies" (Buur 2001, 173).

Bureaucratic state power and transparency exert contrary pulls on each other. Transparency relies on holding state representatives accountable for their actions by publicizing government paper archives that supposedly reveal who took decisions, and how. Individual agency runs into trouble with banal bureaucraft, which confuses it or deliberately stages it. The same procedures that depersonalize decision-making and perform complicity with the machine are also used to help frame individuals for actions that they may not have taken. Making a bureaucratically organized state transparent through the very techniques that keep power faceless or give it a misleading face, are bound to ultimately run aground.

Furthermore, these techniques can be bent or altered by state agents. Rule boundedness does not take discretion off the bureaucratic table as long as official behavior is guided by what Weber (2006) calls "the ultimate and highest lodestar"—that is, the "strictly 'objective' idea of *raison d'état*" (59). The reason of the state, of course, references the principle of sovereignty—that beacon of illiberal, prerogative state power (Brown 1995; Hindess 2004) that can be "expressed as the armed force of the police or as vacillating criteria for obtaining welfare benefits" (Brown 1995, 191). In other words, discretionarily applying and arbitrarily changing rules and policies demonstrate powerfully the sovereign will of the state. A section of the Indian bureaucracy used precisely this logic to justify watering down the RTI law, arguing that transparency was anathema because "government would become too rigid and rule-bound as no officer would like to exercise discretion which could later be questioned" (Singh 2010, 12). Officials want to preserve the sovereign authority to amend rules while remaining anonymous and unquestionable. But they also want to force citizens to divulge their reasons for requesting information and meticulously follow procedures when filing RTI applications. Indeed, on July 31, 2012, the government issued new rules that dictate that petitions cannot exceed five hundred words, and appeals to information commissions must contain all required documents to prevent delay or rejection.[14] Significantly, these rules were not debated publicly. Nitpicky rule following and unpredictable rule tweaking work well to frustrate rights claims.

These bureaucratic challenges to the RTI law show how fiercely state secrecy is guarded. "The concept of the 'office secret' is a specific invention of bureaucracy," asserted Weber (2006), and there are "few things it defends so fanatically as this attitude" (64). Secrecy is not the mark of bad or corrupt governance but of government as usual; it is the backstage of the apparently open democratic state, as those Indian officials who opposed legalized transparency knew well. Secrecy, they argued, is "the bedrock of governance" (Singh 2010, 12). This connection between secrecy and sovereignty is also institutionalized in the RTI Act. Section 8 of the law excludes from disclosure any information that "would prejudicially affect the sovereignty and integrity of India [and] the security, strategic, scientific or economic interests of the State" (Government of India 2005, 7). This clause establishes sovereignty as the limit of transparency and as an exception; it cannot do otherwise.

Even though the RTI law does not dismantle state secrecy, it destabilizes it enough to be perceived as a threat by powerful actors. The Commonwealth Human Rights Initiative website keeps an ongoing tally of RTI-related violence in India since 2005. A total of 488 RTI users have been attacked up until June 2023, of whom 106 were murdered and seven committed suicide.[15] These numbers are a chilling reminder of the dangers of demanding state transparency. The RTI law threatens to respatialize the state's separation from and domination over society by allowing those on the outside to question and partake in inside decisions. This gets to the heart of state sovereignty: that backstage recess, which symbolizes the why of rule and the sheer "prestige of domination" (Weber 1978, 910–11), and which must be kept invisible. This is where the state goes to hide— where illiberality, arbitrariness, and unaccountability reign. It is this face of the state that citizens threaten to unravel when they retrieve official records as information. Escape hatches are needed if the state's sovereign prerogative is to be maintained in the age of participatory and transparent governance. The exemption clause in the RTI law, the expanding bureaucratic procedures that citizens must follow to actualize their right, and both established and emergent forms of bureaucraft that routinely frustrate disclosure all serve as those escape hatches; they keep the how, who, and why of state power muddled, if not illegible, despite the appearance of democratic good governance.

4

Whose Law Is It Anyway?

The Common Man as Subject of Rights

I met Rita Anand, a Delhi-based female journalist from *Civil Society* magazine, at Arvind's apartment in March 2009. She was there to interview him, and I was there to follow up on the food rights case Parivartan had filed on behalf of a handful of camp residents in Delhi's consumer court. Upon discovering that I was a U.S.-based academic exploring the workings of RTI, Rita remarked that this law was unique in capturing the imagination of the urban middle class. "Usually they think that legislation is meant for the poor—like welfare—and not for them." But RTI was a law that the middle class was using liberally. I nodded, having conversed with someone earlier who fit Rita's description of a robust middle-class RTI user: Mr. Divan, a retired army officer and a member of his local resident welfare association. RWAs are mostly elected groups active in middle- and upper-class colonies in Delhi, which interact with government agencies to address the needs of area residents. RTI has become a vital part of the RWA tool kit. Mr. Divan told me he routinely filed petitions to obtain information about poorly maintained public infrastructure and to pursue legal and bureaucratic avenues of redress. He also used the RTI to resolve personal disputes over property encroachment matters.

Rita Anand was interested in people like Divan and commended Arvind for reaching out to RWA members as well as slum dwellers. "With RTI, one doesn't have to work hard," Arvind shrugged, because everyone is curious. "We educate [people] about procedures and how to draft petitions—the right questions to ask, etc. But now some problems are emerging with the RTI. The information commissions are the biggest bottleneck," declared Arvind, describing the backlog in adjudicating on appeals. "The Central Information Commission doesn't function as an independent agency.... There is no activist input or people's participation in the appointment of commissioners. And without that, the RTI might be a lost opportunity." Rita nodded sympathetically: "That's a general problem with the implementation of any act, the institutional collapse." But Arvind considered this weakening intentional rather than inevitable. "The central and state governments want to make this law ineffective by appointing the wrong information commissioners," he stated, stressing the need to follow the RTI Act's rules regarding such appointments. These rules mandate "people's input in choosing eminent persons as commissioners." "Eminent persons" did not necessarily mean individuals unaffiliated with the state, he clarified. "This is not a question of bureaucrat versus nonbureaucrat. There are good bureaucrats and bad bureaucrats; there are good nonbureaucrats and bad nonbureaucrats. If good people are appointed as information commissioners, then RTI will succeed. It is a good law." Rita asked him to elaborate on the bureaucracy's response to the RTI. "The response of a bureaucrat depends on the side he is on," replied Arvind. "When he suffers some injustice at work, such as delayed promotion or medical reimbursement, then the RTI becomes the best law. But when the same bureaucrat has to provide information to someone else, the RTI becomes the worst law." Does that make the RTI "a people-versus-bureaucrats law?" Rita probed. "No. It is not about versus," Arvind emphasized, pointing out that the bureaucracy comprised middle-class people "like you and me" who use the law too. "The RTI Act is not against anyone. It is about people seeking information. It is about making the system accountable. And it can really provide relief to the common man."

I was reminded again of Mr. Divan, who described the RTI law as "the most powerful social legislation to come to India after the right to vote. Today every citizen has the right to ask questions and hold public authorities accountable. In the first few years, 70 percent of the usage [of the RTI law] was by government servants for personnel issues. Now 70 percent of its usage is for social issues that concern the aam aadmi. The RTI Act empowers the common man. Today, every person feels like an investigator and auditor."

Arvind also emphasized the universal appeal of this law. When Rita asked him about the popularity of the law among the middle classes, he corrected her. "The RTI Act is for everyone. It doesn't discriminate against classes." That said, middle-class people were especially captivated by it because "they feel that nothing works in our country. For sixty-five years, nothing worked in governance. The middle class was cynical, and it is difficult to break out of that cynicism. But when they saw success stories with the RTI, they [became] active users."

In her published piece, Rita Anand (2009) would write,

> By and large, the middle class views . . . most laws . . . as populist measures thought up by governments . . . for the poor somewhere out there. . . . With the RTI things have been different. . . . For the first time in sixty years, well off people sought to use a law to improve governance . . . [and explore] the delicious possibility of getting the recalcitrant bureaucracy to mend its ways. In reality, RTI bridged the rural–urban divide. The . . . movement originated in villages. . . . The RTI Bill too was drawn up by grassroots activists. . . . In Delhi, it was Parivartan with its leader, Arvind Kejriwal, who bridged the rich–poor divide. . . . The group chose Sundernagari, a slum in east Delhi, to change the sorry surroundings of residents. . . . Arvind and Parivartan [also] reached out to Delhi's Residents' Welfare Associations (RWAs) offering help in using RTI.

The RTI seemed like a magic bullet and a universal medium (like water, as Aruna Roy put it to me) linking regions and classes: a law for all citizens, in common.

⁓

"The RTI Act empowers the aam aadmi" was a stock phrase repeated by activists, petitioners, and even bureaucrats I encountered during fieldwork. It conveys the idea that the law bridges social divides to produce a generic citizen shorn of any particularity, and enables this common man to audit the state.

The trope of the common man was not invented by the RTI law; indeed, it has had a flourishing public-cultural and political life in postindependence India. It is often identified with one of the longest-running Indian political cartoons, *You Said It,* whose star was the Common Man.

Created in 1951 by R. K. Laxman, this strip was a satirical, critical commentary on everyday life from "the perspective of the Common Man and his experience of the modern state" (Khanduri 2012, 305; Laxman 1998). Laxman's icon was a balding and bespectacled middle-aged man dressed in simple clothes. He was deliberately and ambiguously "middling"—a nondescript person who switched from riding a bicycle to driving a car over time but remained ordinary and humble. He had a name—Wagle—but that individualized identification did not matter because he stood as a symbol for the universal "everyman" (Baviskar and Ray 2011, 1). His encounters with state injustice narrativized everyone's experiences and incited recognition across classes. Laxman's Common Man was depicted as a bewildered and mute witness to mundane corruption and ironies that chip away at democracy and development (Khanduri 2012). This public-cultural symbol of political critique did not, in fact, protest at all. He iconized incredulity about a present so ridiculously pathetic that words utterly failed.[1]

While this cartoon character dropped out of the daily pages of the *Times of India* after five decades, the common man has continued a powerful life of its own. Television series and movies have been made on the subject.[2] The satirical "secret literature" of *Holi gaali* from Uttar Pradesh has invoked the figure of the aam aadmi (Cohen 2022). Political parties have routinely bound their electoral calculus to the plight of this downtrodden citizen. The Indian National Congress has claimed proprietorship over the common man as its constituency since at least Indira Gandhi's times, well before the Aam Aadmi Party, named after the Common Man, was established in 2012. Indeed, it was the Congress Party–led United Progressive Alliance regime that enacted a slew of laws in the early twenty-first century to empower the common man. These included the rights to livelihood (NREGA), education, food, forests, and information. No longer a *bechara* (wretch) or a defeated fatalist of the Laxman variety, who ruminates about the status quo and a venal state but can't change it, the common man of today appears as a doer who questions the state and demands good governance.

But is the common man a universal subject of rights? To what extent does this equalizing figure, invoked so often in political and public-cultural discourse, produce equal citizenship, mending a riven and hierarchical sociopolitical field in India (Mehta 2003)?

In this chapter, I use the truism that the RTI law empowers the common man to critically parse citizenship. The term "common man," as a stand-in for a standardized citizen, is neither self-evident nor agreed on (quite like the word "empowerment"[3]); it is also attached to projects and groups that share nothing in common. I juxtapose the narratives of two Delhi-based people involved in RTI-related good governance activities to illuminate the fractured landscape of citizenship and rights in India: Ravi, an upper-middle-class man and RWA member residing in a gated community, and Pushpa, a working-class woman living in a camp. Though both may fit the empowered common "man" character, Ravi and Pushpa embody class and gender fractures that refute a shared status or experience of abstracted citizenship (Cody 2013). Shining light on their experiences of the RTI law and democratic good governance allows me to unravel the split subject of rights in India. Indeed, not only does the RTI law not create an even political field, but it itself becomes a point of contention in disputes over who should ideally possess and exercise this right and participate in improving governance.

Subaltern studies scholars have shed invaluable light on the fractured political landscape in India, exploring the dynamic between subaltern and elite groups during the colonial period and focusing especially on the former—those considered lacking in political agency or showing prepolitical consciousness and needing tutelage by the nationalist elite (Guha 1982, 1983; Guha and Spivak 1988). Partha Chatterjee (2004) has more recently examined the postcolonial manifestations of this rift, recoding it as a divide between political society and civil society.

Chatterjee coins the term "political society" to parochialize "civil society," an ideal that dances as a universal but is in fact a Western particular representing a minority of people and institutions worldwide. He argues that the dominant liberal view of civil society as an institutionalized and contractual sphere separate from the state where rights and freedoms operate and citizenship is realized does not capture the existing political realities in the postcolonial world and beyond, where communal and kin identities complicate individual rights, inequality undercuts the ideal of equal citizenship, and illegalities transform legal norms. Even though liberal states uphold formal legal equality, large swaths of people in these nations have never been considered enlightened enough to merit inclusion as rights-bearing members of civil society. Chatterjee calls these swaths political society, which consists of groups targeted by developmental, welfare, and pedagogical efforts to modernize them.

Political society majorities articulate a subjectivity distinct from abstract liberal citizenship and a politics distinct from the participatory, civil deliberation of the conventional public sphere (Cody 2015). For subaltern groups, the focus of political engagement is not rights but entitlements, argues Chatterjee, with the one guaranteed and the other transient. Their everyday survival politics consist of breaking laws (squatting or "stealing" water, for example) and hustling to access temporary entitlements by positioning themselves as subjects deserving of state largesse but not deserving of the contractual reciprocity or accountability due to citizens. This makes for an unpredictable politics in that outcomes are not given. Chatterjee (2008) writes,

> In political society . . . people are not regarded by the state as proper citizens possessing rights and belonging to the properly constituted civil society. Rather, they are seen to belong to particular population groups . . . which are targets of particular governmental policies. Since dealing with many of these groups imply the tacit acknowledgement of various illegal practices, governmental agencies will often treat such cases as exceptions, justified by very specific and special circumstances, so that the structure of the general rules and principles is not compromised. . . . All of this makes the claims of people in political society a matter of constant political negotiation and the results are never secure or permanent. Their entitlements, even when recognised, never quite become rights. (58)

Chatterjee's idea of political society as a sphere distinct from elite civil society is helpful when considering the split subject of rights in India; however, it is limiting in its binary framing, as several scholars have noted (Baviskar and Sundar 2008; Menon 2010; Nigam 2012).[4] A clean divide between civil society as an arena of a liberal politics of rights and citizenship versus political society as a domain of a governmentalized politics of needs and entitlements that is informal, exceptional, and often beyond the pale of law is not tenable on the ground. In India, the "manifest disdain for the Constitution and for the legal process" among elites and middle classes, and the routine suspension of "labour, environmental and procedural rules" by corporate actors (Baviskar and Sundar 2008, 88), shows that civil society is as enmeshed in rule-bending, law-breaking, and negotiating exceptions for itself as a political society. Likewise, and most relevant for my work, political society groups do not just operate outside of legality but are deeply entangled with the law and rights. Subaltern subjects have long deployed constitutional rights in India (De 2018; Shani 2022) even as they dwell in the gray zones of the law; they are also active participants in recent campaigns for expanding the scope of rights (Baviskar and Sundar 2008). The hard-fought struggles for the rights to information, livelihood, food, forests, and education are hardly forms of unpredictable subaltern politics; indeed, these campaigns succeeded in taking entitlements out of the realm of transience and legislating them as permanent rights. Thus, food and livelihood are no longer just matters of accommodative policy beholden to regime change. The RTI is an enabler and enforcer of these other entitlements as rights, as I explained in chapter 1. The politics of political society, like that of elite civil society, unfolds on the terrain of law and rights as much as governmental policy and exceptions.

In this chapter, I approach civil and political society as overlapping and entangled terrains as well as forms of doing politics. As Nivedita Menon (2010) suggests, they are "two *styles of political engagement* that are available to people—the former style is more available to an urbanized elite, the latter to the rest. The availability is fluid and contextual and not fixed by class" (11–12; see also Nigam 2012). Furthermore, these styles and realms are gendered. Civil society is a masculinized mode and arena of politics with the liberal (male) citizen as its normative subject, as feminist scholars of Western democracies have long contended (Brown 1995; MacKinnon 1989). In contrast, political society as a "welfarized" realm is feminized and centered around dependent actors, not ideal citizens.

I now juxtapose the narratives of two people with distinctive experiences of the RTI law and good governance to draw out the classed and gendered nature of political and civil society politics. My analysis reveals the limitations of the popular view of the RTI law as empowering all citizens-in-common. In fact, this law is struggled over as different groups stake claims over who can own and use it rightfully. What becomes apparent is not a leveled political playing field but a split subject of rights, and indeed a divided landscape of rights.

"People Like Us": Ravi at the Cha Bar, Delhi

He ordered whole-leaf Darjeeling tea—first flush. I ordered fresh lime soda. Drinks in hand, Ravi and I settled into conversation in a quiet corner of the humming Cha Bar. Ravi had chosen this upscale café, nestled inside the Oxford Bookstore in central Delhi, calling it his de facto office, where he could be spotted on any given day conducting his daily business. This energetic, wiry, and relatively wealthy man sitting across from me introduced himself as a "middle-class activist," a rare breed in his view; people in his class cohort were generally content in their apathetic bubbles, but he was not. He was an RWA member who organized others like himself to demand better municipal governance.

I first encountered Ravi at an RTI meeting for RWA representatives. I knew I wanted to speak with him when I observed the ease with which he embodied a leadership role and the space he took up at that meeting. When I asked if he would agree to an interview, Ravi shrugged, as if he were used to being sought after, and said yes. Having encountered several RWA office bearers in my mother's neighborhood beforehand, I had an inkling of what to expect from our meeting. I expected Ravi to position himself as a citizen frustrated with corruption, entitled to rights and upward mobility, and soldiering to make democratic governance work. But how he performed as a poster child for liberal democratic citizenship while also making a case for illiberal and authoritarian rule, as if there was no tension between the two, suprised and rankled me. There was little room for dialog as he launched into a tirade at the Cha Bar.

Ravi saw himself at the forefront of middle-class political advocacy and used his professional experience in the business world toward that end. "Middle class—people like us, you know"—he gestured toward me and himself—"need to understand that they can really be the engine of change and demand more from governance. That is why I started working in middle-class bastions. Naturally, because of who I am, and because I [saw] a huge potential there—this being the silent majority [that] nobody was paying attention to. RWAs were an untouched group. Their role was limited to looking after the colony affairs. But if we can get together, then we can add value and strength to issues of concern, which touch all of us." That was his calling: to reverse the apparent silencing of the urban middle class and get the state to cater to its needs.

When I asked Ravi what got him interested in advocacy, he shrugged. "I was one of those millions of young men who are angry. I decided that I will bottle up this anger and use it sensibly." He channeled his energy toward governance-focused activism, which, in his words, "requires an attitude and the ability to use resources. Also, the ability to get people together to agree—on anything!"

Ravi got his feet wet in 2005 by protesting against increased electricity tariffs in Delhi in the aftermath of privatization and getting the government to reverse the increase. "The media helped us. Not because we speak English, but because we had people like you and me standing on roads holding placards, which they had never seen before! Public meetings in India happen differently. Normally you send truckloads of [poor] people—you give them five hundred bucks, you put them in trucks, they land up wherever, [and] they say whatever they are supposed [to say].... But we had people quitting offices and standing at crossroads, demanding '10 percent less' tariff." Middle-class protests were unique—not only because people joined of their own volition and skipped professional commitments, but also because they were "civil" (read: classy). Ravi brought up "candlelight vigils" organized by middle-class Delhi-ites during the late 1990s to protest rape and murder cases of young women in their class milieu.[5] Their extraordinariness garnered the attention of the media and state actors, making success possible.

I asked Ravi about other avenues of middle-class participation in improving urban governance, mentioning the Bhagidari scheme in particular. This program was implemented in 2000 by then chief minister Sheila Dixit, directly targeting RWAs and merchant groups. As productive consumers of city services, whose businesses and professional lives are directly affected by inefficient, unaccountable state agencies, RWAs were seen as ideal partners—*bhagidars*—in effecting change.[6] The Delhi government touted this public–private collaboration as innovative good governance. Many RWA members jumped onto the Bhagidari bandwagon to work with the chief minister's office. Not so Ravi. He refused to cooperate with what he saw as a sloughing off of governmental responsibility.

"You can't have a public participation program which is run by the government! It is a strange thing. It is like having a trade union which is controlled by the management," he scoffed. "We have to be on opposite sides—that is the nature of the business [of politics]. The consumer can't be the manufacturer. Bhagidari has a clever modus operandi. You go to the chief minister with a complaint. The chief minister says, 'Gee, why don't you join us? Why don't you solve the problem?' But man, that's why I pay taxes! If I am going to solve the problem, then you need to pay me. My views are clear. Governance is a deal. Um, as a service provider, whether . . . in public sector or private sector, your relationship with a customer is [bound] by a certain contract. Let's say you go into a restaurant and you get a bad dish. What do you do?"

"Either eat it or not," I replied.

"Or you create a ruckus," Ravi retorted. "And the owner has to apologize. He gives you a free ticket; he says, 'I'm so sorry; come back again.' We have to treat government like that—as a servant! You don't let the servant start dictating. At least at the restaurant, I pay after I eat. [The government] takes my money in advance, and then doesn't do what [it] is supposed to do!"

I was struck by the financialized business-speak that laced Ravi's narrative, reading it as a sign of the neoliberal "economization of political life" (Brown 2015, 17). He compared government to a service-sector business. Real citizens were taxpayers, consumers, and middle class, and citizenship was an economic contract between a provider and consumer rather than a political relationship of rights and duties. Partnering with the government as a *bhagidar* was not Ravi's cup of tea. He saw it as a mechanism for controlling RWAs and channeling middle-class anger about governance in the direction of collaboration instead of agonism. Rather than being served by the state, this group of citizens was co-opted to serve the state, and for free! Like other RWA members I interacted with, Ravi insisted that government servants or *sarkari naukar* should serve the public, for the public was the real *malik* (master) in a democracy. Good governance meant righting the skewed master–servant and public–state relationship and getting officials to respond to citizens' commands. Both the public and the citizen in this view were classed, because "only some . . . people can speak the malik–naukar [boss–servant] language of ownership politics" (Roy 2014, 53); Ravi asserted that enunciative privilege unequivocally.

"The middle class actually thinks life is pretty good. But we have no city planning. We have malls and tall buildings but lousy maintenance. We have small, encircled places like this," Ravi continued, gesturing to the café. "But the moment you step out, you step into the rough. We are small islands of prosperity surviving in villages." Ravi pointed to the bustling street scene observable from the Cha Bar, where motorized and nonmotorized vehicles jostled for parking and driving space; where a sea of people walked by or huddled around makeshift food stalls; where plastic cups, paper plates, and banana peels spilled out from garbage bins onto all available surfaces; where decrepit buildings, desperate for renovation, sat amid shiny glass and steel facades; where street peddlers conducted business outside fancy stores. Was this the rough that Ravi wanted me to see? The unsightly backwardness and chaos that abutted and marred Delhi's urban modernity?

"We live in a city in which a posh area flat costs more than probably a flat in Singapore. We pay the highest taxes, the highest rents, and we don't ask a single question. We draw water from Sintex [brand] tanks! Have you ever gone to Singapore and seen plastic Sintex tanks on the roofs of apartment buildings? Or Malaysia? Forget Europe. And we have no [public] transportation. . . . Total madness. If we only had a decent bus which a decent lady like you and maybe a decent guy like me—[who] don't really want to be packed in like sardines and probably want air-conditioning—if you had just given us that option, there would be no need for cars! We'd have a decent city to live in."

The decent and the rough in Ravi's narrative vision were classed codes that signified contrasting ways of life in the city. The first represented the middle classes, who aspired for an aesthetically and functionally modern urban life but were forced to settle for less because of poor governance. The second represented migrant masses who were slumifying Delhi. Creating a decent Delhi meant regulating the inflow of poor migrants, stated Ravi. "All the people who are moving into the city are actually dragging it down, not raising it. And yet you keep letting more people in all the time. You need to block them! . . . You need to change governance, essentially."

"Do you find the RTI law is a useful tool to change governance?" I interjected, mentioning the online chatter among RWA members about the law—tips, tricks, success stories—that I occasionally scrolled through.

Ravi chuckled. "I participate in these online groups. They are completely haywire! I am reminded of the adage 'Do not mistake activity for progress.' There is a lot of activity.... RTI activism in our [RWAs] is self-congratulatory. It's like someone likes the challenge, the kick of getting that *babu* [bureaucrat] to respond to him. 'You won't talk to me! I'll show you!' It's like a lovers' tiff in a romance has just begun."

Calling the state's relationship with the middle class a lovers' tiff seemed curious, but it captured the agonistic, confrontational political stance that Ravi wanted the professional elites to take toward the state as well as the pro–middle class lovers' bias of the state itself. Not only has this class benefited from liberalization policies, but they are also overrepresented in state institutions as politicians and bureaucrats.

Ravi continued. "The important thing is that [RWAs] see RTI as a mechanism of acquiring power.... Information is power.... The fact that [a person] can find information is the cake. What he does with it is a different ball game. RTI has opened up a channel. You know, the genie is out; we just don't want it bottled up again."

He provided an example of this genie's powers. The local municipal authority had informed residents in his neighborhood that they were planning to construct a *samudaay bhavan,* or community center, to be used for weddings and celebrations. "The municipality never bothered to ask the *samudaay,* the community that lives there, whether they wanted such a center," chuckled Ravi. "We are the guys who are paying the taxes. You are not doing this gratis! It is our money, and [things] should be done per our requirement. See, we don't actually need a community center for weddings. Because people in affluent colonies never get married in community centers. We rent [expensive] hotels." One of Ravi's RWA colleagues filed an RTI petition to gather information about municipal plans for the empty lot and used it to obtain a court order in their interest. "We said we want a library and reading room, a hobby center, a yoga center, meeting hall, and an RWA office. Not a community center. The court order says these facilities should be provided.... But tell me, why did we have to go through all of this! What for!"

Although successful, Ravi read this example of legal rigamarole and the fact that his RWA had to use the RTI at all as a sign of bad governance in an immature, underdeveloped democracy. "We are still a nascent democracy, you know; we haven't crossed over. There are not enough public-spirited foundations that are powerful enough to take on government. People have not formalized a system of aggregation at civil levels or invested in institutions. And we inherited a system of governance we didn't invent." Ravi sniggered. "Frankly speaking, the right to information belonged to us the moment we became a nation in 1947 [and] chose to call ourselves a democracy. It is a universal law—a natural corollary of democracy.... Information has to be shared. It is a right—something which is due to you and which you merely acquire by filing a document. There is nothing bombastic about it. There should be no activism required for it. We basically have a sad, lousy system. The RTI is a step, and I absolutely think it is necessary because that is the only way we can put any pressure."

"So the RTI is helping make systemic change?" I probed.

"No!" retorted Ravi. "It can't! Systemic change requires quantum. You can't impact the system by being a minuscule change agent. This instrument has to be picked up by a very large number of people. And that it is not going to happen very soon."

"Why?" I queried. "If RTI is an 'empowerment tool' for all citizens, what prevents its widespread usage?"

Ravi had a ready answer. "What we need to understand is that it is going to be used first by people who have access or who have an interest in information. RTI has more power to work in the middle-class level— the people who know how to do this, the people who persist. To start at the lowest level is good, but it is not going to be effective. The man who is uneducated has to depend on somebody who can fill and file an RTI form.... Even educated people have difficulty in phrasing an [RTI] query." He paused. "I have never personally filed an RTI application, by the way." Of course he hasn't, I thought to myself. "There are other people who file RTIs for me. And I have access to information through different sources." He gave me a pointed look, presuming that I needed no explanation about how elites use networks, privilege, and money (bribes) to access information and make government work for them. "So, I don't think RTI is something that will go from down there [grassroots level] upwards but actually go from up here [elite level] downwards. The RTI Act came out of rural agitations and was intended to help rural folk, marginal farmers, and the dispossessed in cities. But rural areas haven't seen much use." I wanted to tell him otherwise—that a study had shown that in the first two and a half years of the RTI Act, around 400,000 applications were filed in rural areas (compared with 1.6 million in urban ones),[7] even though national media and civil society did not pay much attention to these "marginal" stories. But Ravi gave me no chance to counter his claim. "The have-nots in cities are filing RTI applications, but only with the help of NGOs," he continued. "Our system takes resources and perseverance to access. And questioning a higher authority is alien to our culture. Only the enlightened person is asking questions." This enlightened vanguard transforming governance was middle class and male.

Ravi further asserted that RTI was an appropriate tool for the privileged classes because they tended to prefer bureaucratic over electoral avenues for political participation (Lama-Rewal 2007). His involvement in voter registration drives in Delhi gave him firsthand experience of the middle-class aversion to voting. "'Vote for whom?' [RWA members] tell us when we approach them. 'This politician is a crook, and that politician is a crook, too!' In my colony, some [people] do exercise their individual right to vote . . . but most are absolutely indifferent. Therefore, this [RTI] interaction is necessary." It was different for slum dwellers, who mainly interfaced with governance during elections. "People from the *jhuggis* [slums] vote. . . . The whole lot, they cast their vote to a particular party. So the parties and politicians like to pacify them. Politicians utilize their funds for their vote banks. Unfortunately, the vote bank in this country is not commensurate with the people who . . ." Ravi trailed off momentarily. "You know, 60 percent of Delhi doesn't even stay in authorized housing. And because they don't hold legal status, these people are so manipulable. Because you can negotiate with them, offer them alcohol or saris for votes. To expect them to lead this movement for governance change is not very practical. . . . See, democracy works best when there is some homogeneity in the sense of how people are educated and how they think . . . or [they] speak the same language in terms of ethics, morals. You could argue, really, whether democracy is the best option for a country like ours. Think about it. We just accepted that democracy is the best thing in the world. I don't think so. Not necessarily. If the function of governance is to deliver a better quality of life to people, I am willing to look at any other system which does it quickly . . . Look at the Singapore model. I mean, what democracy!"

"Um, authoritarianism . . ." I began, but Ravi didn't let me finish.

"Yeah, what does it matter! Today it is all about delivery, and the smoother, the faster, the quicker it is, the more justifiable the mechanisms are. There is somebody out there, even as you and I have a cup of tea in Cha Bar, who is dying in . . . say Kalahandi, Orissa [a generic symbol of an impoverished place].[8] Are we so in love with the beauteous concept and model of democracy that we are willing to sacrifice his life, his health?" Funny how the plight of marginalized groups can be used to make a case against democratic rule, I thought. Ravi took a deep breath. "Democracy doesn't suit us, frankly. A country like ours, you know—it is cacophony. It's noisy. It doesn't listen. There's just too many people. There's no discipline. I think we are getting too straitjacketed by ideas of democracy. It is not a deity."

~

How does one situate Ravi and make sense of his narrative? I begin with how he positioned himself: as a middle-class man and a spokesperson for his peers. Given the social and political capital he bore, it may seem odd to call someone like Ravi middle class. Yet this is how elites in India name themselves (Baviskar and Ray 2011, 7) because the moniker "middle class" is broad and imprecise (Deshpande 2003; Fernandes 2011; Srivastava 2015). Rather than being solely tied to wealth and income status or being a hardened structural position, middle classness is a lived social relationship where "some men, as a result of common experiences . . . feel and articulate the identity of their interests as between themselves, and as against other men whose interests are different" (Thompson 1966, 9). It connotes a "particular orientation towards modernity" (Baviskar and Ray 2011, 5) and a habitus (Bourdieu 1984) elaborated through such practices as a consumerist lifestyle, expressed a desire for modernization, and an understanding of the self as a citizen belonging to civil society. The Indian middle class universalizes its interests as "public interest," which governance institutions must protect and serve. Its "power . . . resides in its claim of representing all Indians—the aam aadmi" (Baviskar and Ray 2011, 7).

Ravi embodied this class identity, mind-set, and relationship, performing simultaneously as an "everyman and elite" (Baviskar and Ray 2011, 23) who is "stiffed by state domination and alienated by electoral appeasement of 'vote-banks' [but] can now reinvigorate politics by bringing in efficiency and rooting out corruption" (Baviskar and Ray 2011, 3).

He considered himself part of the "silent majority" that was ignored (oppressed?) by lousy governance and politics—never mind that the Indian middle class is neither silent nor a majority, even though it presents itself as a major constituency that should matter for policy. And never mind that positioning the middle class as a victim of poor governance denies the history of how this class was consolidated by the colonial state and continues to benefit from state policies since independence.[9]

Ravi also saw himself as part of a small vanguard leading the way toward change. His musings on a decent city for decent people reveal a modernist aspiration, albeit one that chooses Asia (Singapore) as its model. "Forget Europe!" he declared. Manifesting this ideal of a decent, orderly, modern city that reflects middle-class desires and lifestyles meant erasing unsightly people and objects—migrants, overhead water tanks, excessive cars—that tarnished Delhi's urbanscape and conjured backwardness, dirt, and danger (Douglas 2002).

Urban studies scholarship on India tells us that Ravi's desire to transform Delhi from a Third World into a world-class city emblematic of middle-class sensibility and civility is shared across his class cohort (Baviskar 2004, 2011; Ghertner 2011b; Srivastava 2015).[10] RWAs have pursued public interest litigation since the early 2000s to remove slums. Ironically, these private bodies allege that slums and slum dwellers constitute a public "nuisance" because they impede the "quality of life and security" (Ghertner 2011b, 287) desired by the middle classes (see also Ghertner 2008). Thus, what appears dirty and chaotic—a slum and its inhabitants—must be illegal and must be demolished for Delhi to emerge as a "world-class" city (Ghertner 2011b).[11]

Ravi projected this sense of ownership of a sanitized city. He wanted to stop impoverished migrants from entering Delhi and "dragging it down" further; the 60 percent of Delhi residing in "unauthorized housing" was bad enough. Urban governance and planning, Ravi believed, ought to center the tax-paying middle class—the only legitimate public—and ensure its expectations of well-being. This decent (civil) group possessed the vision and wherewithal to confront and transform the state and lead the nation toward a better future. It could no longer be ignored or silenced (if it had ever been) because it made up for its lack of electoral enthusiasm with its active use of bureaucratic and legal mechanisms to hold the state accountable and protect its privilege. Ravi maintained that the enlightened citizen-auditors who challenged authority and raised questions through the RTI law were people like him: urban, educated, middle or upper class, resourceful, and male. These were the extraordinary and empowered common men as rights-bearing and -actualizing citizens who constitute civil society. They were the ideal-typical subjects of the RTI law, not the poor.

Ravi's stance toward political society appears conflicted at first glance. He was dismissive of marginalized urban groups for undermining India's modernity and lacking the ability, attitude, and resources to transform governance. Deferential toward those who ruled them and dependent on the sops thrown at them during election time, these urban masses could not be expected to participate in bettering governance. Neither could the rural poor, who were dying in faraway places like Kalahandi as they waited for help to reach them. Ravi's disdain for the undeserving urban poor and savoir-like pity for the rural poor are not, in fact, contradictory; in the end, they work to instate middle class people as both vanguard and common men and argue for efficient authoritarianism over democracy (see chapter 6). Indeed, for Ravi, the very presence of the uneducated, unwashed, and unaware masses, regardless of where they are situated, rendered democracy inconvenient and unsuitable for India. Good governance as apolitical, smooth, and timely service delivery demanded finding alternative forms of disciplinarian rule as exemplified by Singapore. If "dumping democracy . . . [is] the privilege of the Platinum PLUs [people like us]" (Sainath 2011), then Ravi performed that privilege with panache.

"A Slum Woman": Pushpa ji (Her Real Name, as She Wanted It)

Pushpa asked to meet in Sheikh Sarai, a mixed-class neighborhood in South Delhi. I had seen her once before at a public hearing organized by Satark Nagrik Sangathan (SNS),[12] a Delhi-based people's group that promotes government transparency and accountability. SNS helps South Delhi camp residents like Pushpa use the RTI law to access entitlements. The RTI story she shared at that hearing riveted me, so that I asked SNS for her contact information. It turned out that Pushpa worked with them as an organizer.

As I waited for Pushpa on the road that divides the nicely appointed flats from the working-class part of Sheikh Sarai, I heard a voice call out,

"Namaste! Hello!" There was Pushpa, a five-foot-tall, sari-and-shawl-clad powerhouse—rushing toward me. I waved back. "Anu ji?" she checked as she neared. *"Haan,"* yes, I answered. "Namaste, Pushpa ji!" "Namaste, namaste! *Chaliye.*" Let's go.

Pushpa guided me to SNS's basement office in the working-class area. We entered a medium-sized room, which opened onto a tiny courtyard at one end. Eight women were huddled on the office floor, filling out paperwork. From the hum of voices, I gathered that the women were residents of nearby camps seeking SNS's assistance in filing RTI petitions to address survival needs. Pushpa led me to one end of the room to avoid the hubbub.

I settled on the floor like everyone else, laying out my recording device and propping a small, hard cushion that I was carrying against the wall behind me. I must have winced, for Pushpa asked what was wrong. "Back pain," I answered, embarrassed about the class comfort that the cushion probably signaled. Pushpa nodded sympathetically; she offered me a chair, which I refused, and some advice on a massage oil, which I noted. A woman sitting nearby, who had overheard our interaction, spoke up. "*Didi* [sister]," she addressed me, "go to that door between this room and the courtyard. Stand at the threshold, half in and half out, and say out loud, 'Mujhe chhor do!' [Let go of me!]" "What are you saying, Meena?" Pushpa intervened half-laughingly. "Yeh purane zamane ki baatein hain [These are old-fashioned beliefs]." Suggesting that physical pain was a sign of being possessed by evil spirits connoted backwardness. It had no place in the modern, rational worldview and privilege I embodied (and to which the other women in the room were meant to aspire).

The room became awkwardly quiet. All eyes were on me as I rose from my perch. Announcing that my daily dose of ibuprofen offered little respite and my prognosis of spinal surgery was only a desperate hope, I walked to the door. Straddling the frame, one leg in and the other out, I declared, "Let go of me." Gentle laughter followed, and then Meena's encouraging words: "Say it once more, forcefully." "Let go of me!" I repeated, with greater verve and volume. Affirming sounds indicated that I may have relayed the message to the spirits and perhaps cracked the formal veneer that my class privilege and status brought into the room. Meena and the others returned to their paperwork. I reclaimed my cushioned corner and turned to Pushpa.

I began by confessing how moved I was to hear her powerful RTI testimony at the public hearing. Pushpa smiled. "Hum jis desh se hain, vahan to ghar se bahar bhi nahin nikal sakte the [Where I come from, I couldn't even step outside the house]. Women remain behind a *ghunghat* [veil], and so did I. Always." "Where do you come from?" I asked. "Sikar district, Rajasthan." "Oh, that's where the Roop Kanwar sati happened in 1987," I remarked casually, recalling the widow immolation incident where eighteen-year-old Kanwar was burned to death on her husband's pyre.[13] Pushpa's eyes widened. "You know about that? My village is right next to Deorala, where the sati took place. I wasn't there [when it happened], but my sister was. People say that there was something different *[kuch alag]* about Roop Kanwar that day—the look in her eyes." Pushpa hesitated. First evil spirits, now sati. Could our conversation about RTI, rights, and citizenship accommodate such apparent anachronisms? "*Khair, chhoriye* [Anyway, let's drop it]," she said, and we did.

Pushpa married young and moved to Delhi's Jagdamba camp with her husband. Although literate—she and her sister were the only girls in their village who attended school—she was intimidated by city life. "I couldn't talk in front of people in the camp or even say my name out loud. I was fearful, hesitant. Aur ab dekhiye [And look at me now]! I work, I travel alone everywhere, I share information, and I speak in public. I can talk to anyone!"

Pushpa credited this transformation to her association with SNS, whose representatives she first met some years ago, when they visited her camp to talk about resolving local problems relating to food rations, water, electricity, garbage removal, and public toilets (Webb 2012).[14] Pushpa liked what she heard and began attending SNS meetings despite opposition from family and neighbors.

During one such meeting, she learned that private schools in Delhi were required to reserve a certain percentage of seats for children belonging to "economically weaker sections" and educate them tuition-free.[15] Since her daughters were already attending public schools, she decided to avail of this reservation quota for her young son. But the process was challenging. The school administrators questioned her ability to afford expenses beyond tuition. "I told them that I run a small *kirana dukaan* [kiosk selling basic groceries] from my home and my husband is a *raj mistry* [skilled mason] and that we will manage even if we have to go hungry." She put in his application but received no response from the school.

With SNS's guidance, she drew up an RTI petition in late 2005, asking Delhi's education department about the cause of the delay and any redress mechanisms. "I was among the first ones to use the RTI, which was still very new!" Pushpa claimed proudly. "I had to go and submit my application at the education department. But I was terrified because I had never really left my neighborhood until then." The roughly eight kilometers between her home and the education office signified a more profound divide between the familiar and the unknown, the informal and the official. "Will I be able to find the office? How will I talk to the staff there? What is going to happen to me?" Pushpa's husband advised her to take an auto-rickshaw directly to her destination. "I summoned strength from somewhere inside, hired an auto, and went. But when I reached the office, the staff refused to accept my RTI application."

After pleading and waiting, Pushpa finally got one man to look at her application. "'Why do you want to enroll your son in a private school?' he said. 'How will you manage it? You live in a slum.' Anu ji, I didn't even know what 'slum' meant!" Pushpa laughed. "My village education had not prepared me for this." Maneuvering city and government offices required a different kind of literacy and smarts. Despite feeling like a fish out of water, Pushpa gathered her wits and told the official not to ask her personal questions; how she would put her child through school was not his business. "Usually, I am very sweet with people, but this time I was angry. I told the staff . . . not to waste my time. And that if they were going to refuse to take my RTI application, they should give that to me in writing so I could approach a higher officer with my petition." The mention of bureaucratic hierarchy and disciplining did the trick. Her RTI application was accepted.

Within three days, the school admitted her son, but Pushpa never received a response to her RTI query. The law facilitated her access to the right to education, but information remained elusive.

Pushpa's challenges did not end with her son's enrollment. Private school expenses strained her modest salary and her husband's unpredictable, contractual income. "There are so many things that we have to pay for beyond the free tuition. Books. Winter uniforms are so expensive. Then there are school trips. If my son wants to go on a trip, then as a parent, I can't refuse. Dikkat to bahut hai [It is very difficult]. Par koi baat nahin; thoda kam khaa lete hain [But it's OK; we eat a little less]." Pushpa smiled and sighed. Social interaction with class privileged teachers and parents also presented problems. "My husband always says that sitting alongside *bade log* [big people] at school functions feels *ajeeb* [awkward]." They felt like interlopers, transgressing a space not meant for them.

By 2008, Pushpa had helped twenty-five camp children gain admission to private schools and many more families acquire government documents like income, caste, and birth certificates. These documents enable low-income families to access free education, scholarships, and other entitlements. Obtaining them requires police authentication of each applicant's identity, address, and other information. This arena is ripe for bribes, which the RTI helps navigate.

Pushpa told me of the time she assisted eighteen women obtain birth certificates for their children. "Our camp's headman demanded 1,500 rupees for each certificate, which was unaffordable. So I found out the [official] procedure and applied [on their behalf]. The police summoned us for verification. I took all eighteen kids and their mothers with me to the station. The cop at the front desk told us, 'We cannot use women as witnesses. Bring your husbands to vouch for the dates and places of birth of these kids.' What a strange thing to say! 'That is ridiculous,' I told the man. 'Women can't vouch for the birth of their own children? . . . Didn't Indira Gandhi rule this country? If women can't do all this, then why don't you remove Pratibha Patil [then president of India] from her position? Are there rights that women don't have? Can you show me where it is written so I can learn?' The policeman gave me a threatening look. 'Who are you, a *neta* [leader]?' he asked. 'What's your name, and where do you live?' 'I am Pushpa from Jagdamba Camp,' I replied. 'I haven't seen any [vocal] woman like you in that area,' he commented suspiciously. So I offered to show him my ID. But he waved it off and said that verifications for income and birth certificates would cost 500 rupees per head. I questioned him again. 'Why are you asking for money? Is there a written order stating the cost of police verification? You are supposed to come to our homes to conduct this inquiry. But you order us to come to the police station, and then you ask for money. And you also threaten that if we don't pay, our verification will not go through!' The policeman turned red in the face. I told him that if he refused to verify the applications, I would go to his boss, the SHO [station house officer]. 'And what if he refuses?' the policeman retorted. 'Then I will go to the deputy commissioner and then to the courts,' I replied. The policeman made some nasty remark about how women connected with NGOs and *sangathans* [collectives] cause trouble—'*Bhagwan bachaye!* [God save us from them!]' But he processed the applications."

Pushpa chuckled. "My own husband paid a 500-rupee bribe to the police to get an income certificate. He justified it by saying that the policemen shuttle around every day, so a little extra money for *chai-paani* [tea-water] is OK. But I disagree. The police stiff the poor and they use us against each other! 'Your neighbor paid 500,' they tell us, 'and so should you.' Yeh hamara khoon chuste hain [They suck our blood]. We pay taxes on everything from soap to oil to food, which funds their salaries. Why should we give them additional free money? I don't like it one bit and I told my husband so." Pushpa even got the policeman her husband had bribed to return the 500 rupees. "My husband was shocked.... Now he supports what I do. He even went with me to the public hearing that you attended and clapped after I spoke." I smiled and asked her to recount the details of the story that had gotten her a big round of applause.

Pushpa had submitted an RTI petition inquiring about the duties of local elected officials—MLAs and ward councilors in Delhi. The petition asked straightforward questions: how much money these officials get for local development, and how they spend these funds. When she did not receive a reply, Pushpa filed an appeal allowed under the RTI—a first for her—and was summoned to a hearing.

"The appeal hearing was in a big hall full of men, with the magistrate [adjudicating the hearing] sitting at one end. I was alone. The magistrate struck his gavel on the table. 'Silence!' he shouted, and then asked me why I had submitted an application seeking information about the ward councilor. 'What are you going to do with this information? You dress well, and you seem educated. But you live in a slum.' I told him calmly that he was being condescending. Regardless of whether I was educated or not and where I lived, my RTI questions deserved answers. The men in the room were laughing and humiliating me, but somehow I found the strength to say all this."

The magistrate continued to pose tangential, patronizing questions. "He asked if I offer my husband a glass of water when he comes home from work. I replied, 'Alongside a glass of water, I also offer him tea, sir, because I know how hard he works.' The magistrate replied, 'If you run around all day seeking information and working with an NGO, when do you have time to take care of your husband! Take my advice and watch some good programs on TV. Do you have a TV at home?' I was so upset at his question, but I said yes. 'You should watch the Sanskaar [traditional values] channel,' he continued. 'It is very good for housewives. Forget about information. Get involved in *paath pooja* [religious rituals]. Become a good woman.'"

Pushpa looked incredulous. "Anu ji, I run a household. I have children. And this man was trying to teach me! I was furious. I told him that I have no time to waste on offering prayers to idols. I have to deal with sludgy drains right outside my house, a serious drinking water problem, and public toilets that need lighting and properly welded doors. I need to meet my councilor who has funds to address such issues. 'I must get the information I requested,' I told the magistrate. 'And if you can't help me, then give it to me in writing.' I stood up and placed a blank sheet of paper on his desk." The official warned her about overstepping her bounds, but he also stated that she would get the information she sought.

"I was in a closed room with all these men who kept ridiculing me. I was scared.... But I put on a brave face. That magistrate thought I was *moorkh* [stupid]. But in the end, he came out looking stupid. Why shouldn't I ask these questions! Hum apna mat *daan* karte hain [We cast our votes] so that our elected politicians can speak on our behalf and do the work we ask them to do. Sewage, garbage, roads, water, and cleanliness—yeh chotee-motee cheezein [these little things] can be easily taken care of. If I can find out about the development funds allocated to our ward councilor and how they are spent through the RTI, then I can ask him to put some money toward our camp's needs. Then we too can experience some *vikas* [progress]."

"So, the RTI is helping *aam log* [ordinary people]?" I interjected. "Yes, *bilkul* [absolutely]," said Pushpa. Meena, having overheard bits of our conversation, chimed in. "Without RTI, our work just doesn't get done. No government functionary does anything without pressure; this much I know. You either pay a bribe or use the RTI. I have run ragged trying to get caste certificates, income certificates, food rations. You name it. Those who sit in a *sarkari kursi* [government seat] push us around. Voh hamare saath kutton jaisa vyavhaar kartein hain [They treat us like dogs]. Just because we are poor. They don't even care if we have the means to visit government offices. Every time I go to Kapashera [where administrative offices are located], it costs me 100 rupees round trip on a bus. And when I get there, the officials tell me this or that is wrong with my application. 'We can't accept it!' They toss the application in my face. So 100 rupees and four hours later, I come back with nothing. I lose time and wages [as a maid].... I used to avoid going to government offices because I was afraid. But this RTI law has given people like me strength to move forward. I am grateful to whoever implemented it. Today I am not scared of anyone. I no longer plead with officials and politicians, my head bowed and hands folded. Never again! I am not a *ghulam* [slave]."

Pushpa nodded. "These councilors and MLAs only come to our camps during elections. They don't ask us about our dikkat aur pareshani [problems and frustrations] or inform us about funds for local projects. They just throw daroo, kambal, ya paisa [alcohol, blankets, or money] at us and ask for our votes. Once the elections are over, we don't even see them. What do we get in the end? Nothing." Pushpa and her neighbors had taken an unprecedented step for the upcoming legislative assembly elections. Knowing that candidates would visit their camp seeking promises for votes and distributing sops, they hung large banners at each camp entrance that stated, "We want neither money nor alcohol. We want *vikas* [development]. The candidate who solves our problems will get our vote. Our demands are: a proper garbage dump, regular cleanup of drains, water, and functional latrines." These banners got things rolling. The cleaning of the main drain and construction of a garbage dump had started. Public latrine doors were repaired. This was anything but usual, commented Pushpa.

Access to drinking water, however, remained a major problem. The wealthy "colony-wallahs and *kothi*-wallahs [residents of colonies and big houses] near our camps complain that we steal their water without paying for it," said Pushpa. She explained that camp residents sympathize with the water problem that colony residents face but shouldn't be blamed for it. Having no access to municipal water infrastructure, camp-wallahs are forced to tap water pipes illegally; they pay for this connectivity and internal pipe laying out of their own pockets. Wealthy residents routinely cut off these connections out of spite. "We are ready to pay for the water, but at least give us that facility," Pushpa stated in frustration. "We are *insaan* [human] too. Hummein jeene ka adhikaar nahin hai kya [Don't we have a right to live]! Are we not allowed to live? Kya paani jeene ke haq ka hissa nahin hai [Is water not part of the right to life]?"

The issue, Pushpa implied, was not poor people stealing water but bad planning and governance alongside deep inequalities between those citizens who deserve to thrive and those who are let die (Foucault 2003). The majority are "rendered abject citizens of the city" (Anand 2012, 487)—not because they do not have rights but because they are routinely denied those rights, and even, perhaps, the right to have rights that makes us human (Arendt 1958).[16] Meena tutted sympathetically on hearing Pushpa's plea for water. In her camp, they had some access to municipal water because they had a crematorium that required water for rituals. "The municipality can't cut off water to our area so easily," she scoffed. Ironically, the rites of the dead could secure what the rights of the living failed to do.

Thus, state representatives, middle classes, and elites all invisibilized the poor and endangered their survival. Meena recalled a wealthy lady who had spoken at the end of the public hearing where Pushpa had shared her RTI story. "Do you remember that Mrs. Lal or whatever her name was, Pushpa ji? She said something very upsetting to our faces. 'You people come from [backward] states like U.P. [Uttar Pradesh] and Bihar to beg or to find employment.' I really wanted to give her a piece of my mind." Pushpa nodded, adding that Mrs. Lal had later clarified that "what she really meant was that village people should not migrate to cities. Instead of living in slums and participating in RTI activism to access entitlements and rights in Delhi, they should focus their efforts on improving their own villages so that they never have to leave." Pushpa and Meena shook their heads in mock disbelief. Being repeatedly reminded by officials and colony-wallahs that the modern state and city were privileged enclosures and common people like them "matter out of place" (Douglas 2002, 36) was tiresome. Refusing this elitist naming and emplacement required strenuous daily work: visiting police stations, reasoning or fighting with colony-residents over survival needs, struggling for recognition and care from state officials, filing RTI petitions, gathering certificates, fighting for inaccessible rights and improved governance, and so on. Citizenship was anything but an equal and secure status handed on a platter. It was a form of hard labor (Das 2011) that Pushpa and others like her performed daily.

This is what political society politics looks and feels like.

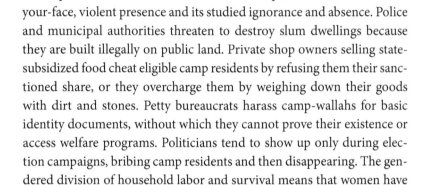

It is impossible to avoid the state in Delhi's camps, both in terms of its in-your-face, violent presence and its studied ignorance and absence. Police and municipal authorities threaten to destroy slum dwellings because they are built illegally on public land. Private shop owners selling state-subsidized food cheat eligible camp residents by refusing them their sanctioned share, or they overcharge them by weighing down their goods with dirt and stones. Petty bureaucrats harass camp-wallahs for basic identity documents, without which they cannot prove their existence or access welfare programs. Politicians tend to show up only during election campaigns, bribing camp residents and then disappearing. The gendered division of household labor and survival means that women have to constantly encounter inimical, alienating state agencies and bear the brunt of their daily contempt and violence. The official adjudicating on Pushpa's RTI appeal, for instance, advised her to stop seeking information about local governance that affected her daily life and focus instead on being a properly domesticated woman. Other government representatives impugned her for daring to exert her rights and question their authority. This vividly illuminates how the state's classism and masculinism (Brown 1995; Menon 2004; Sharma 2008) is performed through commonplace bureaucratic interactions with subaltern women.

As if these forms of violence were not enough, RWAs in adjoining middle-class and affluent neighborhoods file complaints and legal cases against camp residents for poaching water and electricity, encroaching on land, and being nuisances that mar the look and functioning of modern Delhi. These civil society associations function like extensions of the disciplinary and policing arms of the state, and their actions reproduce precarity in camps; never mind that RWA members routinely extend their properties onto public land without authorization. Though they criticize the special treatment, "reservations," and entitlements that political society denizens receive from elected representatives, Platinum PLUs also use political society negotiation tactics with state agencies to carve out their entitled status and protect their interests (Menon 2010).

These are the manifestations of classist, patriarchal statist power and structural violence that Pushpa, Meena, and other migrant subaltern women live with. They make up the constitutive outside of the modern city: the inside that is cast outside, and without which the inside would not function. In the permanent temporariness of their life and politics, things like entitlements, rights, and survival are not guaranteed. As interlopers in the city, they navigate the boundaries between formality and informality, legality and illegality, and labor to survive by any means necessary. Sometimes this means tapping into "networks of illegality, such as stealing electricity, water, [and] bribing their way through Kafkaesque bureaucratic structures to access civic amenities that the legal city takes for granted" (Liang 2005, 6). Sometimes it means using the language of legality and rules, and invoking the RTI. There exists no other effective means of habitability amid persistent threats from indifferent or vicious state agents who treat them "like dogs" and middle-class people who think they own the city and would rather not share it at all.

Pushpa's stories challenge Chatterjee's (2004) claim that subaltern subjects almost always rely on negotiation, not law, to make life possible at the margins. Indeed, the law is as important to political society tactics as going beyond it is.

> The slum dweller . . . has little choice but to ignore the law in order to carry on with the rather difficult task of surviving a hostile city, challenging the idea that it is the natural role of law to ensure public good. At other times, you follow the pores . . . [that are] a part of the structure and design of the legal order itself . . . created to benefit the elite few who know how to manipulate the legal machinery in their favour, and enter these pores to access an otherwise stubborn institution. (Liang 2005, 15)

Lawrence Liang (2005) describes this kind of flitting in and out of the sphere of law as "porous legalities." It is a transgressive mode of survival shaped by the "schizoid relationship between legality and illegality in postcolonial cities" (8) and a "distrust of the usual normative myths of the rule of law, such as rights, equality, access to justice, etc." (15). It constitutes a political society form of politics that marks both elite and subaltern domains. Where elites selectively flout and invoke laws to secure privilege, subaltern subjects, like Pushpa, use porous legalities to "create avenues of participation and make claims to the city" (Liang 2005, 7).

At once using and exceeding legal frames, urban subaltern politics is not restricted to claiming rights from the state. It is also not about rights construed narrowly as discreet instruments that are held or exerted but something more accretive. Pushpa's narrative indicates a more encompassing politics of ongoing rightfulness that faces state and elite actors, and spills outside the tight confines of the law.

Consider the issue of water, for instance, which both Pushpa and Ravi raised, albeit differently. Ravi used poor water infrastructure—unsightly water tanks on top of buildings—to decry a compromised modernity that choked off the aspirational horizon of Platinum PLUs (and, by extension, the nation) to claim world-class status. Meanwhile, Pushpa's complaint about water was not a matter of infrastructural aesthetics but of dire lack, a constant reminder of a denial of one's biological needs, political standing, and humanity by the state and the haves. Yet this cannot be read as an instantiation of a politically stripped "bare life" status (Agamben 1998), for Pushpa explicitly called on her right to live. Veena Das (2011) writes that among India's dispossessed, it is not the "splitting [of] life into the biological and the political . . . [but] their mutual absorption that comes to inform the notion of rights in the sense of *haq*" (320). Pushpa invoked this prior biopolitical right to life to challenge her invisibilization by powerful others and demand her share in a common resource: water.

James Ferguson (2015) uses the term "rightful share" to describe the politics surrounding redistributive welfare policies in Southern Africa. This politics concerns

> a kind of claim-making that involves neither a compensation for work nor an appeal for "help." . . . [It] relies less on the liberal idea of rights "held" by individuals than on the principle (more moral than legal) that material distributions must answer to some idea of the proper, of the just, of the "rightful." . . . Such distributive claims do not take the form of exchanges at all (neither market nor gift) but instead something more like demand sharing—a righteous claim for a due and proper share grounded in nothing

more than membership (in a national collectivity) or even simply presence. (183–84)

The idea of a rightful share resonates with Pushpa's understanding of her political subjectivity. When Pushpa articulated her right to life, she made a moral demand of rightfulness grounded in presence and cohabitation, not neediness. However, she simultaneously referenced the economic frame, positioning herself as a taxpayer who contributed to government coffers through commodity purchases. She also alluded to the logic of the gift when speaking of voting, using the phrase *mat-daan*—a gift of one's opinion—and specifically emphasizing the word *daan* (gift).[17] The gift of a vote demanded reciprocity from elected officials. Indeed, the right to life references obligation. In the Indian constitution, this right extends beyond "the right not to be deprived of life without due process—it [has] included the obligation of the State to provide the means for pursuing livelihoods" (Das 2011, 325).

Although invoking the logics of the market and the gift, Pushpa referenced her deservedness beyond these frames as well. Perhaps this is the politics of *haq* as rightfulness. It calls on the state to fulfill its legal, social, and moral duty. It also articulates a fierce critique of existing social relations to illuminate a different vision of a "good" life beyond middle-class decency and the governance reforms needed to make it possible.[18]

In Closing: A Fractured Commons

Pratap Bhanu Mehta (2003) reminds us that representative governance in India has always been a classed project, given that it "came to be characterized as simply the outcome of a negotiation between India's elites . . . and colonial powers" (5). This makes for what he calls the "central paradox" (22) of Indian democracy: the continued flourishing of social inequalities and domination despite decades of formally equal political representation (see also Chandoke 2005).

This dynamic between legal equality and hierarchical difference unsettles the normative ideal of citizenship as a generic and identical rights-bearing status applicable to everyone. As Julia Eckert (2011) argues, "differential citizenship has always been the norm" in India and elsewhere (309).[19] Narrating Pushpa's and Ravi's RTI stories side by side allows us to see how differential citizenship is borne and enacted by groups across civil and political society. The point is not so much about having rights in common—Pushpa and Ravi share the RTI—but how those rights are invoked, accessed, and experienced. Put another way, "even though the formal act of claiming a citizenship right is [supposed to be] identical, the modality of claims-making, the meaning of the right, and the imagination of citizenship . . . are quite different" (Roy 2014, 52) for differently located people. Focusing on how rights are mobilized reveals the varied "interpretations that occur in the practices of citizenship, the translations of one's projects, needs and desires into claims on the state" (Eckert 2011, 311).

Differential citizenship generates distinctive modes of political engagement that shed light on the political and civil society relationship in India. They are not merely separate spheres populated by different subjects living on different sides of the law, as Chatterjee (2004) suggests, but forms of political participation with leaky relationships to legality (Liang 2005) that are available to all classes but unevenly distributed (Menon 2010). Juxtaposing Pushpa's and Ravi's narratives illuminates these political modalities in urban India and helps us better understand the split landscape of citizenship and rights.

Ravi projects a "proprietary citizenship" (Roy 2014, 53): a branded consumer and taxpayer status that asserts possessive individualism (MacPherson 1962) and masterly ownership of the servant-like state through a privileged and masculinist style of civil society politics. It exhibits "a particular vision of democracy . . . where the central demand is not so much to join but to claim and own governing practices and arrangements; not so much to share but to scrutinise power and regain 'control' over government officials and elected representatives" (Roy 2014, 53). This agonistic style of politics enables the middle class to reorder governance to protect its interests as public interest and to remake the city and nation in its own image. The place of rights in this politics of proprietary citizenship is secure. There is nothing bombastic about rights like the RTI, as Ravi put it; they need not be fought for, only filed for.

Political society modes of citizenship are different. Pushpa performs citizenship as labor (Das 2011), which is directed at rightfulness, enfranchisement beyond voting, and redistributive justice. It is based in a shared precarity of biological, community, and political life. Here, rights are not owned but owed by virtue of membership in a place and polity. Moreover, rights like education and water are not "gifts for which one should feel grateful but . . . something that one has coming—something that is delivered to you because it is your due" (Ferguson 2015, 179). Thus, feeling obligated and begging—hands folded, heads bent in slavish subjugation, as Meena described it—is unnecessary. Rightfulness is a matter of persistent demand from below, not benevolence from above (Ferguson 2015, 177).

This form of citizenship politics is deliberative and deliberate. Though it may be enacted individually, it transcends an individualized relationship between the state and citizen (Eckert 2011, 314). It doesn't just ask for admission into existing democratic structures but imagines a differently democratic state, polity, and polis that centers the lives and well-being of those who are peripheralized. While such citizenship may need the law to flourish, it cannot be reduced to the law. It is moral and legal, mobilized as much through the figure of the *insaan* or human in relationship and copresence with others, as through that of the *naagrik* (citizen). Das (2011) suggests that subaltern "claims to citizenship are crafted not . . . only through formal legal procedures. Instead, it is the actual labor [they] put in . . . of learning how to deal with legal spaces of courts and police precincts as well as the labor of securing objects [like birth certificates] on whose agency they can call on to establish incremental citizenship that creates new forms in which citizenship can be actualized" (330). Pushpa's narrative illuminates this iterative, layered citizenship that is not an ensured status but a laborious and ongoing political praxis of rightfulness without guarantees.

The expansion of rights made available to Indian citizens through grassroots movements in the past two decades has opened more interfaces for subaltern engagements with the law. At the same time, it has brought into focus the limits and frustrations of such engagements. The person using the RTI is not a generic or abstract citizen-auditor but a gendered and classed subject (see also Cody 2015). The dominant discourse on good governance legal reform, however, avoids confronting these identity intersections and hierarchies. It assumes that the state is a gender- and class-neutral entity, that governance is a technical process, and that both can be changed through laws. This leaves no room for reflecting on the fact that in Delhi, for example, poor women make up the majority of the clientele of NGOs who work on RTI and governance issues; that these women bear an unequal burden of the political labor of survival and rights; and that they routinely face hostile patriarchal state structures and policies. Gendered class identities, relations, and struggles are not incidental to democratic rule and state structures but integral to them. Pushpa's narrative reveals that it is not that subaltern women aren't aware or empowered enough to demand rights; rather, officials and middle-class men don't see these women (and other impoverished groups) as fit to bear rights like the RTI.

Platinum PLUs claim the status of empowered aam aadmi, whose interests, opinions, and actions are the only ones worth their political salt. They simultaneously view themselves as extraordinary leaders who can "act politically in the name of the ordinary" (Roy 2014, 52) because they are enlightened and unencumbered by state dependency. Indeed, it is through the "ideological interplay of its conception of itself as both Everyman and elite vanguard" (Baviskar and Ray 2011, 23) that the middle class positions itself at the center of good governance projects, laws, and rights.

The common man of RTI discourse, then, is not anterior to political projects but is elaborated through them. This common man, moreover, is not inclusive and is unable to suture the split subject of rights. The issue is not whether subaltern masses can or cannot exert rights; they can. Rather, it is that a right like RTI is not viewed as theirs at all. This brings me to my final point, which concerns the tiered landscape of rights itself.

If one disaggregates the new rights passed in India over the past two decades, one can see that they are of two different kinds. On the one hand, we have livelihood, education, and food, which are entitlements reconfigured into rights. They take basic human needs out of the realm of negotiation and government policy priorities and give them a legal force and stability that welfare provisions lack. On the other hand, we have "good governance" rights. The RTI, Lokpal (ombudsperson) law, Whistleblowers' Act, and Nagar Raj law, for example, provoke administrative reforms. These rights are meta in scope; they make up a universal medium in and through which other rights can be effectuated. Activists, like Aruna Roy, view these two streams of rights as inseparable, arguing that entitlement-based rights cannot be realized without bettering governance. The picture is more complicated in practice.

These two sets of rights are gendered, with the first set of entitlements-turned-rights being feminized and the second set of good governance rights masculinized.[20] Relatedly, even as the two sets of rights include all citizens, they tend to interpellate different kinds of subjects.

Members of urban, middle-class civil society position themselves as the ideal-typical subjects of good governance laws, worthy of possessing these "educated" rights. They see entitlement-based rights as targeting marginalized groups and as a new form of corrupt "dolenomics."[21] As BJP politician and former chief minister of Rajasthan Vasundhara Raje put it: "Everybody knows that [NREGA] has been a failure at the state level. I mean, you can't find labor to go into the fields anymore.... I mean it's literally a dole because [people] don't work anymore.... [And] now you've brought in the right to food."[22] Elites decry emergent entitlement rights as a form of populist vote-bank appeasement, which sustains dependence on a *mai-baap sarkar* (welfare state). They cite the "'problem' of the slum voter" (Roy 2014, 51) as a subversion of real democracy, where herd behavior trumps individual choice and where negotiation over state handouts overrides the exertion of rights. In other words, these "simulated" rights threaten to dilute the very idea of liberal rights based in property and self-reliant citizenship. Transforming entitlements into rights transgresses the boundary between rights and the dole, ownership and dependence, and classes and masses—worlds and politics that must remain separate and unequal because they share nothing in common. According to the Platinum PLUs, the RTI law is exclusively theirs because it is not the dole.

While these recently legislated laws do not heal the class and gender rifts in the field of citizenship rights in India, they do signal shifts in the style and language of civil and political society politics, altering the balance between needs and negotiation and rightful claims. Pushpa's stories speak of rightfulness and citizenship as matters of unrelenting democratic struggle, offering a powerful corrective to Ravi's narrative of entitled, enlightened citizenship better secured by authoritarian rule. These stories do not present the RTI law as a neutral, accessible medium, equally empowering for all citizens-in-common. Rather, the RTI is a mechanism through which gendered class is performed and policed. It is a contentious, dense thicket within which contests over what counts as a thriving, good life beyond economic and legal logics, and indeed beyond formal democracy, take place (see also Tidey 2022). The usage of this law by dispossessed urban women alerts us to the fact that any analysis or policy of "radical democratic transformation . . . cannot remain in the rarefied realms of 'civil society' where [political society struggles] may be dismissed as uncivilized" (Menon 2010, 14). It is precisely from the standpoints and experiences of women like Pushpa and Meena that any project of governance reform and structural change must begin.

5

"A River That Starts Small and Grows Big"

Corruption, State, Culture, Law

In August 2010, less than a month after RTI crusader and whistle-blower Amit Jethwa was killed in Gujarat for exposing illegal extractive activities in protected forest areas in which a local politician was involved,[1] Arvind convened a meeting with prominent activists, civil society leaders, legal experts, and retired bureaucrats in Delhi. On the agenda was a discussion of how to address the deadly undoing of the RTI law and how to contain the unabated impunity of state and corporate corruption. The venue was the India International Centre. Permitted to attend this meeting as an observer, I took my place on the sidelines, along with a few others. Our eyes and ears were focused on the long table around which sat the real participants, all men.

The meeting began with someone proposing assistance for families of murdered RTI activists as well as whistle-blowers inside the government who face "professional harassment and victimization": "they deserve protection." Another person suggested scrapping the requirement for state approval to initiate probes against those who hound and kill whistle-blowers. Perhaps they could propose activist-led "public hearing platforms" within investigative agencies to oversee their work and hold them accountable. Vigilance bureaus, the group agreed, had been corrupted and "captured by politicians." Even the Central Vigilance Commission, the apex anticorruption body, was not insulated from executive meddling. "We need to take away political interference in bureaucratic functioning and break the nexus between bureaucratic and political bosses," stated an attendee.

Another participant brought up the ubiquity of corruption within state agencies, where both petty and large-scale bribes are routinized. He laughingly shared a story about a clerk in his office who had become a "big man" after years of taking bribes. Lower-level functionaries like clerks can spend their entire working life taking a "1 percent cut," whereas MLAs (that is, elected politicians) only get five years to fleece the system and take a larger, "10 percent cut." "Corruption is like a river that starts small and grows big," this man concluded, adding that it was impossible to pinpoint the exact origin of something so widespread. "Corruption is not limited to bureaucrats and politicians. Doctors, accountants, lawyers, media—it is spread all over." His comment garnered nods from around the room. "It happens all the time," asserted another attendee, "because we have socially accepted it."

"The social acceptance of corruption is [because] . . . we have a weak Prevention of Corruption Act," offered someone else. "We need the Lokpal law!" he declared, implying that a better law would do what one lacking teeth could not: make corruption legally, and presumably socially, unacceptable, ending it for good. The proposal at hand was to create, in law, a fully independent, federal-level ombuds body—the Lokpal—that would sit above existing vigilance agencies and investigate and adjudicate all charges of government corruption. Everyone agreed that this agency must include "diverse categories of people who are not easily manipulated," a mix of insiders and outsiders appointed with great care and without political intrusion.

How do you create an institution that is a part of government but also sits autonomously atop it, I wondered? How do you ensure that this new anticorruption agency stays incorruptible? What seemed to me as intriguing questions and potential contradictions became, for those attending this meeting, technical issues to be hammered out in the upcoming months.

This preliminary meeting in summer 2010 set in motion processes that led to a national-level anticorruption movement, which Arvind spearheaded alongside Anna Hazare in April 2011. Indeed, Arvind had long expressed frustration with the bureaucratic stonewalling of the RTI law. "We have a great RTI Act, but if the people who are supposed to enforce it don't act . . . then the law will not work," he had stated one afternoon in October 2008, as we sipped 9-rupee coffee at the Indian Coffee House, a popular activist *adda,* or den, in Connaught Place. "There are huge pendencies on RTI appeals. Officials are not giving information. They are not scared. RTI is a *behtareen* [excellent] tool. It is necessary but not sufficient for changing the system. Even if RTI works, it is just one small part.... If money has been siphoned off or there is corruption, [RTI] exposes all that. What do I do with that information? You make a complaint to the vigilance agencies, to the Central Bureau of Investigation, to the police, to the chief minister, to the president, to the prime minister. No action is taken. Anticorruption agencies don't work. RTI just gives information.... That is not a guarantee that the system will work better. So that brings us to the larger issues of what ails governance.... The ordinary citizen, in his day-to-day functioning, has no control over governance. And this is not democracy. It is a sham. The real change would come when people are directly able to participate [in governance]. And for that you need better understanding of our system, and you need a different campaign altogether."

IAC became Arvind's new campaign. It called for the passage of an anticorruption law, the Jan Lokpal, or People's Ombuds bill. This law sought to establish a suprastate agency to punish graft and purify governance in the name of saving the nation. Movement leaders organized Gandhian protests and hunger strikes (Sharma 2014), drafted the new law, invited public discussions about it, and negotiated with the ruling Congress Party–led government for over a year. However, their proposed law was rejected. In August 2012, Anna Hazare quit and the movement broke up, but Kejriwal vowed to carry on the good fight through other means. He founded the AAP and entered the electoral fray. With a broom as its symbol, the party represented a continuation of Kejriwal's technomoral mission to "change the current corrupt and self-serving system of politics forever"[2] and to establish swaraj as good governance. I delve into AAP's populist promises and politics in chapter 6. Here I take up the vexed issues of corruption and the anticorruption law that Kejriwal and his associates brought into focus during the Indian Spring.

The Conundrum of Corruption

To undo the limits of one law—the RTI—with an apparently more perfect law—the Jan Lokpal bill—in order to end state corruption sounds awkwardly circular, but it captures well Kejriwal's judicialized, technomoral politics, which pivots on the law as a force for changing the "system." It also begs some key questions, which I probe in this chapter. First, if corruption represents a systemic breakdown, then which system needs amending—the state, society, culture, or something else? Second, how is corruption defined, and who is to blame for it? Finally, what are the constraints of uprooting it through the law?

Corruption, as the meeting I describe above suggests, is a messy social practice and a category of transgression (Muir and Gupta 2018; see also Sharma 2018). It is full of gray areas, which make it difficult to study, let alone eradicate by legal fiat. Although many in India accept corruption as a truism, they disagree about its spatial borders and its beginning and end. While many see it as a state disease that seeps into society, others view it as a wider cultural malaise that gets reflected in state institutions as much as in society. Then there are those who argue that corruption is not the real problem; the political, economic, and social inequality that lies at its root is what should be tackled.

Defining what counts as real corruption and identifying its true perpetrators and victims is tricky. Exceptions to the rule of corruption abound. Legal acts may be disparaged as immoral and antisocial, while illegal ones may be considered necessary, fair, and socially tolerable (Gupta 2012; Scott 1969) because legality and ethical legitimacy do not overlap neatly (Pardo 2018; Tidey 2022). Moreover, questionable practices, such as the "stealing" of water or electricity by the urban poor, may be entirely disentangled from personal virtue (Das 2015), for illegal acts do not always a criminal, dishonest person make.[3] This fuzziness is why de Sardan (1999) urges us to consider a "corruption complex in a wider sense," which includes a range of "illicit practices" that people use to survive and navigate state institutions and logics; these practices share a "family resemblance, a certain relationship of affinity" (26) with corruption but cannot be reduced to it. David Sneath (2006) contends that bribery and other practices of gifting are situated on an ethical spectrum. And Das (2015) goes a step further to suggest that corruption practices are always contextual and perspectival, given that they are located in particular normative worlds where the modern logics of bureaucracy and law have settled in uneasily among other cosmologies.

The lack of consensus about what corruption is, where it resides, what it does, and the kind of threat it poses to society complicates any easy legal resolution. Corruption evades the discreet classification of practices into legal and illegal demanded by law. Indeed, I propose that law and corruption, as situated social fields, are inverted mirrors of each other, intertwined and coconstitutive: one is a symbol of rationalized liberal modernity and the other of its dangerous, unwieldy underside, and both center on the public–private boundary.

The law, together with bureaucracy, embodies and enforces the public–private separation that is central to liberal state power. To quote Weber (2006), "The complete depersonalization of administrative management by bureaucracy and the rational systematization of law ... realize the separation of the public and the private sphere fully and in principle" (67). The law not only protects the overlapping, public–private, state–society, and formal–informal distinctions but also produces corruption as a criminal contamination of these sacrosanct divides. Dominant technical definitions of corruption see it as a "transgression of the boundaries between the public and private realms" (Tidey 2022, 10). It is a "behavior which deviates from the formal duties of a public role because of private-regarding (personal, close family, private clique) pecuniary or status gains" (Nye 1967, 419). As deviant in-betweenness, corruption reveals the lived miscegenation of categories that ought to be separate, but are not so in practice (Muir and Gupta 2018).[4] Corruption is finessed informality that nestles alongside a stupefying maze of formal rules that make up bureaucratic institutions (Lomnitz 1988), filling their cracks and dysfunctionality. If the law helps reproduce an idealized standard of the liberal bureaucratic state, then corruption exposes how this state functions as an enclosure (Visvanathan 2008), a privatized public sphere propped up by daily, opaque bureaucraft. Corruption scrambles the rationalized onstage face of the modern state and is a danger that must be contained; the law becomes the preferred mechanism to achieve this under good governance discourse.[5]

However, ending corruption through the law is deeply paradoxical, as I elaborate here. If the law needs and produces corruption as its constitutive outside, then can the law—even a more perfect law—be relied on to eradicate it? My use of "the law" here does not reference an abstract or static system; rather, I follow the lead of my interlocutors in pointing to the classificatory and binary logic of modern, rationalized law. Even when they disagreed on the interpretations and usages of specific laws, the people I worked with saw the law as a system meant to differentiate right from wrong. Where this binary logic requires precision, categorizing acts as legal, illegal, criminal, or not, through formalized application of conventions, corruption resists such simplification and straitjacketing. If the law is a formal economy of rules, then corruption signals the informal, ritually practiced bending of rules.

In this chapter, I offer an exploratory ethnography of corruption that approaches it less as a problem than a problematic that resists consensus and closure and invites analysis. I treat corruption not as a social anomaly but a "social fact" in Maussian terms (Mauss [1925] 1990, 78–80), which is at once political, cultural, economic, legal, and even aesthetic in that there is an "art" to performing corruption correctly (Gupta 1995). I focus on the public discourse on corruption in the context of the RTI law and the IAC campaign, drawing on interviews, observations, and media commentaries.

This chapter juxtaposes vignettes that offer different takes on corruption: where it exists, who is to blame, and how to tackle it. Juxtaposition is a powerful methodology for studying contentious social issues like corruption in that it allows me to tease out the messy indeterminacy that colors public debates about corruption and probes the constraints, and even the impossibility, of cleansing the system with the law. In reflecting the matter at hand, my analysis seeks neither neatness nor classificatory precision. Moreover, I am interested in approaching corruption in its everydayness and generativity while keeping in view the structural inequalities that not only produce such acts but are often propped up by the very system of laws that are meant to resolve them.

Before I proceed, I offer a word about the translocality and masculinism of the public discourse on corruption. Although my focus here is contemporary, urban India, corruption is neither a recent problem nor solely an Indian one.[6] Indeed, neoliberal good governance proponents consider it a global menace and offer universal solutions for tackling it, including emphasizing the rule of law and downsizing states. As Chicago economist Gary Becker famously put it, "If you want to cut corruption, cut government."[7] That said, however, this malaise is considered unevenly spread and more insidious in the Global South. Such "racialized sociogeographic distinctions of development and modernity" (Muir and Gupta 2018, S11) are iterated annually in ratings produced by institutions like Transparency International that rank countries according to standardized metrics of corruption (Sampson 2015; Tidey 2022).[8] There is back-and-forth traffic between these international benchmarks, national-level debates, and local social activism against corruption; articulation is unavoidable. Hence, the stories I tell here are both specific to India and translocal. They are also gendered. The views I document appear to offer neutral analyses of how graft affects everyone and expert advice on how to end it, but they instantiate a middle-class male standpoint. It is these privileged voices that define the terms on which the problem is debated and challenged. Moreover, what makes corruption discourse masculinist is the troubled and deeply gendered nature of the public–private divide that overdetermines this issue. This binary, which also lies at the heart of liberal law and statehood, has been profoundly consequential in securing patriarchal authority and inequalities (Brown 1995; MacKinnon 1989; Menon 2004). Discussions about corruption and legal reform cannot escape the structuring masculinism of liberal state power.

"The [State] System Is Corrupt, Not People": Corruption and Its Exceptions

"There are two forms of corruption: mutual and extortionist," Kejriwal told me one afternoon in his no-nonsense, self-assured style. It was July 2009, and we were sitting in his office, trying to converse amid constant interruptions. "Mutual is when the giver and receiver are both happy. . . . [It is] generally related to corporations vying for government contracts. Extortionist is when people have to pay bribes to get legitimate work done." Kejriwal considered the latter as more rampant than the former, "big ticket" type.

Indeed, extortionist, or retail, corruption is what got him involved in good governance activism in the first place. In 2000, he took a two-year leave from the Indian Revenue Service and set up an NGO, Parivartan, to help people avoid having to pay bribes for their everyday needs. Parivartan began by targeting Delhi's income tax department and the Vidyut (Electricity) Board. Kejriwal and his associates would stand outside the gates of the Vidyut Board from 11 AM to 1 PM daily, telling people entering the premises not to pay bribes for an electricity connection or for other issues: "Just tell us your grievance, and we'll get your work done free of cost." All the cases that went through them were resolved. However,

Arvind realized that they were reaching very few people, and their intervention was neither scalable nor sustainable in the long run. So he decided to test the state RTI Act passed by Delhi in 2001 to see if it could work as a mechanism to curb graft. He recalled drafting his first RTI petition under the Delhi law on behalf of a man who was asked to pay a 5,000-rupee bribe for an electricity connection. Within ten days of filing that petition, the man was connected to the grid. "We thought this was amazing," recalled Arvind, and he began encouraging people to use the Delhi RTI law for "any grievance pending anywhere." His group assisted people in drafting queries and spread the message about the law so that others could petition on their own. From "middlemen," as Arvind put it, his colleagues and he became "facilitators," helping resolve around two hundred cases in three months. "This was magic for us."

The passage of the national RTI Act in 2005 gave Parivartan more ammunition to tackle retail corruption. In July 2006, Parivartan collaborated with NGOs and media houses to launch a nationwide "Drive against Bribes" that urged people to "use RTI [because] it is more effective than bribery," as Arvind described it. During the fifteen-day drive, approximately 22,000 RTI applications across fifty-five cities were filed, and activists found that "RTI was very successful against extortionist bribe." However, this law was being actively subverted by officialdom and was "slowly becoming nonfunctional." Moreover, the transparency law was simply not equipped to handle the scale and dogged persistence of corruption in India.

"Almost every single individual in this country is turning corrupt," Arvind asserted. "The entire psyche of the nation is turning corrupt." Such a sweeping claim, of course, says both too much and too little. While rhetorically effective, it proves ineffective where the law is concerned, and a new anticorruption law is what Arvind was after. So I asked him to clarify why everyone was turning corrupt and who or what was to blame. "The system," he answered. "Nobody is born corrupt. They are made corrupt. The system is corrupt, not people."

He would expand on this claim during the IAC mobilization, equating the system with the state. In a published interview, Kejriwal (2011) stated:

> Till now, in this country, we have not paid any attention to governance systems. . . . There are very small departments in the government with less

than . . . 200 people. And even some of them are corrupt. You have the Delhi Metro which has more than 7000 people but it is performing very well. Why? It is not that E. Sreedharan [the managing director] sits on each and every person's head; it is because he has developed the right kind of systems. . . . Many of [the] officers in Delhi Metro come on deputation from the railways. When they come to Delhi Metro they behave properly. I think we need to talk of the right kind of systems and it is precisely these systems that we are attempting to put in place through the Jan Lokpal bill. . . . It is the system that will govern the character and the performance of the people.

Kejriwal loved to use the Delhi Metro as an example of an exceptional and atypical bureaucracy, one well organized and efficiently managed. E. Sreedharan had designed a good system that produced disciplined, responsibilized subjects (Barry, Osborne, and Rose 1996; Foucault 1991) and deterred corruption. Systems were good or bad, not people; people simply acted out internalized systems (Bourdieu 1998).

In this dominant (middle class) and populist view, corruption "belongs to the domain of 'the political' (in the popular sense, i.e., ministers, MPs, MLAs, bureaucrats) . . . [and] can never touch 'the people'" (Chatterjee 2011). When it touches people, it is because the system is rigged to bring out the worst in the public. If corruption is a symptom of an immoral and bad state system, then the ideal solution is a technomoral one: a law that can enact a rationalized good governance system, which in turn provokes ethical behavior across society.

IAC followers toed this line. I met a small group of IAC youth at a *nukkad naatak,* or street theater, performance about corruption near Delhi University in March 2012. This performance urged the audience of around 150 people to consider how everything, including the country, was up for sale; how state officials loot the public; and how to change the system and cultivate *naitik mool* (moral values). I commended the team after the performance and expressed an interest in talking with them. They suggested meeting the following day at a dormitory-style building where many of them who had traveled to Delhi from other places to participate in the anticorruption movement were staying.

The next afternoon, I found myself sitting in an open space lined with mattresses across the floor. While some people napped, others huddled around electrical outlets, charging their phones and chatting. I joined one such group of three. Shalini, Kamal, and Sameer greeted me with warm hellos and a few yawns. "We don't get much sleep," Shalini smiled apologetically. These twentysomethings belonged to lower-middle-class families. Like many other young people I met, they had quit jobs or school to join the IAC. Sleep or no sleep, they were charged up for *vyavastha parivartan* (systemic change).

When I asked them why anticorruption efforts aimed transforming the system should focus on the state, Kamal had a ready answer: "Because everyone knows that all *netas* [political leaders] are thieves, and the main orders come from above." He rattled off a list of recent the scams—2G spectrum allocations for cell phone service, Commonwealth Games infrastructure, and so on—in which state and corporate actors had siphoned off billions. "Our system is rotten. There is too much corruption." But what about commonplace bribing? I pushed. "We all do it, no?" Kamal nodded. "It is partly our own fault. When someone asks for a bribe, we give it." He told me that Arvind had asked his followers to "introspect" about their complicity in graft—an ethical self-cultivation of sorts—and to seek the help of "priests, pundits, and *maulvis*" to address immorality within society. "If one person changes for the better, others start changing too," remarked Shalini. "This is how fashions catch on, like the stylish sunglasses you see everyone wearing these days!" We all laughed. "I hope morality doesn't become a passing fad," I added.

Now Sameer joined in. "Nobody is saying that the *aam janata* [ordinary public] is paak, saaf, aur imaandaar [pure, clean, and honest]. But the bureaucracy is sabse zyada bhrashtachari [the most corrupt]. Seventy percent of corruption [in India] can be attributed to the bureaucracy. The peon, the clerk, the officer, and on up. They are all in it together. They get their own share *[hissa]* of the spoils. You can't even complain to the topmost officials because they too get their cut. . . . And this bureaucratic corruption compels me [to pay bribes], even though I am honest and want to follow rules. . . ." Sameer trailed off in frustration.

"Oopar se hi main hai [The main corruption is at the top]," offered Kamal, agreeing with Sameer. "It forms a chain, from the top to the bottom," he explained, gesturing a downward flow with his hands. "That is why corruption is increasing down here [in society]. . . . So you have to first target the government, and then it will trickle down." The top, for Kamal, meant politicians, whom he described as "a breed unto themselves... [with] no fear of repercussions." "But these politicians have emerged from society, haven't they? Like you and me?" I queried. "*Bilkul* [Absolutely]," he answered. "Arvind says that the *kursi* [chair] is so powerful that it corrupts anyone who sits in it." Kamal reminded me that students active in radical and alternative politics during the 1970s had turned corrupt when they entered the government and occupied seats of power. "We need an efficient system, which has controls, checks and balances; then people will change *apne aap* [automatically]."

A "good law," asserted Sameer, would accomplish that. "Not normal laws like those in the Indian Penal Code of 1860, which treat a 500-rupee bribe taken by a train conductor and a 2,000,000-rupee bribe taken by a senior officer on par and designate the same punishment! Existing laws have no mechanism for recovering money stolen by officials. And our system is fragmented. We have multiple investigating agencies that don't coordinate with each other. In the end, nothing comes out of these investigations. We need a single and complete authority that has the power to oversee audits, vigilance, and punishment. And that is the Lokpal."

The commentary of these young activists reflected the narrative of the IAC campaign, which commonly deployed phrases like "the top," "the chair," and "the system" to discursively construct the state as the fountainhead of venality. Skilled and honest men who understood the system had to stop the venom at its source and establish a better governance system through the mechanism of law. Stopping the filth at the mouth of the river would have a multiplier effect downstream of morally cleansing society.

By defining corruption as state immorality and inefficiency, Kejriwal and his associates were able to turn an apparently undifferentiated "India" against corruption: a morally outraged nation rising against a venal state, looking to be saved by ethical technocrats. This was the technomoral and populist good governance mission of the IAC (see chapter 6).

The movement had an impact in the corridors of power, given the media coverage and the cross-class public support it received in Delhi and in other cities and towns across the country. The issue of corruption could not be ignored by the political establishment. Although the Congress Party–led regime at the center did not pass the IAC's Jan Lokpal bill, and it heavily criticized the movement's use of moral arm-twisting and subversion of parliamentary institutions and procedures (Sharma 2014), it was on board with the basic idea that ending corruption required a top-down legal approach. Manmohan Singh, then prime minister, proposed amending the existing Prevention of Corruption Act. The law, he asserted, required a "clear and unambiguous definition for the term 'corruption,' covering both the supply and demand sides," and had to also address the issue of "consensual bribery [where] the supplier of the bribe goes scot-free.... We need to ensure that even while the corrupt are relentlessly pursued and brought to book, the innocent are not harassed."[9]

The trouble, however, is that corruption eludes such absolute delimitation and clear-cut winners and losers. At issue is not simply whether supply and demand should be treated on par, legally and ethically, but also what forms of bribery are corrupt and dangerous, and what kinds of transactions are considered reasonable and excusable. These are knotty and contentious issues.

～

"Corruption as controlled activity is tolerated" is what an RTI activist told me, offering the following example. A junior engineer—a government employee—is taught to expect envelopes full of bribes each month in addition to his salary. However, he is also expected to "do the right thing" (see also Tidey 2022). That is, he might use materials that are "a bit substandard but not so bad that a bridge might fall. That would be unacceptable." But otherwise, the bribe-taking engineer would not be considered a criminal. So how does one begin to narrow the field of what and who counts as truly corrupt, to reach a classificatory clarity that the law demands and generates? Which unscrupulous actions and actors should be taken to task legally?

Indeed, Arvind Kejriwal also acknowledged the thorniness of classifying corrupt acts during a television show. It was November 2012, just after the IAC campaign had disbanded, when he appeared on NDTV alongside his then associate, Prashant Bhushan, RTI campaigner Shekhar Singh, and public intellectual Pratap Bhanu Mehta.[10] Anchor Barkha Dutt queried Kejriwal about his "unsparing focus on the issue of corruption," which particularly targeted state and corporate actors for perpetuating large-scale scams and stashing black money in foreign accounts. "Many people now say that for you and your party, private enterprise is a bad word, business is a bad word, corporate has become an abuse." Kejriwal disagreed: "We have never said that corporates are bad.... What we are trying to say is that if you try to subvert the system and make gains by indulging in corruption, by indulging in *hawala* [parallel underground banking] operations, I think that is bad."[11] Bhushan concurred: "Today... we are seeing... a version of crony capitalism in this country where some large corporates have become so huge by virtue of bribing their way into getting all kinds of illicit gains—such as 2G licenses, coal allocations, mines,... and so on—that they have become a threat to democracy itself.... This is what... we are against.... I don't say that all corporates are corrupt.... In fact, I believe that most corporations are also the victims of corruption. When Kaushik Basu said that the bribe giver should not be penalized and only the bribe taker should be penalized, there was a half-truth in that.[12] If the bribe giver is giving a bribe in order to get his legal entitlements... [such as] his ration card or his driving license [or] a corporate [actor] who gives a bribe merely to maintain his license... [which the government is] threatening to cancel illegally, they are the victims of corruption because they are... being forced to give a bribe in order to get their legal right."

Shekhar Singh, another guest on the program, added a different "class of people" to Bhushan's list of legitimate victims: Fair Price Shop owners, who are part of the government's notoriously corrupt Public Distribution System and sell subsidized food and cooking oil to the poor. "A ration shop owner who gets seven *paise* [commission] per liter on kerosene... can't run his shop [and] is forced into taking things, which are technically not his entitlement because you create [such] systems" stated Singh. "There are a whole lot of people who... are giving bribes for their entitlements [because] they... don't have real options."

Watching this debate on television, I was reminded of an interaction I had with a *rationwala* during my research.

~

In late 2008, I accompanied Arvind to the food commissioner's office to discuss the lawsuit Parivartan was filing in the Delhi consumer court against ration shopkeepers for defrauding customers. As we waited outside his office, we were joined by two other gentlemen, one older and one middle-aged, both dressed in simple cotton kurta-pajamas. The older man recognized

Arvind immediately—"I have seen you on TV!"—and introduced himself. He ran a Fair Price Shop in the city with his son, seated next to him. They came from a family of farmers who used to own a small plot of land in what is now the part residential, part industrial West Delhi neighborhood of Naraina.

"Naraina?" I remarked with surprise. I had grown up near there and could not imagine this overbuilt and bustling area's past as a farmland. The gentleman smiled. "Hanh [Yes]! Our land produced the sweetest carrots ever." But in 1947, his father decided to sell the land to resettle refugee families arriving after the partition of India. "Jawaharlal Nehru had asked everyone to help," and they considered it their patriotic duty to heed the prime minister's call. "Our land sold for 1 rupee and 90 paise a yard, in the heart of West Delhi!" Delhi was a small city then, he reminisced, cupping his hands as if to hold the entire city in them. He used to travel everywhere on a bicycle. "These days, no one wants to exercise. They overeat, move around in AC [air-conditioned] cars, live in AC homes. No wonder so many suffer from sugar [diabetes]." He distinguished his ethical way of life from these immoral others. "I wake up at 3 AM, do yoga, sweep my street, teach yoga to neighbors, have my breakfast, and then take a one- to two-hour nap." This disciplined and simple routine, alongside "imaandari ki kamai (an honestly earned living)," kept him healthy.

Arvind nodded, but he also pointed out that there was an inconsistency between widespread corruption in ration shops and the man's personal commitment to an "honestly earned living." The rationwala, however, saw no contradiction at all. "Shop rents have increased tenfold, and wages of store helpers have also increased five to six times. But the rate of commission that the government provides has remained the same. This is what encourages corruption among shopkeepers." The system compelled him to behave dishonestly sometimes in order to survive. Yet these acts did not take away from his dedication to simple, clean living and to fulfilling his moral duties toward his family, community, and nation. He was not corrupt, and his actions were not illegitimate (Das 2015; Tidey 2022).

⁓

These limit cases tell us that corruption confounds clarity; it is a discourse teeming with exceptions (de Sardan 1999). Fine-tuning corruption into a precise classification system is tricky, and defining and pointing fingers at who is corrupt is contentious. Bribe givers are not considered immoral to the extent that they must pay money to access their rights and entitlements. Bribe-accepting bridge engineers and cheating ration shop owners are seen as legitimate casualties of an unruly system, cogs in an "evil"-generating, dysfunctional wheel.[13] Daily survival in this encumbered and oppressive system of governance becomes a narrative of *majboori* (helplessness) and harassment rather than what Shiv Visvanathan (2008) views as creative "play" and bending of indecipherable bureaucratic rules.

In the abovementioned NDTV program, Pratap Bhanu Mehta concurred that most people "are victims in the sense that, over the years, the Indian state has created such a labyrinthine structure that it has become very difficult at the individual level for people to be honest all the time." Anchor Barkha Dutt, however, was skeptical: "This society that all of us are a part of, they [sic] are not victims necessarily." She described how people often evade taxes and conduct real estate deals using black money, as she connected rampant corruption to the public's "*chalta hai* [anything goes] attitude." It is this very attitude that critic Anuj Chopra (2011) also picked up on to offer a classed reading of corruption as a cultural malaise.

Corruption as Cultural Pathology

In a *Foreign Policy* article responding critically to the IAC campaign, Anuj Chopra (2011) called corruption in India "a deeply engrained cultural neurosis that exists on every level of society." Although acknowledging that India had a "stagnant bureaucracy and opaque power structures" and that "widespread corruption is corroding the foundations of governance and damaging public trust in institutions," Chopra alleged that the problem could not be blamed on the state alone. He saw the IAC's Jan Lokpal bill as a "palliative measure," not a "cure for the disease of corruption," which needed more than the simplistic belief that "ferreting out crooked politicians alone will bring about a cataclysmic change." Chopra brought into focus "private corruption" whose "tacit approval . . . is common across India's social classes." As examples, he referenced people selling their votes in exchange for cash and other handouts, or paying bribes for low-paying, lower-rung government jobs because of the potential for earning "extra" income through bribes. He described an election-time raid "of private houses and private vehicles hired by campaign workers" in Tamil

Nadu that uncovered millions in cash plus alcohol, wristwatches, saris, and so on, meant to be given to voters for the promise of their votes. "You'd expect the masses—outraged by rampant government corruption—to reject this kind of electoral bribe. Instead, many of them bickered about the quality and quantity of the handouts received," lamented Chopra. Therefore, he concluded, "The Lokpal bill, if it works, might take down a few corrupt politicians. But the battle to slay corruption begins at home," in the private recesses of society rather than in public institutions.

To see corruption as a cultural malaise afflicting everyone is problematic in how it reifies the very idea of culture and normalizes a middle-class standpoint. It makes an argument akin to the culture of poverty thesis, which blames the poor for reproducing their poverty and deficient values from one generation to the next rather than engaging political-economic histories and structures (Lewis 1969). Chopra played on this idea, claiming that far from being innocent victims of corruption, Indians were active participants in perpetuating this filth; the classes and masses both needed a thorough washing. Interestingly, however, he singled out the masses in his choice of examples: people selling their votes and paying bribes to obtain low-paying government jobs that guarantee additional income through corrupt means. Thus, those dependent on the state for handouts and jobs were particularly prone to proliferating corruption. This aligns with the middle-class perspective I expounded on in chapter 4, which views the welfare state's nods to the poor as a source of venality and evidence of the weakening quality of citizenship. Although the middle classes are deeply entwined with the corruption complex, paying bribes willingly and evading taxes, they tend to blame the rot on poor governance and lower-income groups instead (Chatterjee 2011).

My friend, Jaydeep, a privileged civil servant, displayed exactly this classist dynamic of complicity and disavowal. Like Chopra, he disagreed with the IAC's charge that the government was the fount of venality. "Why point fingers at only the state!" Jaydeep exclaimed as we sat in his office one afternoon over tea and biscuits. He brought up examples of corrupt aam aadmis: *dhoodhwalas* (milk vendors) who supply milk diluted with water, and auto-rickshaw drivers who charge more than the metered fare. "Aren't they corrupt?" asked Jaydeep rhetorically.

I offered him a counterperspective. Surely a poor *dhoodhwala* making a few extra rupees off his upper-middle-class clientele is not a criminal.

"We can afford to pay a little extra." I also shared the example of Shahid, a rickshaw driver who had just deposited me at Jaydeep's office and who refused to take the metered fare of 54 rupees. Why? Because I had seen an IAC sticker on his vehicle and mentioned Kejriwal's name. Shahid had looked at me in his rearview mirror and smiled, telling me that he attended as many rallies as he could afford to and avidly supported what Kejriwal for was doing for the country, because "there is no other option." At the end of the fifteen-minute ride, he insisted on not charging me any money. I insisted harder, and he relented. "What about people like Shahid?" I now probed Jaydeep. He shrugged dismissively; there would always be exceptions. The fact remained that the very aam aadmis the IAC represented and who backed the campaign were corrupt, and therefore, singling out the state was wrong.

Jaydeep's take on private corruption and his condemnation of the working poor reflected a classed standpoint, quite like Chopra's.[14] Das (2015) asserts that "the problem with a middle class hankering for a society free of corruption is that there is very little understanding of how the very process of securing life for the poor can be made to appear as corruption" (335). Indeed, Shalini, the IAC campaigner I introduced earlier, offered a different explanation for the predicament of milk sellers and auto-rickshaw drivers who scam the public: "If you ask the milk seller why he mixes water into the milk, he will tell you, 'Inflation has increased so much; what am I to do?' Auto drivers face the same problem. It is the government, after all, that passes the budget." Working people were victims of the government's policies over which they had no control. Their small-scale transgressions, like charging extra for their services, were therefore forgivable. But the middle and upper classes, who have benefited disproportionately from the state's liberalization policies, do not empathize with this predicament. Blaming the working poor, as Jaydeep did, and blaming culture at large, as Chopra did, offer easier ways of explaining away everyday corruption without reflecting on structural inequalities.

Someone else I met also offered a "culturalist" perspective on corruption. Like Chopra, he blamed rampant depravity on a pathological "mentality" in society and raised doubts about the effectiveness of the law in curbing it. Ramesh Singh was a PIO for his department in 2009, and meeting him turned out to be more challenging than I expected. During our initial conversation over the telephone, he checked my credentials to make sure I was not from the media. Once satisfied, he agreed to meet, only to fail to show up at the appointed time and place. After waiting for over two hours while his secretary kept informing me of serial delays, I left. To his credit, he called me later to reschedule. The second time around, I was the one who caused a delay, having foolishly chosen to drive to his office near central Delhi. Frustrated by the city's notoriously bad traffic, and distracted by Singh's text message telling me that I was late, I missed the final turn that would have brought me to my destination. I pulled over, dreading the long loop I would have to take, thanks to my mistake. When an onlooker suggested that I could reverse into the street leading to Singh's office, I complied willingly, going the wrong way on a one-way street for about twenty-five feet. The onlooker guided me, ensuring that my illegal maneuver would go smoothly. Now fifteen minutes late, I was shown to a room where two men sat. The man on the telephone waved me to a sofa, while the other barely glanced up from his desk.

This government office was as banal as any other, with fluorescent lighting, steel cabinets, dull furniture, and impersonal, askew paraphernalia on white walls, including a dry-erase board with alphanumeric codes that only an insider could understand. And there were stacks upon stacks of files. The only personal effect in that room was a picture of Sai Baba, an Indian holy man. Before I could decide which of the two officials in the room was a devotee, the man on the phone hung up. "Ramesh Singh," he said, walking over to where I sat. Aware of my interest in the RTI law, he launched right into a monologue.

"The intention of the RTI Act is very good: transparency, accountability, and decreasing corruption. It is in the interest of democracy. It has increased the role of the public in the form of participation. But in order to participate properly in a democracy . . . a citizen needs to be educated [and] informed. The general public is unaware and therefore unempowered," bemoaned Singh. "Ninety-five percent usage of the RTI law is wrong. It is self-interested. Blackmailers misuse it," he said, recounting the litany of complaints I had heard from many other PIOs (see chapter 3). "Aise log RTI ka band bajaa denge [Such people will ruin the RTI]." He alleged that citizens tended to use this law to get back at officials. "People think that all government employees are thieves; that we are born to create trouble for the public. That is not true! Corruption is everywhere, not just in government departments. . . . You see, every system has positive and negative aspects, and these things affect the people who are part of the system. I will tell you about a Japanese man who came to work with us for a year. He was trained to be a model citizen who did not dirty his surroundings. He was a smoker and even flicked ash in his cigarette case!" My eyes widened in surprise. Singh nodded vigorously, expecting that reaction. "But after one year of living in Delhi, he had no compunction about urinating in public!" He laughed loudly. "Here people spit in public places but won't do it inside their houses. Log gandi cheez mein gand dalte hain." Dirt begets dirt; a dirty environment invites filthy behavior. "Our system is like that."

Which dirty system was Singh referencing, I wondered? Was he echoing the partly critical, partly celebratory middle-class viewpoint that India is corrupt, but that is just the way things are—the "anything goes" attitude that Barkha Dutt had mentioned on NDTV? Or was it something else? Singh interrupted my rumination: "There is a general disrespect for laws here." I squirmed, recalling my traffic violation that morning. "Even the Supreme Court's directions are not obeyed." Converting cabs and auto-rickshaws to natural gas or getting people to abide by the seat belt law presented challenges, he reminded me, and attitudes toward the transparency law were no different. Everyone was part of the problem. "People know about their rights, but hardly anyone knows about duties listed in article 51(A) of the constitution. That is the tragedy of our mentality. We need public awareness and education. Government awareness is also needed. But, see, politics is a reflection of society. Society changes, and so does politics."

Although there was some overlap between Singh's ideas and the IAC's perspective that the system shapes individual behavior, the system that Singh referenced was not the state as much as it was society. In his understanding, society cradled the state, blurring easy above–below, inside–outside, clean–dirty distinctions, especially where morality was concerned. The values nurtured in society were mirrored in the state: disrespect for public spaces and the law, and a lack of civic sense. Like Anuj Chopra, Singh believed corruption could not be resolved by passing laws or targeting the state alone. The need of the hour was to change the hearts and minds of citizens and officials. Cultivating civic values and citizenship required a moral education about duties and obligations as social facts rather than abstract legal ones. Technocratic legal appeals would not go very far if people were uninformed and prone to breaking laws.

~

Chopra's and Singh's laments about corruption as cultural pathology or dirt are examples of a "modernist complaint" (Chakrabarty 1992, 542) anchored in developmentalism. Venality becomes a sign of traditional backwardness and signifies India's incomplete, even rogue, modernity. Such complaints, of course, are not new. They have long justified and guided governmental interventions. Colonial public hygiene projects, for instance, sought to change bad cultural habits and create new kinds of clean and governable subjects and spaces (Anderson 1995; Chakrabarty 1992).[15]

At the heart of such colonial projects lay the public–private divide and how to police it. This liberal divide, which Visvanathan (2008) calls one of modernity's most "lethal dualisms" (52), and its accompanying assemblage of ideals (the state, civil society, citizen, individual, rights) never worked as they were supposed to in colonial India, where other understandings of personhood, community, and social worlds prevailed. In Bengal, for instance, it neither mapped onto nor captured Hindu Bengali understandings of the world and the home, the outside and the inside (Chakrabarty 1992, 2000; Chatterjee 1989; Kaviraj 1997). The "outside," in this worldview, constituted an "exposed and interstitial" (Chakrabarty 1992, 543) space of adulteration, distinct from a familiar and secure feminized "inside."[16] This outside–inside split did not align comfortably with the public–private one but instead signified a different ordering of social space. Indeed, colonized subjects routinely confounded the public–private distinction, messing up the orderliness of colonial cities, streets, parks, and markets. These areas were commons that were shared but not "public" in the liberal vein—that is, they were "civic space[s] with norms and rules of use of [their] own, different from the domestic values of bourgeois privacy" (Kaviraj 1997, 98). Furthermore, many private acts, like washing and urinating, took place in the streets, raising hygiene and other alarms for the colonial state.

Singh's concern about dirt and Anuj Chopra's criticism about corruption at home rather than in the state reflected colonialist-developmentalist norms anchored in the liberal public–private distinction. Indeed, in their own ways, both suggested that India's culture of corruption could be tamed by cultivating civic citizenship and moral uplift through social awareness raising rather than through top-down statist policies or laws. Chopra highlighted ipaidabribe.com, a site that asks bribe givers to confess their transgressions to an online public. In the act of truth telling—how much they paid and to whom—they exonerate themselves, help others avoid making the same mistake, and educate. "T. R. Raghunandan, a former civil servant who spearheads ipaidabribe.com," wrote Chopra, "recently told me that the best way to break the cycle of bribe paying is to combat ignorance. If Indians don't know their rights, they're more likely to accept that bribes are simply the only way to get things that are rightfully theirs."

It is hard to miss the middle classness of an initiative like this, for it speaks to those complicit in corrupt acts but also lets them off the hook. A virtual confession—as a practice of modern ethical self-positioning—allows those who break and bend the rules to wash their sins without owning them as theirs alone. "I paid a bribe (but I am not corrupt)" operates as a disclaimer that expresses a shared condition and sentiment at once practical and moral. Everyone has corruption stories, which are simultaneously intimate and out in the open, unique and general. These stories interpellate an "I" who is a subject of and subjected to a venal state, and also constitute a "we," an intimate public (Berlant 2008) bonded as victims of a system gone wrong. The moral force of these stories lies in innocent victimhood ("I am a casualty of the system") and sometimes trickster pride ("I have the resources to work the system"). Either way, the purported benefit of confession is a public good.

～

I confess: I paid a bribe to get a driver's license (but I did not realize that I had done so until after the fact).

I arrived in Delhi in 2008 with an international driving permit alongside my Connecticut license, but was unsure whether these documents would carry any weight if I got into an accident—an unavoidable fact in the city. My civil servant friend, Jaydeep—the same one who criticized milkmen and auto drivers for being corrupt—recommended getting a local license because lower-ranking traffic cops, whom I would likely encounter, would not be familiar with international permits. He advised paying for the services of a driving school rather than taking the required tests on my own: "Trust me on this one." The school would arrange everything for me, even if I opted to skip taking lessons, and I would get my license quickly. Following regular procedures would take longer. I took Jaydeep's advice.

When I asked my mother about local driving schools, she told me that there were many. She turned to Rajeev, our neighbor, who had recently learned to drive and was eager to help. "I will take you to a school tomorrow, didi [sister]," he said reassuringly. "I know Bhaiya, the guy who runs the school." Rajeev's chosen terms of address—didi for me and bhaiya for the owner of the driving school—are generic terms of respect for older female and male persons, which signal kin-like relationality.

Bhaiya turned out to be a portly man in his thirties. He sat in his tiny, ramshackle office when Rajeev and I arrived there the next morning. I explained to him that I needed a license but no driving lessons. He informed me that he charged 2,000 rupees per student for the entire package of tests, lessons, and license fees. But because I knew Rajeev, I would get a discount: "Only 1,600 rupees for you." He scheduled the written test for me, handed me a booklet to prepare for it, and instructed me to bring the required paperwork and photographs to the test location. "Before you go for the test, please come and see me," he stressed, nodding in Rajeev's direction. "Zaroor," responded Rajeev. Of course.

Three days later, I was ready for the test. Rajeev, who decided to take me to the test center despite my protestations, pulled out his motorbike. When I thanked him for his help, he brushed aside the formalities: "Please, didi, you are embarrassing me." He kick-started the bike; I hopped on sidesaddle. As promised, we stopped at the driving school, where Bhaiya rattled off instructions for me. "You will only answer eight out of the twenty multiple-choice questions and leave the others blank." Huh? I knew that I had to answer twelve questions correctly to pass.[17] So why tackle only eight? What if I know the correct answers to the questions? I queried. Bhaiya looked frustrated. "You are free to choose any eight and even pick B as your answer to all eight if you want." But what if I know that B is the wrong answer, I prodded. "Well, then you can choose all Cs or Ds instead." Both indignant and amused, I gently protested this strategy: "I know my road signs and rules, Bhaiya, and am well prepared." He looked up from texting on his phone and huffed impatiently. He was probably not used to students questioning his test-taking strategy, and here I was, a self-assured older woman bearing cultural and economic capital, doing just that. He relented a little. If I was that confident in my preparation, I could answer eleven of the twenty questions. "Bas [that's it]. Not one more."

Rajeev explained Bhaiya's strategy to me on the way to the testing center. "He has a 'setting' with the Transport Department people." According to this unofficial pact, Bhaiya paid someone a cut so that they would pass his students. The students were asked to partially complete the written test so that there was wiggle room; presumably someone would fill in the correct bubbles for unanswered questions. Ah, a little cheating. I smirked inwardly, knowing full well that Bhaiya was not alone in managing settings and enabling success.

When it came time for my written test, I transgressed Bhaiya's script. Maybe it was self-righteousness, or maybe I wanted to create a semblance of honesty for my own sake. I answered sixteen questions, sure that my answers were correct. I left four questions blank, just in case. The informal economy of settings had its dos and don'ts and unknowns, and I had to tread this terrain of relations and unwritten rules carefully. If Bhaiya's contacts in the Transport Department could make his students sail through, they could surely report back to him about disobedient ones who filled not eleven but sixteen bubbles—and I needed Bhaiya's assistance for the driving test.

I passed.

When the day of the driving test arrived, both Rajeev and Bhaiya accompanied me in my mother's car. Rajeev sat in the front passenger seat while Bhaiya chatted away on his mobile in the back as we awaited our turn in a long line of cars. A uniformed male officer of the Transport Department, notebook in hand, instructed test takers to do various maneuvers. When it was almost our turn, Bhaiya asked Rajeev to switch places with him, moving to the front passenger seat. He needed the official to see him, he explained. The car in front of us pulled up to the testing spot, leaving us in direct sight of the evaluating official. Bhaiya exchanged a slight nod with the official. "I know the guy," Bhaiya announced. "Koi chinta nahin [No need to worry]. You will only be asked to drive forward and in reverse." And that is exactly how the test proceeded. In less than five minutes, the official waved me off. "Ho gaya [All done]?" I asked Bhaiya. "Yes, all done," he replied with a smile.

I passed.

I thanked Bhaiya as I dropped him at his driving school. He shrugged off the formalities, tutting in feigned discomfort as he scrolled on his cell phone.

I never found out Bhaiya's real name. I didn't need to. "Brother" was good enough.

~

My package deal with the driving school was partly legitimate and partly a bribe. Of course, I could have just skipped the legitimate part and paid a tout to do the work for me, as another one of my neighbors had suggested: "No need to go to the transport office at all! I know a *dalal* [tout] who will charge you 2,000 rupees and bring the license to your home." Alternatively, I could have opted to navigate the process independently, as I had initially planned, and likely received my license. Or maybe not. Or perhaps the process would have been lengthy. I expunged these perhapses and maybes by participating in an informal network and paying a go-between to help accomplish my task. The informal webs of relations, both known and unknown, and transactions, both economic and social, that I had to mobilize in order to obtain an official document that provided me with a legible local identity and entitled me to drive a vehicle in Delhi seems absurd: my friend Jaydeep, my mother, her neighbor Rajeev, and finally Bhaiya, one of Rajeev's knowns, who ran a driving school and who used his contacts inside the Transport Department to ensure that I succeeded in my quest.

This network of informality (Lomnitz 1988) relied on "performative rituals" (Visvanathan 2008, 54) that confronted the world of expertise, rationality, bureaucratese, and the written word with artful orality, visuality, and bodily gestures. In my driver's license story, the written word mattered less. Indeed, I was asked to leave my test partially blank. All interactions between Bhaiya, Rajeev, and me were conducted in person and no contracts were signed, for I had Bhaiya's word. Visual cues and gestures also played a critical role; Bhaiya's insistence on sitting in the front passenger seat of my car and exchanging a slight nod with the testing official was recognition enough. This was a dance of speech acts ("you have my word") and embodied signals, at once out in the open and surreptitious. Trust was key.

The predictability that rule following should have offered but did not was made possible by practiced rule bending and cultivated familiarity. Larissa Adler Lomnitz (1988) argues that Weberian understandings of rational bureaucracy miss the plethora of "informal networks following principles [of] . . . patronage, loyalty, and *confianza* (trust). . . . [that] grow in the interstices of the formal system" (42–43). Bhaiya brokered my link to a world of formal unknowns through his web of personal relationships and informality. He guaranteed me timely success, and he delivered.

This kind of informality cracks open and greases a labyrinthian bureaucracy and makes it work where official rules might hinder, frustrate, or fail. It is "an intrinsic element of 'formality' . . . [and] an adaptive mechanism that, simultaneously and in a vicious cycle, reinforces the shortcomings of the formal system" (Lomnitz 1988, 42–43). In other words, this informality is coeval with the formal hierarchical system and not an equalizing alternative per se. Although it provides access and functionality, it does so selectively; financial means and cultural capital make a difference. The informal economy of corruption and middlemen—the constitutive outside of the state—depends on systemic dysfunction to survive. It does not address the structural inequalities that underwrite differential access to the state. Rather, in assisting individuals to overcome bureaucratic hurdles one person at a time, this informality reproduces the very systemic problems it navigates. This vicious cycle that Lomnitz (1988) describes points to the exploitation and violence that formal bureaucracy and informal networks coproduce, and that the law participates in, willy-nilly.

Corruption beyond Culture and the Law

Finally, I introduce Sumit Jha, who highlighted the structural inequalities that lie at the heart of corruption and state secrecy, and who moved the discussion about sociopolitical change away from culturalist arguments and legalized framings. "No law is going to change structural inequality," he declared plainly, offering a nuanced take on what I view as the liberal limit of the law—that is, its inability to deliver the kind of transformation that good governance experts and activists like Kejriwal promise.

I encountered Sumit by chance at the cafeteria at the Alliance Française in Delhi; a journalist I was supposed to interview brought him along. He sat at our table, slurping a steaming bowl of Maggi noodles, listening to our exchange about NGOs and law-based activism and piping in from time to time. He delivered sporadic sound bites with a deadpan obviousness that I had come to expect from those involved in people's movements and radical politics. His perspective intrigued me, and I requested a one-on-one conversation. A few days later, we met at a roadside *dhaba* (food stall) near the Delhi University campus, where he was a regular. He placed his "usual" chai order with the *dhabawala* while I specified, "No sugar, please." We sat under a gulmohar tree, on fire with its red blossoms. Sumit lit a cigarette, I turned on my iPhone's recorder, and we began talking about transparency, corruption, and the recent upswing in judicialized politics.

His main issue with law-based projects of change was that they lacked a critique of the state. Those involved in such efforts believed that all that was needed was "a knowledgeable person, who knows everything about procedures and laws, [and whom] no one would be able to fool. That means that there is nothing wrong with [the state]. If you have a good person, he will make everything right." Kejriwal appeared as such a messianic figure.

Sumit did not trivialize activists' growing reliance on the law to effect change but refused to see it as a silver bullet. "Pro-people and left forces should use the law as a space, but one should not be under the illusion that this is going to make a radical change in society. How are all these laws going to affect the feudal mind-set, or the patriarchal mind-set, or Brahminical ideology? I think those are the basic problems of Indian society—feudalism, patriarchy, capitalism. See, one has to understand what the system is. The system has a kind of class and gender logic that cannot be cleaned up by laws. You need total abolition of [the] caste system and patriarchy in society. You need a radical restructuring of property relations, in old-fashioned socialist terms."

So those who believed in the promise of the RTI Act were wrong, I probed. This law was supposed to provoke a sea change in governance, instituting transparency and accountability and ending corruption. Sumit chuckled. "It is not that easy that you get a law and you get access to everything. I don't think transparency is a problem. Today's modern state is very complex. We have an extremely centralized state with a very sophisticated intelligence apparatus—a state within the state. [Even] if the state becomes totally transparent, so what! The inherently exploitative apparatus will stay . . . as is. The police will still shoot you. Now they will say, 'OK, I am shooting you.' To put it more bluntly, supposing capitalism becomes transparent. So what! A person will say, 'OK, I'm transparent and I am exploiting you legally.' But does it answer the structural exploitation in society? Capitalism needs the state to enforce contracts and to maintain law and order and to repress any possible rebellion. Supposing that state becomes totally honest and efficient and transparent. People may get some administrative relief, and in a class society that counts. Because the way our bureaucrats behave—it is a feudal country, a decadent, corrupt society. So naturally it will make things slightly better for the people. But I don't think the exploitative system is going to go away."

Sumit took a long drag. "Now, corruption. Corruption is not an issue!" he declared, turning the modernist complaint of people like Anuj Chopra on its head. "India is very famous for corruption. You know, 'the Third World.' Countries which don't have legal corruption—the U.S., for example—have lobbying, etc., etc. Do you think those are . . . perfect, nonexploitative societies? No! Take the NREGA. You get all the information through RTI that the NREGA is implemented 100 percent according to the spirit and letter of the law. So what! You fix a minimum wage of 100 rupees per day. A business executive gets 10,000 rupees per day. Does that mean it is an ideal system? Even if the government implements all its schemes in a transparent and noncorrupt way, are we going to have an egalitarian society only through schemes?"

Sumit readily admitted that the RTI law was partially successful in providing people with access to information—no mean achievement "in a society with widespread illiteracy and widespread disinformation [spread by] mass media." But to therefore think that "the law is a magic wand, which will cure all the diseases—therein lies the danger." When I asked if there was an alternative to a law-based politics, Sumit replied: "It is not either-or. Our system is very corrupt, very callous, so you need some kind of cleaning up. . . . My problem is [that] one should not create too many illusions . . . , so that all your activists are busy writing petitions. . . . I call it 'extra legalism.' It is depoliticizing people. Like, I'll tell you my experience. I was part of a radical group in Bihar. I saw that the village health center and the public distribution system were not working. So I started writing petitions. I put in at least half a quintal of petitions to make one village health center ... [or] one ration shop work. Nothing happened. The senior members [of my group] laughed at me: 'You are so stupid! Politics is not petition writing!' So we found other ways. If a health center was not functioning properly, we would blockade the subdivisional officer's office for forty-eight hours. He would come, get the doctor, and get the center opened. It was a practical political training for me. But social movement people, morning to evening, write applications—to the executive engineer, to the block development officer.... This is the attitude! You put so much faith [in] writing applications [and] knowing everything about procedures and laws. Every day, India gets truckloads of applications. The prime minister's office has around twenty five officers just to reply to these applications! Petitioning should be part of the whole activist process, not everything. Because ultimately you are strengthening the status quo [and] in the long term it can be dangerous. Writing applications may help marginalized groups access government programs, but they will always remain marginalized."

Sumit took another long drag and blew out smoke, away from my face. "If applications could change a society, then why struggle? Let us give a memorandum to the prime minister for implementing socialism in this country!"

I burst out in raucous laughter. Sumit joined in.

A Ballooning Labyrinth

This chapter has offered a rumination on corruption as a limit phenomenon and on the limits of the law in wiping it out. Corruption at once transgresses the idealized limit between the public and private realms that undergirds liberal law and defies delimiting. There is avid disagreement in the Indian public sphere about which system to target, how to separate innocent victims from wrongdoers, and how to distinguish clearly between "bonafide mistakes and colorable exercise of power,"[18] as former prime minister Manmohan Singh put it. The discourse on corruption teems with contentious and irresolvable gray areas. Legal and vernacular social understandings about what is good and bad, legitimate and illegitimate, do not map neatly onto each other. Exceptions muddle the apparent truism, the rule, of corruption.

The IAC attempted to control this unwieldy corruption complex by framing it morally and locating it in the state system. Even if it could not be traced to a singular source, like an intricate and evolving riverine system, its main site of multiplication was the state. If that key node could be targeted and diffused legally, then it would have a ripple effect downriver. This thinking lay at the heart of the IAC's technomoral mission of cleansing governance, empowering a victimized public, and restoring a proper democratic order through a strong law.

Kejriwal and his associates faced pushback for their strategy. Prabhat Patnaik (2011) located the IAC among those "'fuzzy' middle-class movements of a moralistic kind that touch a chord among large sections of the people and draw participants from other classes" but offer little, if any, political-economic analysis or recourse; he rued the lack of reflection on the part of the leadership on why corruption in India had increased under neoliberalism (see also Roy 2011). Someone I encountered at the IAC campaign's headquarters endorsed this view. "The logic of development [vikas ki avdharna] is the main issue, not corruption," he said. "The rise in economic disparity due to liberalization is disastrous. Ye vikas hai ya vinash [Is this development or destruction]! Aadmi shaitan ho gaya hai—paise ka ghulam [Man has become the devil—enslaved to money]." But, he lamented, "Nobody is talking about development post-1991, not even the IAC."

Critics of the anticorruption campaign also questioned the efficacy of taking a state-focused, legal approach (Nigam 2011) and asked if this represented a problematic "over-judicialisation of resistance" (Sundar 2011). Taking a judicialized route to ending corruption is complicated in postcolonial contexts where the relationship between legality and illegality is anything but settled. Perhaps corruption is a sign and outcome of "porous legalities" (Liang 2005). As a morphing spectrum of social practices, corruption confounds the precise boundaries, the dos and don'ts that the law demands.

Global good governance discourse ignores this complexity in its judicialized anticorruption approach, arguing that the law "assures that governments are truly accountable. . . . [And] when there is no way to enforce accountability, the result is autocracy and widespread corruption" (Boeninger 1992, 278). Mathematical equations, like "$C = M + D - A$ [or] Corruption equals Monopoly *plus* Discretion *minus* Accountability" (Klitgaard 1998, 4), and laws based on such exact definitions work well as aesthetic exercises in simplification, which deny "the tenuousness of the connections between legality, legitimacy, and ethics" (Tidey 2022, 16). Legal measures based in simplification impose formulaic systematicity on what is "an inherently untidy experience" (Douglas 2002, 5) and fail to contain the chaotic social life of corruption. For corruption is not an object or disease agent that can be isolated and neutralized. Rather, it is a "relation between official–unofficial, formal–informal, public–private" (Visvanathan 2008, 53) as well as a proliferating effect of these modern categories.

A technical, legalistic approach to eradicating corruption can only go so far before stalling. If corruption "stems from taxonomy, the power to classify and declassify" (Visvanathan 2008, 53), then the law, as an institutional embodiment of the modern will to classify, can hardly be relied on to cure what it in fact generates. New laws will produce new transgressions—exceptions that erupt at the law's limit and fray its seams. These impasses will in turn provoke interpretive wrangling over what is and is not corrupt, ongoing refinement of existing laws, and/or calls for new laws in a never-ending chase for perfection and control.

Perhaps it is not corruption that is a problem, as Sumit suggested, but structural inequality propped up by the state and laws. Corruption is not the fallout of a poorly designed system but is paradoxically produced by the logic of bureaucracy itself—the hierarchical and unfamiliar system of regulations, routines, and relations typified by the state and law as public institutions—that seeks to realize a rationalized social and political utopia but fails to do so (Graeber 2015; Weber 1968). If we suspend the ideal of the liberal state as perfectly public, civic, and rule-bound, then what we confront is a much more unruly, even threatening arena that is unequally accessible. Here I find Dipesh Chakrabarty's (1992) ideas about the complexity of the public realm in colonial Bengal provocative. He argues that the street and the bazaar, for example, functioned not as ordered and civic public arenas but as dangerous spaces where the known touched the unknown, and where local worldviews encountered strange knowledges and practices, such as those of the law and bureaucraft. The "spatial complex" of the outside "has a deeply ambiguous character. It is exposed and therefore malevolent. It is not subject to a single set of (enclosing) rules and ritual. . . . It is where miscegenation occurs . . . [and it is] a place against which one needs protection" (543).

I suggest that we might want to see the state similarly. Like the street and the bazaar, the colonial state in India functioned as an eclipsed public or an "inverted commons" (Visvanathan 2008, 54). The Official Secrets Act went a long way in privatizing the state by cocooning administrators and their practices from scrutiny by the colonized. It even forbade the colonized from being in the vicinity of, photographing, or sketching places classified as sensitive by the government, let alone accessing them; that the category of sensitive was infinitely malleable needs no emphasizing.[19] Colonial governance reinforced the outside nature of public spaces for native subjects.

Independence from the British did not bring freedom from the privatization of state sites and records or from the sovereign logic of the liberal state, which yokes power to secrecy, as I argued in chapter 3. The postcolonial Indian bureaucracy, writes Visvanathan (2008), remains "an enclosure" (54) full of gatekeepers and forms of knowledge that are "monopolized, secret, changing, and manipulative" (52). It is an arena of faceless rules and impenetrable strangers with whom one must transact and haggle. Corruption becomes an assemblage of ingressive and transgressive practices, which renders maneuverable an inhospitable terrain of bureaucratic unknowns and incomprehensibles, affording "a sense of security" (54) for some. It vernacularizes the formal "grammar of a bureaucracy" (55), allowing the power-laden rituals of gifting to infuse the equally power-laden, rationalized rituals of contract and relationality to transmogrify impersonal rule. It explodes the myth of the clean binaries underlying the liberal state and law.

To be clear, I am not endorsing a one-sided, celebratory view of corruption. As the liberal state's ineluctable other, corruption mimics the exclusions and structural violence of the state (see also Gupta 2012). Even as it enables people to navigate through abstract rules to get what they need, corruption does not restructure, simplify, or even decenter the state. It perpetuates violence because, while it makes existing structures work, it does not change them. Rather than deprivatizing state institutions and procedures, corrupt practices like bribing perpetuate new, partial forms of re-enclosure, allowing access for some, and in some contexts. For it is in the interest of those both on the inside and outside—officers of the state and middlemen—to keep alive the messy tangle of formal and informal rules. Their survival depends on it. As Visvanathan (2008) argues, while the "clerk and tout blunt the insensitivity of the bureaucracy, make it user friendly . . . [they] also make sure . . . that the state remains a labyrinth" (55).

If corruption is not a symptom of poor bureaucratic and legal infrastructures but instead their product, then instituting more and better laws to control it will not only expand an already distended state but also proliferate bureaucratic rules, lifeworlds, and mazes that generate corrupt acts in the first place. This is what Visvanathan (2008) terms a "Baroquization" of the state enabled by an unending dance wherein each "reform recycles corruption in a renewed form" (55).

Dismantling corruption through laws is bound to fail at its limits because new laws will continue to produce corruption as an unruly excess. While such laws might provide relief to some, they will not materialize an equal society. They will also lead to a further judicialization and bureaucratization of social and activist life, as Sumit pointed out, where deciphering and negotiating ever-expanding procedures, writing petitions, appealing to the state, and fighting in courts become (liberal) ends in themselves. Judicialized good governance activism reinforces faith in a bureaucratically rationalized liberal state and the law as neutral and good rather than as power-laden, classed, and gendered phenomena. While such faith enlivens and moves politics, it also narrows the scope of alternatives beyond the law and the state.

6

On Good Governance Populism

The questions *[sic]* is not about changing the system but [to] make the existing system work and deliver effectively.

—NARENDRA MODI, keynote address, Mumbai, June 5, 2010

We are not here to do *rajneeti* [politics or rule]; we are here to change it.

—ARVIND KEJRIWAL, keynote address, Mumbai, June 21, 2013

I begin this final chapter with a provocation. Liberal democratic good governance, I contend, serves as a hotbed for authoritarian populist politics. This statement may appear counterintuitive, given that the international development industry positions good governance as a remedy against the illiberality and irrational excesses of populism and authoritarianism.[1] This understanding makes good governance populism seem like a contradiction in terms. I offer a different perspective. Rather than being inherently antagonistic, good governance as a state-making project and populism as a people-making one (Chakravartty and Roy 2017) share a discursive affinity. Although the former is technical/political and expert driven and the latter is moral/political and popular, both are undertaken to better the lives of the public. Both discourses are capacious, ideologically flexible, and Manichean in form (Laclau 2005), deploying good-versus-bad and us-versus-them dualisms. Indeed, good governance offers an opportune and productive vehicle for a populist politics that can take authoritarian, majoritarian forms as easily as pluralist ones.

The world has seen many good governance populists recently, including Donald Trump, Tayyip Erdogan, Jair Bolsonaro, Hugo Chavez, and Victor Orban, who, despite their ideological and political differences, have taken an antiestablishment stand and pledged systemic reform in the name of the people and the nation. India has two such leaders, Modi and Kejriwal, who are rivals. As different as Modi's right-wing, divisive Hindutva politics may be from Kejriwal's more inclusive, secular-leaning one, both leaders converge on the good governance stage as prominent faces of technomoral populist reform. Both divide the "population into a valorized majority us—the people—and a demonized minority them" (Mazzarella 2019). Where Modi's "us" is adamantly Hindu, Kejriwal's is a loose collective of "common men" wronged by corrupt political actors. Both leaders use "a folksy or vernacular tone" (Mazzarella 2019, 47) to garner popular appeal. Indeed, the malleable and accommodative quality of good governance discourse allows for overlaps between ostensibly distinct forms of politics, alerting us to the paradoxes and unpredictable risks behind its proclaimed goodness.

If Modi can assemble an antidemocratic, dictatorial regime in the name of good governance, can Kejriwal's swaraj mission tend in the same direction? I suggest that it can. Although Kejriwal's good governance strategy is more focused on public welfare measures and is less lethal than Modi's, it shows a similar inclination for nationalist and patriarchal authoritarianism (Sharma 2022).

To parse good governance populism and expose its paradoxes and risks, I first describe how the World Bank conceptualizes the relationship between good governance and populism as antagonistic. I challenge this framing using political theory and anthropological scholarship. Next, I focus on Kejriwal and a group of his volunteer associates to elaborate ethnographically on the affective friction and dilemmas that his technomoral good governance strategy generates.

Good Governance and Populism: Antithetical or Aligned?

By the early 1990s, World Bank experts had named good governance as critical for the success of neoliberal economic restructuring. They also saw it as a weapon to counter the rise of populism and authoritarianism worldwide. They claimed that the prior decade of decelerating growth, structural adjustment disasters, and collapse of planned economies had exposed the adverse effects of poor and corrupt governance. The resultant increase in economic strife, inequality, and political uncertainty had further damaged the legitimacy of state institutions and leaders in their citizens' eyes. "In such circumstances, the authority of the governments over their peoples tends to be progressively eroded" (World Bank 1992, 9), and they "tend to veer either too far in response to political pressures at the expense of economic reforms (the trap of populism), or too far in the support of economic reforms at the expense of consolidating democracy (the trap of repression)" (Nelson 1992, 292). Populism and authoritarianism were "equally inimical to good governance and sustainable development" (Landell-Mills and Serageldin 1992, 305). Multilateral agencies could help states dodge the "evil" of populism on the one hand and of "political regression" (Boeninger 1992, 275) and on the other by actively promoting liberal democratic reforms. If populism was a reaction against neoliberal restructuring gone wrong because of corrupt and clientelist states, good governance was a counterbalance to this populist tide.

It is not surprising that populism came up in discussions at the World Bank in the immediate aftermath of the Cold War, when political and ideological gauges were being recalibrated and the world respatialized: "'Populism' is a word that we reach for when we sense the possible breakdown of . . . the liberal settlement" that divided the globe "into a zone—the 'free world'—where the norms and forms of liberal democracy were presumed to be hegemonic, and a zone—the communist countries and the 'developing world'—where they were not" (Mazzarella 2019, 48). While the post-1989 moment shone a particularly harsh light on populism as an illiberal and ideological force in a world where liberal Western political-economic ideals had finally emerged triumphant, populism has long been relegated to the margins of politics proper (Frank 2018). Since "the mid-20th century, mainstream political theory has worked to erase the link between democracy and assertions of the popular will, to highlight instead liberal norms, institutions, and procedures" (Samet and Schiller 2017). Ernesto Laclau (2005) critiques this tendency to "demote" and "denigrate" populism as a deviant, irrational "other" of the liberal political order (19). Bank deliberations displayed these biases in positioning good governance as an antidote to populism.

I challenge this oppositional framing of good governance and populism, arguing that they display striking discursive and structural affinity. Furthermore, rather than stemming the tide of populism and authoritarianism, good governance can promote both, often simultaneously.

What, then, are their structural similarities? Martin Doornbos (2001) describes good governance as a "flexible carrier" whose "intrinsic open-endedness, vagueness, and inherent lack of specificity tend to generate a good deal of . . . debate as to what is or should be its 'proper' meaning, prompting multiple efforts to appropriate it" (95). This description easily applies to populism as well, which is similarly amoeba-like and promiscuous as a concept and strategy (Frank 2018; Mazzarella 2019). Laclau (2005) argues that populism is not an "it," a delimited phenomenon with specified content, but a "dimension of political culture" (74), which tells us "something about the ontological constitution of the political as such" (67). In other words, it is a structuring principle that brings the political into being.

As a capacious and pliable vessel, populism refuses ideological or class attachment (Laclau 2005). Historical and existing populisms worldwide are labeled as left, right, or center; working class or agrarian; movement or party based; nationalist or regional/communitarian; authoritarian or democratic; reactionary or progressive; or any combination of these (Laclau 2005; Mazzarella 2019; Rancière 2014). Moreover, populism is not a pathological deviation from liberal democratic politics, per the Bank's discourse, but constitutive of it (Samet 2013); indeed, it could well be "an illiberal democratic response to undemocratic liberalism" (Mudde 2015; see also Hindess 2004; Mudde 2007).

If good governance rests on a Manichean politicomoral worldview structured around easy binaries, so does populism. Laclau (2005) contends that as a "a political logic" (117), populism bifurcates the social field into antagonistic positions and ties together the grievances of different groups into a singular platform to craft popular appeal and identification. It creates "the people" as a good majority whose collective will it then claims to ventriloquize against the entrenched interests of a corrupt minority—the system, the ruling elite, and so on. Binary framing lends both populist and good governance discourses an antiestablishment vigor. Jacques Rancière's (2017) description of populism as an "attitude of refusal" of existing politics applies equally to good governance in that its core becomes elaborated through what it is not: bad institutions and policies, and dirty politics. Although populism mobilizes a charismatic, affectively charged vernacular and good governance a language of morally inflected rational expertise, each pledges to transform things as they are into things as they should be.

These overlaps make possible the contemporary phenomenon of good governance populism. It is a bundling of disparate discursive, symbolic, and historical elements into a shifting assemblage of technomoral strategies whose ideological bases, cultural groundings, policy tactics, and political effects are neither fixed nor predictable. Indeed, Modi and Kejriwal represent varied but overlapping clusters of populist elements in their good governance missions.

I now examine the complicated dynamics of this technomoral politics in Delhi using Kejriwal's swaraj mission from 2009 until 2014 as my primary ethnographic focus. I analyze how he vernacularized and moralized political reform with Gandhian and nationalist ideas, symbols, and tactics; invoked the plight of the common man, which could be bettered by virtuous trustees; and took an avowedly nonideological, even antipolitical, stance. The intermixing of the charismatic and the rational, the moral and the technical, and the democratic and the authoritarian that good governance populism symbolizes makes it unsettling; it is neither self-evidently good nor bad but rather dangerous in the Foucauldian vein (Foucault 1982). I sit with this messiness as I consider the possibilities and perils, the hopefulness and betrayal, of Kejriwal's populist swaraj agenda.

Pitching Swaraj

On a Sunday afternoon in May 2009, I found myself cramped in Aman's tiny living room with three other women and thirteen men. Some were Parivartan old-timers; others were unknown. We had gathered for a strategy meeting that, unbeknownst to me, would prove consequential.

Arvind Kejriwal had convened this meeting to discuss how to propel forward Parivartan's swaraj mission. Since I began working with him in 2008, Arvind had been toying with the idea of swaraj to breathe new life into the RTI Act and manifest participatory, clean democratic governance. He called formal democracy, where people vote once every five years and then are largely left with no say in how they are ruled, a "sham." "We want *azaadi* [freedom] from representative government, like Gandhiji [demanded]," he told me on one occasion. "What India needs is . . . swaraj," or local self-governance.

In late 2008, Arvind began experimenting with the Nagar Raj (town/city governance) law to put swaraj into motion. Passed in 2006, this law extended decentralized governance mechanisms already present in villages to urban areas, allowing city residents to participate in local decision-making.[2] Indian cities consist of municipalities subdivided into wards and wards into areas. Most decisions about urban development are made in a top-down manner at the municipal and ward levels, with little or no input from areas. The Nagar Raj bill inverted and innovated this structure based on the idea that residents of an area know its problems best and should be involved in improving public services and deciding how development funds are spent. Furthermore, given that residents routinely encounter local government representatives, such as public schoolteachers, beat cops, health staff, and sewage workers, they should be empowered to discipline these functionaries for nonperformance. To achieve bottom-up, participatory urban governance, the Nagar Raj law proposed creating Mohalla or Area Sabhas (neighborhood assemblies), which would be given information about government programs and funds to help them make development decisions. They would convey their decisions to elected ward councilors, who would forward them to the respective municipal bodies; the latter would simply execute decisions taken at area levels. The central government framed a "model" law institutionalizing local self-governance, leaving it up to the states to modify and implement it.[3]

The law looked elegant enough on paper, but it raised issues for socially dense and diverse urban contexts like Delhi, where the idea of the local is complicated by large groups of settler and itinerant populations living on the edge of survival, and where shanties abut wealthy colonies. What would collective, area-level decision-making entail in such a milieu? Would municipal officials be amenable to taking orders from area assemblies, particularly those consisting of people living at or below the poverty line?

To test the Nagar Raj bill's potential to actualize swaraj, my colleagues at Parivartan organized assemblies in two low-income areas in Delhi. They mediated meetings between residents and local officials to resolve infrastructural and social issues. Although hesitant to work in middle- and upper-class areas—which, as one colleague put it, "are controlled by RWAs . . . [that] are completely against any 'power to the people' and want the government to work with them, not with the *aam janata* [ordinary public]"—Parivartan's activists also recognized that professional and elite classes could not be overlooked. "This section of society," reasoned Arvind, "happens to be the most vocal [and] also controls the media [and] civil society institutions in this country."

Widening swaraj's appeal and cobbling together a bigger, cross-class coalition to fight for participatory, decentralized governance was on the table when Arvind called the meeting on that Sunday in 2009. He opened by describing the successes of Parivartan's neighborhood assemblies, where residents were actively taking up issues and holding officials accountable. He also relayed encouraging feedback from various middle-class forums, where his exhortations about swaraj struck a chord. "We [need] to bring swaraj everywhere!"

A male participant interjected: "Swaraj seems like an idealist utopia. Does it even exist anywhere?"

"There are many examples," responded Arvind. He told us about an elected representative from Chhattisgarh who included his constituents in decision-making. Accused of running a "parallel government" by other politicians, this man argued that the elected government of the day was, in fact, a parallel government and what he was practicing was real, direct democracy. Arvind commended him for emulating Gandhi's idea of swaraj—a liberation from colonial-style, distanced "representative" rule (Gandhi 1997). Many heads nodded. "Gandhi and swaraj" was an intimate, familiar association. But Arvind tweaked this coupling, arguing that rather than inventing swaraj, Gandhi had revived an older Indian tradition. He gave the example of the Buddhist kingdom of Vaishali (ca. sixth century BCE), hailing it as the world's first democratic republic in the world, where the king consulted his subjects on various matters, and where collective decisions were binding on him (see Kejriwal 2012). One day, some people in Vaishali decided that a young woman in their midst should become a courtesan. She agreed on the condition that she be given the king's castle in exchange. The king was unhappy with this decision; however, the people reminded him that the castle was not his—their "tax" money had built it. So the king deferred to the "democratic" process and relinquished his castle to the newly appointed courtesan. Arvind praised this indigenous parable about swaraj, where a ruler obeyed his subjects; this is exactly what contemporary India needed.[4]

Why would Arvind use a patriarchal monarchy as an ideal example of democratic rule, I wondered? Who were "the people" of Vaishali who deemed that a woman should become a courtesan? Could the woman refuse this command without reprisal? Although he did not endorse the practice of courtesan-ship (Kejriwal 2012), Arvind did not reflect on the patriarchal underpinnings of Vaishali's swaraj—or, for that matter, of Gandhi's praxis.[5] Gandhi's (1997) call for swaraj in India condemned Western rule in gendered terms: he likened the English parliamentary system to a "prostitute" and a "sterile woman" (30), arguing that India needed to rid itself of such unethical and unproductive modern institutions and worldviews.[6]

No one attending the meeting that day questioned Arvind, as if the revered stature of his examples precluded criticism. Gandhi is idolized as the father of the nation and a paragon of virtue. Vaishali has connections to Buddhism and the legendary state courtesan Amrapali, celebrated by Hindi popular culture. References to ethical practices during Buddha's time and Gandhi's have a powerful resonance in public memory, serving as apt "allegorical modules that speak to the possibilities of making a cause heard" (Tsing 2005, 227). Arvind was on comfortable moral ground.

He continued, "The building blocks of swaraj are already there in the Nagar Raj bill. The question is, will the government agree to implement our amended [version]? We are asking for things which they won't give us easily—control over local police and governance. Will they give us power?"

"Yes, they will," averred an older Sikh man, "if the people demand it."

But how to go about demanding swaraj from inimical and entrenched state institutions? Our host, Aman, presented two options—"a revolutionary approach or an incremental approach"—between which he advocated for the latter. "A revolution is overnight, but we need to reform existing governance structures and try to build a groundswell among the public *dheere, dheere* [slowly, slowly]." Arvind disagreed. "Incremental change and lobbying won't get us anywhere. In two or three years, we will tire out of frustration. The RTI law is an example of an incremental change, and look at what has happened to it today." The buzz for swaraj "would fizzle out" if they did not act quickly to generate and expand revolutionary fervor.

Now a woman seated on my left raised her hand and introduced herself as Ayushi. She was a twentysomething with a hip, posh, socially conscious vibe—expensive smartphone, branded clothes worn unselfconsciously, and a thoughtful, engaged energy. She spoke in English. "Our messaging about swaraj to different classes should be different because the issues that face a teacher or doctor are not the same as those that face a sweeper. We need to woo the middle-class person who wants to do something." Using terms that sounded like an advertising pitch, Ayushi suggested a "slick, upmarket campaign" to sell swaraj[7] and to give it a frictional grip (Tsing 2005) among "apathetic and unenthusiastic" middle classes. "It must have a coolness factor," she asserted. "Right now, it looks like we have hatched a hasty campaign in someone's garage." Ayushi did not care for the unimaginative swaraj decals she had seen on auto-rickshaws, which listed a number to call for information. "People will not use these stickers [on their vehicles]," asserted Ayushi. By people, she meant the professional and elite classes. If these groups aspired to coolness, then political involvement had to be pitched to them as cool, something to exhibit proudly, like a brand. Boring decals wouldn't cut it.

Aman agreed and recommended different "stickers targeting two or three broad classes." Ayushi added that they could also invite English-language TV anchors to do segments on swaraj. "That won't reach a lot of people," pointed out Arvind, who wanted to capture a wider audience. He suggested airing clips through independent, neighborhood-level cable providers who offered locally moderated content in various languages. They could produce short films—"but not boring documentaries"—to get the message out in accessible terms.

A young man seated across from me joined Arvind in advocating for less urbane strategies. This was Viresh. It was hard to miss his embodied distinction from Ayushi's cosmopolitan cool (Bourdieu 1984). Sporting a crumpled kurta and pajamas, ordinary *chappals* (flip-flops), and an aging, nonsmart cell phone, Viresh exuded a lower-middle-class, earthy vibe—intelligent and street-smart. He spoke regionally inflected Hindi with a smattering of English. Viresh suggested grassroots strategies like songs and street theater "to provoke a '*bheed* [crowd] psychology'" and motivate the public. "Once we create the right *mahaul* [environment, buzz] around swaraj, then it will not be difficult to increase our following from seventeen people to seventeen hundred." He also proposed conducting surveys: "We can ask people about their experiences with government structures. Are they working to their benefit or not? How to change these structures can come later."

Aman jumped in. "OK. First, you get people to admit that the current system is not good, and then you ask them for an alternative. Rather than providing them with a ready-made swaraj solution, you facilitate that demand from the ground up."

"Exactly!" replied Viresh. "We can offer swaraj as an option and ask people what form it should take—a new law or something else."

Ayushi interrupted. "Surveys are very resource intensive. There are only seventeen of us here. A signature campaign or an internet campaign would work better. We need a mass communication strategy."

Viresh disagreed. "If we are interested in bringing about a revolution, it won't be hatched in a drawing room." He glanced pointedly at all of us. "In-person surveys can and should be done to form a direct attachment with the people. We can't say, 'I sent you an email and now you must join me on the streets for a revolution.' Humein sadakon pe uttarna padega [We will have to descend onto the streets] and connect with people first," he asserted, countering Ayushi's mediatized understanding of public relations with a more intimate, visceral one.

Arvind interrupted this back-and-forth. "Thinking that people will take to the streets and succeed is a dream; it will never happen." But he offered "a wild idea": "Should we nominate candidates for ward councilor elections in all 272 wards in Delhi? Will it fly? It is important that movement people come to power once, pass the necessary resolutions and laws to give all power to the people, and then leave."

A lull descended over the room as people looked at Arvind and at each other, agog.

Arvind broke the silence. "Can we become a third force in Delhi [beyond the Congress and BJP parties]? If we lose the elections, we will still have made swaraj an issue and will force other parties to adopt the concept. If we win, we will need to draft and pass resolutions [to institutionalize swaraj]."

Now everyone began speaking at once.

"We will have to make a party."

"We will not win the next elections. Conveying the message of swaraj by losing an election? It doesn't make sense to me."

"But if we come forward as a party, then we will be more successful in attracting people to our cause."

"No. A political party equals centralization equals corruption."

"We would need to maintain internal democracy in the party."

"If we make a party, power will begin to concentrate, and we will become corrupt. That goes against the idea of swaraj."

"One party [the BJP] promises Ram Rajya; another will promise swaraj. What's the difference! I think it is better to call a general strike. Dilli band karo! [Shut down Delhi!]."[8]

Arvind interjected. "Right now, we are running the swaraj campaign in the style of an NGO [and] have done some public meetings. . . . Logon ko swaraj chakhne do [Let people taste swaraj]. They will be convinced. . . . Let's jump in and get out. We can dissolve the party after elections."

"Swaraj will not come about without a political movement," countered Aman. "Why convert a people's campaign into a political party?"

Ayushi agreed. "A political movement is real democracy, not a party."

Viresh weighed in once again. "Only 50 percent of the people cast their vote in elections. And that has undermined democracy. We have to talk to those 50 percent who don't vote and mobilize them. We need to build a movement first. . . . Let people demand swaraj from other parties, and if they don't relent, then people can decide whether we should form a party or not." Many heads nodded. Ayushi suggested that before considering next steps, they needed to demonstrate the tangible outcomes of swaraj: "We need to organize more area assemblies at the grassroots [level], so we have a prepared ground if we decide to fight local elections."

Arvind agreed. "We need a huge mass base, which is not there right now. Let's create that and then decide whether a political party is needed or not. We have to take the idea of swaraj to every household . . . and create a demand for it. Then [we can] initiate a debate among people and refine our ideas. Let them decide: *kranti* [revolution] or party."

～

This meeting choreographed and foretold the kaleidoscopic sequence that unfolded over the next three years: an NGO-like body (Parivartan) grew into a social movement (IAC), which morphed into a political party (AAP). The agenda grew from RTI to Nagar Raj to anticorruption, all leading up to swaraj.

The friction I observed in Aman's living room in 2009 also hints at the key issues that Kejriwal faced in mobilizing a mass following for his techno-moral swaraj project: first, how to engender a cross-class coalition where people like Ayushi and Viresh would both find a voice; and second, what political form to take—a movement, a party, or one followed by the other. Kejriwal addressed the first by using the symbol of the common man in an attempt to encompass everyone. He tackled the second by taking a movement route into the electoral arena while declaring that AAP represented not a maturation of a movement into a party but a revolutionary transformation of party politics itself.

I now untangle Kejriwal's populist technomoral assemblage, focusing on how he constituted a moral commons by navigating class and gender divides and repudiating ideology and politics. I also tease out the irresolvable tensions of his good governance strategy.

Cobbling a Moral Commons

Beyond Class and Gender

Laclau (2005) argues that populism condenses two "structural moments": an "equivalential" moment, which links together a plurality of demands to construct a unified "global political subject," and a "divisive" moment, which names "an institutionalized 'other'" to construct "internal frontiers" between us and them (117). Kejriwal's politics illuminates both in that he curated a discourse of commonness to conjure equivalence across social divides and rallied this innocent us against a venal them. This "'we/they' opposition ... [was] constructed according to moral categories of 'good' versus 'evil'" (Mouffe 2005, 75). The issue of corruption provided ripe ground for sowing an illusory yet resonant intimacy among "we the people" as victims of a degraded political establishment. Kejriwal's technomoral populism offered a simplistic certainty: people could end state corruption by demanding a new law and paving the way for swaraj.

The IAC movement used an assortment of popular and patriotic symbols to carve out an anticorruption moral commons. Gandhian idioms and tactics were forefronted as IAC leaders called their fight against graft a satyagraha for swaraj and used civil disobedience, hunger strikes, sit-ins, and conventional and social media techniques to spread their message (Sharma 2014). Their "mediatized populism" (Chakravartty and Roy 2017) relied on nationalist imagery, only some of which was secular: T-shirts and posters with images of Bhagat Singh, a young revolutionary executed by the British in 1931; slogans like "Bharat mata ki jai" [Hail to Mother India], *"Inquilab zindabad"* [Long live the revolution], and *"Vande mataram"* [I bow to thee, mother]; and photographs and videos of murdered whistle-blowers and RTI activists, represented as *shaheed* (martyrs). The IAC also used images of Mother India associated with the Hindu right to project a feminized nation whose honor and sanctity had to be protected. Kejriwal, Hazare, and other male IAC leaders presented themselves as virtuous sons who would save Mother India from debased governance through technomoral means. They spoke for and as common men.

The aam aadmi discourse was key to performatively equalizing the public. Of course, Kejriwal and his team did not invent this discourse. As I mentioned in chapter 4, Laxman's eponymous cartoon character has long iconized the generic "everyman" (Baviskar and Ray 2011, 1), whose familiar stories of injustice meted out by a rotten system transcend class. This symbol also enjoys a flourishing life in political party discourse. The Indian National Congress in particular has claimed proprietorship over the downtrodden common man as its constituency.[9] The most prominent populist electoral slogans coined by Indira Gandhi during the 1970s— "Roti, kapra, aur makaan" (Food, clothing, and housing) and *"Garibi hatao"* (Remove poverty)—hailed the aam aadmi. As a multifaceted sign, it provokes identification among the masses and professional classes who bring not abstracted but differently embodied social and citizen identities into the political sphere (Cody 2015).

The IAC and AAP reinvigorated this sign as they "popularized the classically populist language of the 'aam admi' . . . combating the predatory 'political classes' . . . [to articulate their] demand for legal accountability in governance and a new culture of 'clean and transparent' politics" (Chakravartty and Roy 2015, 315). No longer Laxman's mute fatalist or the needy subject of Indira Gandhi's welfarist discourse, Kejriwal's common man became a campaigner who demands rights and a doer who improves governance.[10]

Nothing conveyed this commonness better than the bodily practices of Kejriwal and Anna Hazare, his compatriot during the IAC days. Both men's figures circulated as signs of ordinariness, representing different kinds of cultural capital (Bourdieu 1984). Hazare was the earthy face of the common man. A wise, aging Gandhian dressed in white, he used simple Hindi and a moralizing tone to convey his rural roots, his ascetic masculinity as a celibate *brahmachari,* and his selfless service to the country as a former army man and social activist. By publicly fasting for the greater common good, Hazare staged unparalleled nationalism. Through his suffering body, India could purge itself of political contamination, excess, and vice (Sharma 2014).

Kejriwal, meanwhile, embodied the urban, modern face of the common man. His association with elite institutions—he was trained at the Indian Institute of Technology and recruited into the Indian Revenue Service—marked his expertise. This privilege was tempered by a relatable style. Kejriwal's direct, unadorned speech conveyed accessibility and transparency.[11] His ordinary clothing reiterated his plainspokenness, but it also drew some ridicule. Commonly outfitted in casual pants, sweaters, and a wool scarf wrapped around his head and secured by a white Gandhian *topi* (cap), Kejriwal earned the epithet Mufflerman during the 2013 election season. Though unstatesmanlike when compared to Modi's meticulously crafted self-branding, Kejriwal was charismatic for those who saw themselves in him. AAP played on his curated ordinariness, turning the Mufflerman label into an affirmative sign during the 2014 electoral campaign.[12] They circulated an image on Twitter (now known as X) showing Kejriwal as a broom-wielding faceless superhero figure who embodied the universal plight of countless muffler- and cap-wearing, nameless people and was ready to clean up the state (Figure 1). "Hum subke andar ek Kejriwal hai [There is a Kejriwal inside all of us]," declared a character in a comedic short produced by All India Bakchod.[13] This line conveyed playfully that Kejriwal operated as a metonym for the people and as a sign that resonated across social divides.

The white Gandhian *topi* worn by Kejriwal, Hazare, and their followers materially manifested populist equivalence. Printed with the slogan "I am Anna; I want the Jan Lokpal bill" during the IAC campaign, it positioned everyone wearing it as Anna (Hazare), the original signifier of nationalism, integrity, and ordinary authenticity. After Kejriwal established his party in late 2012, he kept the *topi* but changed the slogan to "I am Aam Aadmi; I want swaraj." The *topi* appeared to gather the different facets of the common man into a singular marker, simultaneously signaling the grassroots, humble appeal that rural, nonelite people like Viresh wanted and the political coolness that middle-class urban denizens like Ayushi desired. It performed a fuzzy equivalence across class, caste, religious, and gender lines as it attempted to create a universally innocent and morally outraged public. Cap-wearing aam aadmis could claim oppression at the hands of the state; the particularity of their problems and demands did not matter (Laclau 2005, 96).

Or did it?

The common man discourse is tainted in terms of class and gender, and its mobilization as a symbol of an apparently undifferentiated public and a strategy of populist good governance is tricky. Ordinariness, as I discussed in chapter 4, has been appropriated by the middle classes, and Kejriwal also played this up to create a broader base for the IAC agenda. It was small wonder, then, that the IAC was largely represented

Figure 1. Arvind Kejriwal as a broom-wielding common man turned superhero. Image appears in "Mufflerman Returns: AAP's Kejriwal Embraces His Inner Superhero," by Scroll staff, November 21, 2014, and available at https://scroll.in/article/690875/Mufflerman-returns-AAPs-Kejriwal-embraces-his-inner-superhero.

by the international and local English-language media as a "middle-class awakening."[14] The urban professional classes had finally broken out of their apolitical ennui and channeled their rage toward reforming the system—or so the story went. Critics pointed to the irony of this "self-styled revolution of the urban middle class against the corrupt political class" (Joseph 2012): the very class overrepresented in the state system was demanding its overhaul.[15]

The gendered subtext of Kejriwal's mission was less commented on, but its patriarchal underpinnings were and remain apparent. Promising good governance through laws and other technical reforms does not necessarily challenge or change the gendered nature of state institutions and policies (Menon 2004; Sharma 2008; Sunder Rajan 2003).[16] Relying on nationalist symbolism is also problematic in that nationalism, as feminists have long argued, is a patriarchal discourse that uses women as a ground on which to articulate an exclusionary, violent politics (Mani 1998).[17] Kejriwal's unreflexive use of the parable of Vaishali, Gandhian swaraj praxis, and the image of the common man rising to save Mother India as moral allegories to support his uprising came laden with patriarchal presumptions.

His associates downplayed the obvious gendering of the common *man* trope, explaining it away as a language limitation. They argued that *aadmi* operates as a gender-neutral noun, quite like the word "human," which automatically includes woman; she is spoken for when one invokes the common man.[18] AAP ultimately disaggregated the aam aadmi figure, introducing alternative caps for female supporters that read, "Main hoon Aam Aurat [I am a common woman]." That this was a superficial nod to gender inclusivity and equality was laid bare by Kejriwal's tweets from November 24, 2012:

Main hoon Aam Aadmi. Main laoonga swaraj [I am a common man. I will bring swaraj].[19]

Main hoon Aam Aadmi. Main laoonga poorna azadi [. . . I will bring total freedom].[20]

Main hoon aam aadmi. Main banoonga Jan Lokpal [. . . I will establish the People's Ombuds/anticorruption law].[21]

Main hoon aam aurat. Main door karungi mengai [I am a common woman. I will put an end to inflation].[22]

In this populist conjuring of commonness, men are hailed as political subjects shouldering the responsibility of freeing the nation from corruption and establishing good governance, while women become domesticated subjects doing their naturalized duty of ensuring their families' survival by fighting inflation. The common woman is not depicted as passive, but her agency is confined to her reproductive, caregiving role. One would think that Kejriwal would have known better. His past participation in the struggles of slum women ought to have given him a deeper understanding of the gendered division of labor underlying women's political struggles. His tweets belied such a grasp.

Gender inequality remains institutionalized in AAP's leadership. Despite announcing its commitment to female representation, AAP has fallen short.[23] In April 2013, two women were on the party's national executive body; in 2022, women made up seven of thirty-three members.[24] The National Political Affairs Committee—the party's apex decision-making body—had no female representatives in 2013; today, there are two women among seven men.[25] These absences are not coincidental; they are consequential.

The AAP government's 2014 raid in Khirki village in Delhi is a case in point. This mob-style, warrantless raid was led by Somnath Bharti, then law minister, on a group of African women allegedly involved in a drug and prostitution racket. Bharti claimed that complaints from Khirki residents drove him to take action. Several women accused him of assault and molestation. Feminists criticized him and AAP for invoking a racialized and gendered moral order where Black femaleness signifies impurity and deviance that must be policed, and where some (Black African) women could be violated to protect other women's respectability and neighborhood peace.[26] Rather than condemning this style of vigilante justice, AAP used the language of swaraj to justify Bharti's actions. The aam aadmis of Khirki had complained, and their call had to be heeded, regardless of prejudice and majoritarianism. As in ancient Vaishali, so now.

The symbol of the common man is flimsy ground for a populist good governance mission. Quite like the "socially unmarked anonymity of abstract citizenship" (Cody 2015, 51), it constructs an evanescent and fraught public, an us, that remains haunted by class and gender erasures. Experiences of citizenship, governance, state transparency, and corruption are neither generic nor generalizable but shaped by lived social hierarchies. The common man discourse glosses over differences and avoids confronting the split subject of rights. It cannot but fall short in establishing a hegemonic hold that moves beyond simplistic equivalence and turns "a feeling of vague solidarity . . . into a stable system of signification" (Laclau 2005, 74).

Beyond Ideology and Politics

The other tactic that Kejriwal used to assemble moral commonness was disavowing ideological and political affiliation. By strategically staking a neutral, centrist, and outsider position, he presented AAP as a nonideological, antipolitical party.

IAC's and AAP's inchoate medley of moralizing representations—Buddhist Vaishali, Hindutva-associated Bharat Mata, religicoethical Gandhi, leftist atheist Bhagat Singh—served to mark their status as misfits on the political and ideological terrain. Kejriwal claimed a capacious patriotic space that was at once secular, religious, liberal, Gandhian, and accommodative of all common men. He went on record to say that "during the Lokpal campaign, [he tried] to draw on as many patriotic symbols as possible . . . [because] the country . . . was forgetting the importance of nationalism. 'It binds us together'" (Jeelani 2011). This nationalist populism was idealistic because patriotism did not need an ideological anchor.

Indeed, Kejriwal pointedly repudiated ideology. During a 2013 speech, he noted, "Many people are accusing us . . . [of being] leftists. Up until last year, when the Anna movement was on, people used to say that we are capitalists . . . [But] we are not wedded to any ideology. We are basically aam aadmis. . . . [who] just want solutions to our problems" (Kejriwal 2013). In other words, corruption and governance-related issues had no truck with ideological policy agendas (read: neoliberalism). Good governance reform was a pragmatic and idealistic matter divorced from divisive isms. Neither left nor right, this positional politics was morally righteous (Bornstein and Sharma 2016; Mouffe 2005).

While some criticized Kejriwal for framing corruption as a nonideological, "touchy-feely 'moral' problem . . . [around which] everybody can happily rally ... fascists, democrats, anarchists, god-squadders, daytrippers, the right, the left and even the deeply corrupt" (Roy 2011), many were swayed by his ideological refusal. Nikhat, a Muslim professional from Delhi, told me that she joined the IAC and AAP because Kejriwal positioned corruption as a "unifying issue" unhampered by what she called "smoke screen ideologies—left, right, secular. We said, cut out corruption! Don't give us ideological crap. Give us what we deserve as citizens." There was Swamiji, an ex-communist from Uttar Pradesh with gray dreadlocks and a mendicant's bearing and attire, who gave up longstanding ideological loyalty to join Kejriwal. "I don't want to feel constrained by any singular program anymore," he told me. And Neeti, an upper-middle-class former activist fluent in "lefty" perspectives and radical global movements, was drawn to AAP precisely because it rejected pigeonholing. She entered the party as a volunteer because it "doesn't alienate [anyone].... Let's see how long they manage to occupy this center space. I would leave it in an instant if they went toward the right. I'd prefer it to be more left leaning, no doubt. But I hope that this delay in articulating ideology will result in bringing more people together."

AAP's identification as neither this nor that offered a wide, relatable platform for people. Curiously, this anti- (and, dare I say, post-) ideological centrism also sits well with the neoliberal spirit that sees in the defeat of communism the end of ideology itself. Indeed, Bank experts predicted that the triumph of Western liberal democracy and capitalism would result in a global victory for "middle-of-the-road" centrism as economic policies and political perspectives converged toward a natural (read: nonideological) stasis (Boeninger 1992, 272).

Kejriwal's strategy of populist indeterminacy (Laclau 2005) extended beyond ideological avoidance. He also presented his good governance mission as anti-"politics," where "politics" denoted conventional state and party practices and crooked power plays. Indeed, critics called out IAC as a dangerously antipolitical force. As a middle-class formation— "a coalition of otherwise apolitical private citizens" (Sengupta 2011)— that promoted a suprastate Lokpal agency based on the "idea that nonelected institutions that do not involve politicians are somehow the only ones that can be trusted" and converted a "complex institutional question [of governance reform] into a simplistic moral imperative" (Mehta 2011), what could it be but antipolitical?

Kejriwal maintained this moral antipolitics when the IAC morphed into a party, playing up AAP's distinctive social movement origins. Movement actors in India are commonly viewed as nonparty political entities (Kothari 1984) and icons of an ethical politics, as opposed to state actors (Bornstein and Sharma 2016). Kejriwal promised to keep alive movement virtue in party form and use it to clean up the state. "This is not a party but a social movement, a political revolution,"[27] he declared, pledging to continue "the *andolan* [struggle] . . . on the streets as well as in the parliament."[28] He claimed AAP's representatives were "not political leaders [but] common men [who entered politics] because there was no other option. . . . We are not here to do *rajneeti* [rule/politics]; we are here to change it" (Kejriwal 2013). To demonstrate its difference from politics as usual and commonness with ordinary citizens, AAP denounced "VIP culture." Party leaders refused red beacons on official vehicles and elite residences.[29] And Kejriwal continued sporting his Mufflerman outfits.

To some, AAP's identification as a revolutionary misfit inhabiting the edges of institutional politics was refreshing. "AAP is not an NGO, and it is not a movement," remarked Neeti enthusiastically; "it offers a political space like none other." Institutional in-betweenness, for her, was as attractive as ideological centrism.

Others were less sanguine, arguing that by entering politics, Kejriwal had lost the moral high ground. They warned him against confounding the lines between the state and social movements and between politics and ethics.[30] Kejriwal countered: "Gandhiji used to say that politics devoid of spirituality is very dangerous. . . . [People today believe] that politics cannot proceed with morality, ethics, and honesty. . . . We will prove that it can be done." He promised to convert the existing "satta ki rajneeti [politics of power]" into "janata ki rajneeti [politics of the people]."[31] To those who characterized his transformation from activist to politician as a moral downfall, he replied that social service and party work were not antagonistic. To serve the public was a moral duty of the political classes, for they are *naukar* (servants), not masters.[32] This middle-class reframing of who rules and who serves, which inverts but preserves the master–servant hierarchy, is a populist tactic used often by Kejriwal and his party members (Roy 2014).

By defining governance as virtuous public service, Kejriwal refuses to separate the political from the technical and the moral. He evokes a

Gandhian praxis of altruism, social constructivism, and welfare, and counters the neoliberal logic of dewelfarized statehood. However, reducing state politics to service delivery is also antipolitical. By improving the quality and affordability of basic entitlements—water and electricity, for example—AAP has gone against neoliberal directives of privatization and free market deregulation. Yet by disavowing ideology and representing governance as a technomoral act, AAP also removes power from the political equation and depoliticizes rule. It obscures the fact that governance is an exercise of power, and policies and services are political tools that serve to govern (Ferguson 1994).

At once idealistic and anti-ideology, politicized and antipolitical, Kejriwal's good governance populism is paradoxical. It is a politics of indeterminacy and refusal—a politics of *not*. Representing AAP as an actor that is not a conventional party and that does not engage in power politics maintains its ethical superiority. It carves out a conveniently hybrid, nonpartisan space to carry out its idealistic (but not ideological) mission to revolutionize governance through services and policies but not immoral politics.

This alternative politics of not is perilous in a context in which "the platform of the apolitical has emerged as a dangerous ground where the clouds of popular fascisms gather in a language of liberal protest" (Bhatia 2011). In addition to being laced with patriarchal nationalism, it carries the danger of authoritarianism, which gets to the heart of the illiberalism that is entangled with liberal democratic good governance (Hindess 2004).

Dictating Swaraj or Benevolent Authoritarianism

Even though IAC and AAP leaders have positioned themselves as common men and decried elitism, their extraordinariness has never been in doubt. As technocrats and upstanding individuals who cut their teeth on movement activism, they claim to have the skills, authority, and moral bearing necessary to take on good governance. As uncommonly capable, righteous common men, they can lead the way toward betterment for all. This stance has a curious affinity with nineteenth-century colonial trusteeship promoted by liberals like John Stuart Mill. Even though good governance today iconizes a modern developmental imperative rather than a colonial civilizational one (Cowen and Shenton 1995; Hindess 2004), and is undertaken by local leaders rather than occupying powers, it shares with the latter a propensity toward authoritarianism.

Taking a legalistic approach to ending corruption reveals an underlying antidemocratic vanguardism that marks off a rung of trusted technical experts to steer the nation-state. Indeed, critics of the IAC raised this issue, questioning the authority of self-appointed representatives of the people to make laws: "There is a problem when groups not constituted legally cross the line of ... democratic agitation ... [and insist] that their fatwas be written into law ... no matter how well-intentioned they are" (Sainath 2011). Some called the IAC's People's Ombuds proposal "unaccountable," arguing it would create a hypercentralized, Orwellian monstrosity (Chandoke 2011) akin to an elite "council of guardians" (Sengupta 2011) with draconian powers to investigate any state institution but no electoral mandate or oversight. These critics did not buy the IAC's promise that the impeccable technomoral credentials of the individuals appointed to the Lokpal agency—senior judges, national and international awardees, and heads of public bodies—would automatically make this office incorruptible and representative. They accused the IAC leaders of using "coercive moral power" (Mehta 2011) to subvert and vilify the political process (Patnaik 2011). Then again, "bypassing mediating and moderating institutions and procedures in pursuit of an immediate, redemptive and affect-intensive presencing of popular sovereignty" (Mazzarella 2019, 47) is a time-tested populist strategy; mobilizing it in the name of swaraj and in a top-down manner makes it especially ironic.

The specter of authoritarian trusteeship has continued to haunt the IAC turned AAP. It appeared with particular force in June 2014, a moment of reckoning for the party. After resigning from the Delhi legislature as an act of moral outrage because parliamentarians were stonewalling its anticorruption bill,[33] AAP fought and lost the national election to the BJP. Although Kejriwal emphasized that winning was never AAP's goal and that the swaraj cause was much bigger than that, how do you reconcile with a bitter defeat at the polls when the party's full energy had been directed toward elections? How do you continue raising awareness about swaraj and setting an example for others to follow, as Gandhi might have done? Some AAP members raised exactly these issues, accusing the party leadership of not reflecting internally what it advocated for the rest of the nation: inclusive, decentralized organization and decision-making. The party's website avers that "there is no central high command in Aam Aadmi party [and its] structure follows a bottom to top approach."[34] Some functionaries alleged that this was mere rhetoric.

A few AAP leaders resigned out of frustration. Many party volunteers felt restless and deflated after losing an election and key leadership. Some got together and formed AVAM (AAP Volunteer Action Manch [Forum]), urging the party to better organize and recognize volunteer service and to implement swaraj within. Ironically, AAP, a party of supposed rebels, responded harshly to this internal rebellion.

During a Google Hangout on August 9, 2014, Kejriwal accused party volunteers demanding swaraj of making "a mockery of . . . a very powerful concept."[35] Declaring that AAP had "the most inner party democracy and swaraj as compared to all other parties," he clarified what swaraj entailed. "Swaraj does not mean voting. Swaraj means consensus—*aapsi sehmati.*" Furthermore, it did not imply the inclusion of everyone in every decision at every level. "Can you name five organizations, anywhere in the world, in which all decisions are made in consultation with . . . all members?" Kejriwal asked rhetorically. "Is there swaraj in your family? Do all members of your family take decisions collectively through votes? Does this happen in any company [corporation]? In the army?" I flinched at the absurd choice of examples as I listened. Why choose the patriarchal family, a profit-making entity, and a hierarchical and repressive state institution to make a point about democratic decision-making?

Kejriwal continued. "I did not write [in my book on swaraj] that our policy toward Pakistan should be made after discussions with all 121 crore [1.21 billion] people in this country [or] that insurance, banking, currency, national highways . . . will be planned after consulting with 121 crore people." He clarified that swaraj meant that local decisions in villages and neighborhoods should directly involve residents. At the level of municipalities and districts, "people's *rai* [opinion] will be sought. But beyond that tier, it is difficult to even seek opinions." Here Kejriwal offered a scalar, graduated swaraj model, where national and technical matters like finance and infrastructure could not possibly involve public participation or even opinion; never mind that he had previously decried distanced representative democracy. This scaled model of participation is what AAP would follow within the party. Leadership would "take the *advice* of volunteers" on matters such as choosing candidates, but "the final decisions" would be taken at the top, Kejriwal emphasized.

The same man who asserted on other occasions that swaraj was not "rocket science" now suggested that it was profound and could only be handled by the worthy; he used the word *kaabil* to describe these techno-moral trustees. The protesting volunteers did not qualify for this sacred duty because they were misusing swaraj for their own selfish agenda: to get nominated as party candidates and gain political power. Deeming them *desh-drohi* (antinationals), *ghaddaar* (traitors), and rival party moles that threatened AAP's noble mission, Kejriwal expelled these volunteers and blacklisted AVAM. He also expelled party leaders who criticized these decisions for "anti-party activities."[36] Thus, the good "us" functioned as a malleable category that could be narrowed as needed. Kejriwal's autocratic actions, seen as unfit for a party that had embraced a movement spirit, led other leaders to resign in protest.[37]

With these purges of 2014 and 2015, the AAP sent a clear message that only the chosen, *kaabil* trustees deserved to lead the party and that its vertical setup could not be questioned despite references to commonness, equivalence, and direct democracy. Hierarchy and authoritarianism were not at odds with swaraj when the nationalist mission of saving the country from bad governance was at issue. A higher calling made some compromises inevitable, even if they went against AAP's commitment to equality and the devolution of power, and countered its pledge to rule with, rather than over, the public.

Hindess (2004) reminds us that it is "not only that liberal [regimes] will sometimes decide to make use of 'illiberal' methods but also . . . that the need to make such decisions should itself be seen as a central feature of liberal political reason" (28). AAP's actions demonstrate the illiberality constitutive of liberal rule, given its imperial entanglements—that is, the tension between freedom and self-government on the one hand, and the government of the less advanced by the more capable on the other (Hindess 2004). There is a friction between democratic good governance as raison d'état and as a technique of administering a people. The former lends legitimacy to rule, even when the latter may take authoritarian forms. Swaraj is no different.

AAP's sacking of volunteers and leaders who wanted change within the party exposed the swaraj mission's contradictions. It forced many party workers to think through the whys, hows, and now whats of their participation—that is, to reflect on what drew them to Kejriwal's cause in the first place and kept them engaged, even if critically, and where their ethical and political desires lay. Should they join AVAM, stay with AAP, or withdraw from both? This was to be expected, given that a technomoral project works by creating an emotional attachment to its mission and leaders that is intimately and collectively felt (Stewart 2007, 2).[38] Indeed, crafting a populist commons is impossible without affective pull and push. Kejriwal and AAP materialized a shared, unwieldy structure of feeling that relates to "emergent formations (though often in the form of modification or disturbance in older forms)" (Williams 1977, 134)—the older forms in this case being politics as usual.

Below, I narrativize this emergent affectscape, which was thrown into relief as a result of the events of 2014: a layered and evolving mix of "thought as felt and feeling as thought" (Williams 1977, 132) that Kejriwal's swaraj call and autocratic decisions fomented. I describe interactions I had with volunteers in August 2014, which took place in groups and one on one at dining tables, on living room floors, and on stoops outside shanties; on public transportation and in cars; and on WhatsApp group chats and the sidelines of an AVAM press conference. The mood was conflicted as volunteers expressed feelings of rapture, loss, betrayal uncertainty, and resolve. I animate this inchoate complex of affective energies in three composite vignettes,[39] using ethnographic storytelling that defers a "quick jump to . . . evaluative critique" (Stewart 2007, 4) and explores how the promise and risks of populist good governance are experienced in all their "intensity and texture" (4).

Eroding Fantasies, Unraveling Feelings
Take One: Ameera

Madras Coffee House in Connaught Place is an old institution. Once a popular joint, today it is an oddity against the air-conditioned luxury and youthful vibe of the Barista and Costa cafés dotting this central Delhi shopping mecca. But this is where Ameera wanted to meet, and I was game. The café, as I discovered, had seen better days. The green vinyl on the furniture was cracked and the cayenne red laminate on the tables was chipped. Creaky ceiling fans made a ticking sound annoyingly out of sync with the '80s and '90s Bollywood beats playing in the background. Ameera and I were shown to a booth in an otherwise empty room. What was meant to be a quick chat over South Indian–style filter coffee extended into a two-hour conversation and dinner: first, because Ameera's stories about Kejriwal and AAP were riveting, and second, because the servers kept prodding us gently to order food. Out of guilt and growing hunger, not to mention the desire to be left alone, I ordered *idlis* and *sambar* as I took in Ameera's account. I tried to keep up as she jumped between thoughts. "There is just so much to tell. Cheezein khultee ja rahi hain [everything is opening up]."

Ameera had a close working relationship with Kejriwal, who had met her during one of his public meetings and invited her to volunteer with AAP. He gave her many responsibilities, telling her that she was among the trusted few with the *aukaat*—ability and audacity—to take on these tasks. Such "emotional appeals and many heart-to-hearts got me more and more involved."

But Ameera faced pushback from some insiders—not only because she had Kejriwal's ear, but also because she openly criticized internal wrongdoing. "The easiest thing to do is to assassinate a woman's character," remarked Ameera. "I was going through all of that and trying to not let it affect me, thinking that this is not important in front of the larger goal. But I always had this thing in my head that I can sustain this only because of my education, my family's support, my inner conviction; but every young woman would not be able to." So she quit AAP after the Delhi elections in December 2013 and wrote to Kejriwal, confiding that it "is difficult being a young woman in this environment. . . . Every day that I volunteered, main poore khandan ki izzat lekar nikalti thi [I carried the weight of my family's honor]. This is the end for me, with AAP. I don't regret a single moment. There is so much that I have learned but I can't compromise. . . . There is no 'don't get affected.' I can't do the detached-attachment bit."

Ameera got pulled back into the party for the 2014 national election campaign. Some of the very (AVAM) volunteers whom Kejriwal would later expel urged her to return. "Every time I would get disillusioned or saturated, [these volunteers] would remind me, '*Yeh apna* system *hai* [This is *our* system]. We should stay and solve the problems that we see.' That is the kind of crucial role they have played for the party!" exclaimed Ameera, leaning toward me, eyes brimming with tears. "Some people came out of their retirement to volunteer. Some left their jobs. Some gave up their youth. Some left their children—two-year-olds! Everyone gave up something for this cause. And most of these were people who joined the party before any election, when the night was darkest."

Ameera and others periodically broached the issue of volunteer engagement with Kejriwal. "We gave him . . . feedback about the need to collectivize the volunteers. But each time we were told to wait; there was always something more pressing. The biggest problem within the party is that they reduce every feedback to a complaint. But it is not! Pay heed and take corrective measures!"

The 2014 election became a pressing concern that sucked volunteer energy. Even though the party made it clear that "winning elections is not a priority, volunteer roles [were] restricted to that," divulged Ameera, twirling the food on her plate. "It was such a difficult election for everyone," she sighed. "So many of our people were hurt *[ghayal]*—financially, emotionally, physically. Innumerable faceless, nameless people working for [swaraj] day and night. It wasn't just Arvind Kejriwal's charisma! . . . Till date, AAP is equal to Arvind Kejriwal. How is that different from 'India is Indira [Gandhi] and Indira is India'? The party is making Arvind into a *bhagwan* [god]! I mean, he has made a huge contribution. He is responsible for awakening the masses. He may be the first, but he is not the last person to take this forward. What if Arvind Kejriwal is not there tomorrow? This *vyakti-vishesh* [individual-focused] strategy is not sustainable. I mean, you can't rely on Arvind alone. You need a model that breeds leadership. But no one is interested. . . . They would rather have a single god."

Ameera teared up. "I don't want anyone to feel that I am against Arvind. I have learned so much from him. He is a *sachcha* [genuine] person; not was, but is. I have so much *shraddha* [devotion] toward him. . . . But if he compromises even a little bit with his ideals [or] manipulates them, then he will get more and more entangled in the *chakravyuh* [political maze]. It is the capacity to review [self-reflect] that makes you different. I thought that after the 16th May massacre [electoral defeat], we would learn. But that hasn't really happened."

Expelling volunteers for demanding swaraj within the party showed a lack of reflexivity within AAP leadership. "When [volunteers] complain, we are labeled selfish," said Ameera, shrugging her shoulders. Then she looked directly at me, her eyes ablaze. "I am not here out of loyalty for a man or a party, but for a cause. The whole model of swaraj and participatory democracy is very difficult to execute. It needs a lot of, um, energy. Volunteers *have* to be there. When Arvind and others around him say that 'what's the big deal about volunteers; if one leaves, many more will come,' that is wrong! If you are neglecting problems within your party, then what will you do outside.... Selfless volunteers who saw this as an opportunity to save the nation, people who were never interested in getting a photo clicked [with the leaders], who never complained, have withered away. 'Nothing is going to happen,' they say. 'AAP has become a cult, and everyone keeps worshipping Arvind.'" The ones who stayed and organized AVAM were "declared 'illegal'—a group of 'politically motivated people' who were anti-party," cried Ameera angrily. "AAP didn't even think twice about . . . disowning [them]. They cut off their [own] spine. It is nobody's business to kick out volunteers. We are not employees. How can anyone stop us from holding [party leaders] accountable? . . . Why should I resign! I *feel* for the cause. This party does not belong to Arvind. It belongs to each one of us!"

A moment later, she hung her head. "Actually, I am very confused right now. I know this cause—swaraj—is important. But there is this huge majority that thinks that AVAM's strategy is not right, because they worry that the party's image will be ruined [by publicly airing internal challenges]. It seems like AAP is focusing on its image too much.... But are we here to build an image? Every day I have been moving with this thought. I am never at ease. Is our foundation so weak that it will fall apart just because someone raises questions? What used to inspire, now seems like . . . *dilasa* [false appeasement]. I am so confused right now, so directionless." A sob escaped Ameera's lips. "All of us are broken, *so broken*, from inside."

Take Two: Ashwin

"I'm here," I texted Ashwin when I reached the designated Mother Dairy store in his neighborhood. He had offered to fetch me because his flat was tricky to locate. Three minutes later, I saw him walking toward me. We exchanged nods and smiles. A few turns, back alleys, and a steep flight of stairs later, we arrived at the small flat he shared with his two younger siblings. "I think I would have found your place with Google Maps," I quipped. Ashwin chuckled. "Google *zindabad!*" Long live Google!

Originally from Madhya Pradesh, twentysomething Ashwin moved to Delhi for education and employment. He described himself as an aam aadmi from the "lower middle class," adding laughingly that maybe this classification was a convenient delusion that helped poor, struggling people feel better about themselves. As the oldest son, he was responsible for supporting his family. In fact, he had started a new job at an insurance company when his life took a literal detour into the IAC campaign in August 2011. "It was my third day at work. I was on my usual DTC [Delhi Transport Corporation] bus. For some reason, our bus was diverted toward Ramlila Maidan," where the IAC sit-in was in progress. Intrigued, Ashwin got off the bus and walked over. "Mujhe laga jaise andhe ko aankhein mil gayee ho'n [I felt like a blind person had gotten a new set of eyes]! I was fed up [with the system] and convinced of the IAC cause.... See, I am from a village and have seen corporations forcibly take away land from people. I have seen upper castes talk to my father with impunity and disrespect. People want to fight such injustices, but the forces we are up against are so powerful that they can quash us in one go. Activists also tend to work on a small scale, in small groups that are easily crushed. I wanted this system to change!" Ashwin called out of work and stayed at the IAC sit-in for two days.

In 2013, he joined AAP as a full-time volunteer despite financial difficulties. He told me that he was inspired by Daya ji, a middle-aged woman living in the shanties near his neighborhood. "She took on extra work cleaning houses just so she could pay for a mobile phone and transportation expenses for AAP-related work. She makes between 2,000 and 3,000 rupees every month, which goes toward AAP. This is her contribution to the nation, she says. One day she told me, 'Ever since I joined Kejriwal ji, my *aatmaa* [soul] has been on fire. I have an intense yearning. I come back from work, get a call from the volunteer cell, and run over immediately. I haven't had a proper meal in ages.'" Ashwin gave me a wide-eyed look. "I saw people like Daya ji and [other] well-known activists join the AAP—Medha Patkar, Soni Sori, Prashant Bhushan—and I too signed on.... When Arvind spoke about swaraj, it felt right."

"How do you understand swaraj?" I interjected.

"Swaraj is when every *akhri insaan* [last person] from the *antim tabka* [most downtrodden stratum] ... has the right to make decisions about his life, neighborhood, and development. When those on the bottom are included as stakeholders by the rulers. When every last person feels empowered. That is swaraj. I work with people in a nearby slum who struggle for basic toilet, water, and sewage services. Yell and holler as we may, we don't even see the faces of the people we vote for. We should be consulted [on governance matters]. That is why, with AAP, thodi si aasha dikhee [I saw a ray of hope]. When they talked about a right to reject and to recall [politicians], I felt this was *bilkul fit* [absolutely right]. Our country is in a *khatarnaak* [dangerous] place politically, socially, and economically. That is why we need AAP. It has an *aandolanaatmak tareeka* [revolutionary style], unlike the usual party politics of divisiveness, vote banks, money, and *goonda-gardi* [criminality]. AAP threatens that system, that *kachra* [garbage]. So I jumped in, even though I knew I would have to make sacrifices. In an age where everyone is focused on self-promotion and winning the rat race, I saw so many people quit paid work to join Arvind and AAP."

Ashwin was vindicated in his decision to volunteer full time for AAP when the party was first elected to govern Delhi in 2013. "Those forty-nine days! Just ask anyone and they will tell you how much things improved." I smiled, sharing that virtually every auto-rickshaw driver I encountered told me that the traffic became more disciplined and the traffic police stopped harassing them. Ashwin nodded eagerly. "The main source of income of the traffic police is bribes, and that vanished, which is a huge thing—even in government offices. After we started the 1031 Helpline to train people to conduct sting operations on corrupt officials, only a few were caught and suspended, because more than 90 percent of the officials stopped demanding bribes. Unki jaan sook rahi thi [They were scared].... Arvind made it happen overnight! I will give you two examples of things I experienced personally. We have a *subzi mandi* [vegetable market] nearby. The local policemen used to take 20 rupees daily from each stall owner in the market [as graft]. Always. After AAP formed a government, the same policemen went around the *mandi* and announced to stall owners that 'we have stopped taking money from you. If anyone asks for money on our behalf, report it to us.'"

Ashwin continued animatedly: "Second example. At 5 AM one day, I went to grab some chai and a newspaper from one of the roadside stalls outside the hospital [where] my father was admitted for surgery. As I stood drinking my chai, I saw a police van pull up. A policeman got out, picked up a newspaper, and began walking away without paying for it. The stall owner yelled after him. 'Sir, that will be 5 rupees.' The policeman waved him off, but the stall owner persisted. 'Sir, give me the money.' The policeman threw the newspaper back and left! Could such a thing have happened before? Would a poor stall owner dare [to take on the police]? Matlab hi nahin banta [No way]! But this poor guy knew that jo sarkar oopar baithi hui hai vo meri hai [the government sitting up there is mine]. He felt secure enough to speak up.... Different people see their pain in AAP, and they feel empowered to raise their voices—against party leaders too!"

Ashwin told me that he had joined AVAM, which he cited as an example of the empowerment that AAP fostered. "There has been so much negativity directed at AVAM recently. But we are not wrong. AAP is a very new party and it needs better *vyavastha* [organization]. Ever since the Anna movement, so many people have joined. They come from different class, caste, and educational backgrounds.... Even though they all find something in AAP that speaks to them, these divides are not easily bridged. You have someone like Medha Patkar who has sacrificed forty years of her life to the Narmada [dam] movement, and you have a shopkeeper who has lost a few days' income to join AAP. Kya unko ek tarazu mein tolenge [Can they be on the same plane]? AAP needs to figure out the roles that different party volunteers will play and also create a *mahaul* [environment] where everyone feels that this is my party and it will work on the problems I face. People belonging to the bottom rungs of society ... should see [AAP] as their home and feel as connected to it as anyone else." Encouraging personal attachment and building inclusivity required more careful strategizing, opined Ashwin. AAP needed to reorganize its house, as AVAM was asking it to do.

"We are not wrong," he repeated. "Arvind is not wrong either. It is actually a rung of yes-men who have hijacked the party. AVAM is simply following in Arvind's footsteps. He said swaraj; we are only reminding him of it. He said 'sach pareshan ho sakta hai par haar nahin sakta' [truth can be frustrated but not defeated]; we say, so be it. What Arvind is saying about AVAM—that we are traitors, or agents of the BJP or the Congress Party—is exactly what critics said about AAP and Arvind earlier on. He survived this onslaught and so shall we. . . . Our *maun vrat* [silent protest] begins soon. Arvind will have to listen to us. He will. I have hope."

Ironically, AAP chose to ignore AVAM, much like the erstwhile ruling Congress coalition had done to the IAC. The silent protest petered out.

Take Three: Shaan

Shaan, a tall, bespectacled young man from southern India, welcomed me into a small flat in South Delhi, clearing laptops and papers from a sofa to create a sitting space. This flat served as a home office for a group of AAP volunteers who drifted in and out as we conversed. Shaan had a contemplative air. He moved unhurriedly and spoke softly, repeating himself often as he offered a technical, economic view on governance, democracy, and swaraj.

"I believe in capitalism" is how Shaan began when I asked him to describe why he linked up with AAP. "I pay taxes to the government and I see no returns at all. If governance improves, my returns will be better. . . . That is kind of my selfish motive for joining." He was raised to be "a bit socially active. My parents taught me that even if you can't make a huge difference, you can contribute to someone else who is trying to do that. So I thought that I should try contributing a bit."

Shaan had previously volunteered for a small regional party that also promised clean governance, but he quit after a disappointing experience. He found AAP refreshing. "AAP definitely has a few strong points. It has the intent and the will to get things done. There is a lot of enthusiasm to do what [Arvind] talks about. The party agenda may not be wide enough to [address] all the issues of the country—nuclear weapons or Kashmir [for example]. But whatever few points they have started with— like anticorruption—they seem to have the enthusiasm to actually execute them." This energy was due to AAP's youthfulness, asserted Shaan; at thirty-three, he was an older volunteer. "That makes a huge difference. Older people coming from a bureaucratic mind-set think differently, but [in AAP] even older people seem to be young of mind."

Shaan focused on neighborhood assemblies—getting residents to collectively list their local problems and participate in deciding how to spend the development funds allocated to their MLA. "Ninety percent of the complaints would not be necessary if the municipal authority was doing its job—streetlights are out, drains are clogged, there is no drinking water.... Here we have a lot of *jhuggi* [slum] clusters and their requirements are absolutely minimal. Like a toilet [that] doesn't cost much... We file complaints in Kejriwal's name with the municipal department to create a paper trail. I don't know if it is the name that is working or what, but to our shock, things are resolved the same day! So what keeps me here is beginner's luck. We have had the opportunity to actually start getting things done for people."

However, the swaraj model was testy. "Neighborhood assemblies take a huge effort—time, money, people." In mixed-income areas like Shaan's, organizing a cross-class assembly was challenging. "In wealthy parts, just getting across a message about something related to the assembly takes a couple of days. The guards won't let you in. You have to drop a package at the gated entrance, or you have to approach the Residents Welfare Association. Some RWA members tell you, 'If [Kejriwal] is going to ask us to take [decisions] then why did we elect him?' *Arrey* [Geez]! What fools! Are these people ready for swaraj?"

Class issues were also reflected among party volunteers, who were "a diverse group.... There is a divide—the class issue is so inherent." AAP needed to better manage such divisiveness and also consider whether "working purely through volunteers" was viable in the long term. "People are contributing despite financial and family constraints. They are sacrificing a lot. But you can't expect that to continue forever. Um, it is like... [in] an online business, getting a first hit from some random person is a huge task. Once you get a hit, then you make sure that that person sticks to you... [as a] customer who pays money for something you are selling. [In AAP] you are talking about volunteers who are *giving you money and time!*"

Shaan had a solution for how to make volunteers stick to the party and its mission: "AAP should be run like a private enterprise where you have proper recruitment policies, evaluation, compensation.... Because this whole anticorruption, good governance thing—there is a market, a huge public demand. There is also a very good opportunity on the supply side with the [monetary] donations that AAP receives.... But the intermediate part is missing—people who can make sure that the supply side is properly channeled to meet the demand. AAP could consider paying a minimal amount of compensation to volunteers." Shaan paused. "See, I don't actually believe in altruism. Altruistic people have my full respect, but there is nothing wrong in being selfish. There are a lot of people who want to get something for contributing to [AAP's] cause— like social exposure, learning team management, and improving communication skills. And I don't see anything wrong with it." AAP also needed to think about retention strategies for volunteers. "It makes a huge difference because [when volunteers leave] you lose a whole chunk of your supporters!"

Assuming his comment alluded to the recent expulsions, I asked Shaan if he saw the AVAM purge as an antidemocratic move.

"Uh, I personally don't believe in democracy."

My ears perked up. "So you believe in authoritarianism?" I prodded playfully.

"No. I believe in benevolent dictatorship."

"So who would be your ideal?"

Prefacing that he was "an I.T. guy, from the technical side," Shaan asked me if I knew about the Linux operating system. "It kind of runs the world right now."

"Yes, I do," I admitted, sharing that a former student of mine was a Linux coder who had done research on the open-source, free software movement. Guided by the ethic that "information wants to be free," as my student described it, those participating in this movement saw themselves as altruistic enablers, liberating information for the public good. They had leeway, given the decentralized organization of open-source software coding.

Shaan nodded appreciatively. "Yes, Linux is decentralized. But it is also under a benevolent dictator, Linus Torvalds, who started this thing."

"Of course," I laughed and rolled my eyes. I had heard about Torvalds.

"He only contributed a small piece of code, but he still calls Linux *his* code. He is totally dictatorial about the cleanliness and efficiency of the code—the operating system should be of the highest quality, and it should be free. Today Linux is millions of lines of code. It is humanly impossible to go through it to understand what it is doing. So Torvalds has a set of trusted lieutenants [called] maintainers [who] have the full authority to decide about what can be added to the code, what can be removed or changed. There are tens of thousands of developers from all over the world adding code, testing, adding patches for free. If the maintainers think the patches are good, they use them. If Torvalds sees that some bad code has gotten in, he publicly abuses the particular maintainer. But if someone's code serves the purpose of a whole lot of people, then . . . Linus has to allow it even if he doesn't like it. Because people demand it and it is a free market! Linus is obviously very selfish. He wants to have something good, which is free and which he can manipulate. So guys like him are working toward some selfish goal which actually adds to the whole society, indirectly. They are jealously passionate about what they are doing." Lest I think that all dictatorial passion projects were successful, Shaan also gave "parallel examples in the UNIX universe that fizzled out even though they were technically far superior than Linux. They died because the leaders weren't benevolent enough. They were antisocial sociopaths and so coders weren't contributing much. So, if AAP doesn't have that benevolence part . . ."

"Wait, do you think AAP should run like Linux?" I interjected.

"If it does, it would be fortunate. India would be very lucky. But, uh, I haven't observed Arvind long enough to know if he is a benevolent dictator or not."

"So benevolence has to be there alongside dictatorship?"

"Yeah. Because democracy is a fantastic concept. A full 100 percent democracy would never work in India, in my opinion, because to get one thing done you have ten different ways to go forward. Which one would you give preference to? You could [decide by] vote. But what kind of voting would you go with? First past the pole? If 490 people voted for one thing and 510 for the other, then are you going to suppress the voices of the 490? Full democracy is a fantastic fantasy."

"Couldn't you say the same about swaraj as well?"

"Exactly. It is a fantastic fantasy. . . . If you go and lecture about swaraj to people, they won't even give you ten seconds. People are busy and have their daily sufferings. You have to dumb it [down] and sometimes make wild claims to get people to pay attention," said Shaan pointing to a disjuncture between swaraj's ideal and its practicability. That said, however, "swaraj is definitely required. You need interaction between government servants and the people. . . . But that is going to work only up to some level. Swaraj doesn't mean deciding about matters of national interest at [the] level of the neighborhood. Things that can be decided [on] are restricted and localized," said Shaan, echoing Kejriwal's notion of scaled swaraj that justified authoritative hierarchy. "We can't leave everything to the people. I have campaigned in some rural constituencies for AAP where the alcohol problem is so bad that any kind of benefit [people] get—rice or food, under [the] Food Security Act—gets sold off for alcohol. So you can't leave everything to the [community]. . . . People need to be brought to a certain level for swaraj, so they can take decisions and think objectively about what is right and wrong. There has to be someone who can monitor and maybe have some power to veto things. . . . Hierarchies are not something that can be done away with. Even animals have hierarchies, a leader of a pack. You can't have 1.2 billion people. . . . Someone said this—maybe Henry Ford—that if it were left to the people, then we would still be sticking to a horse cart with faster horses. You do need people who can think about the future."

"Visionaries?" I queried, recalling Kejriwal's comment about the *kaabil* trustees.

"Yeah. And in this process of thinking about the future and taking out-of-the-ordinary steps, you will make some horrible mistakes—like Arvind did when he resigned [after forty-nine days of his first term as chief minister] and put a brake on something that was going relatively smoothly. Or when the AAP said that they were not going to use red beacons on cars or demand bungalows. That was kind of silly. But they course corrected! People don't actually care about where [elected leaders] live as long as their work gets done. They actually idolize heroes. They need heroes. Arvind needs to control. He should put his foot down and be a 'my way or the highway' guy, at least for some time. But he also has to be careful about becoming a dictator without the benevolence."

─────

"Fantastic fantasies"—this is how Shaan characterized democracy and swaraj. The resemblance between his words and Lauren Berlant's is hard to miss. Berlant (2011) sees liberal capitalist democracy as holding out a "fantasy bribe" (7) of a good life, security, and justice, which ignites affective optimism that "moves [people] out of [themselves] and into the world" (1). Fantasies, though, inhere im/possibilities: they wax and wane, magnetize and attenuate, promise and betray. "What happens," asks Berlant, "when fantasies start to fray—depression, dissociation, pragmatism, cynicism, optimism, activism, or an incoherent mash?" (2). Her term "cruel optimism" gathers this mash of sensations that results from the dismantling of fantasies (cf. Bonilla 2020). Berlant (2011) writes that "the *affective structure* of an optimistic attachment involves a sustaining inclination to return to the scene of fantasy that enables you to expect that *this* time, nearness to *this* thing will help you or a world to become different in just the right way. But again, optimism is cruel when the object/scene that ignites a sense of possibility actually makes it impossible to attain the expansive transformation for which a person or a people risk striving" (2). Perhaps good governance populism provokes just this kind of cruel optimism among those striving for it. It offers a promise of a flexible and pure goodness and improvement that seduces people. It is that which you cannot not want; it is that which speaks in your name and keeps you attached (stuck?) even when you know that it is problematic and ultimately impossible—an unraveling, fantastic fantasy.

The three composite stories above point to the structure of feeling, the cruel optimism, unleashed by Kejriwal's good governance endeavor. They portray what impelled some people to answer his call and their intense process of reflection and contention as they faced the contradictions that surfaced in mid-2014. These were the tensions between decentralized, participatory self-rule and authoritarian decision-making; between Kejriwal's cult of personality and the impersonal bureaucratic organization of AAP; between AAP's self-positioning as an oppositional, alternative political force and its desire for mainstream dominance; between swaraj as an emergent ethical praxis and calling, and swaraj as an institutionalized practice; and between moral authority and dictatorial leadership, even if of a benevolent kind. These tensions manifested as a dis-ease among volunteers, an ongoing figuring out and feeling one's way through something simmering and shifting: nostalgic reveries, shrugs, surprise, adoration, pragmatic certainty, downcast eyes, and disenchantment, which convey "a generative immediacy" (Williams 1977, 133) that is irreducibly complex. This is the messy and disjunctive affectscape associated with Kejriwal's swaraj, where deep attachment, inspiration, drive, and loyalty thrive alongside equally deep confusion, disappointment, hurt, exhaustion, and betrayal.

This is what the powerful tug of a fantasy and the agony of its erosion feels like: the sensation of being tied to the ongoing dialectic of promise and deferral that one cannot entirely break out of, because doing so raises "the fear . . . that the loss of the promising object/scene . . . will defeat the capacity to have any hope about anything" (Berlant 2011, 24). Perhaps nurturing fraying promises and cruel optimism feels more bearable than hopelessness in a context of dangerously narrowing democratic possibilities in India today.

Epilogue

*I*t is January 2023, nearly nine years after Kejriwal's AAP lost the national election and Modi's BJP came into power. Both good governance icons are in Delhi, one as chief minister and the other as prime minister. I can't help but notice Modi's images and messages plastered all over the city's center. But just in case I miss a billboard or a vehicle decal with Modi-related iconography, I have Manjeet Singh with me to point it out. "Look, over there and there," says my taxi driver. "There is no escaping the leader," he quips in Punjabi. I have known Manjeet ji since 2005, when this Sikh migrant from Punjab made Delhi his home. His beard has turned gray over the years and his face grows a little more gaunt each time I see him, but his voice has lost none of its spiritedness. We talk politics as we drive through central Delhi in his well-worn diesel cab. He is as engagingly opinionated as ever, expressing how "ruinous" the BJP has been for the country. "These people are sowing hate. Today the enemy is Muslim, tomorrow it will be someone else. They have sold our country to corrupt businessmen—Adani and Ambani," he asserts animatedly, naming two billionaire beneficiaries of the regime. He notes proudly that his home state of Punjab helped stop the "BJP–Ambani–Adani combine" during the 2020–21 farmers' protest against the corporatization of agriculture. Punjab also voted for AAP in 2022, the only state besides Delhi where the party is in power currently. "How do you feel about AAP?" I ask Manjeet ji, noticing an image of Kejriwal on the back of a public bus on our left. He doesn't miss a beat. "Saanu umeed si, par ay vi nakli nikle [We had hope, but they also turned out to be fake]!" He pauses for effect. "AAP is BJP's B-team. Modi says he is a Ram bhakt [devotee];

Kejriwal says he is a Hanuman bhakt. What's the difference!" Manjeet ji *sniggers as he alludes to the affinity between both leaders. If worshipping a different Hindu god enables a "softened" Hindutva[1] politics, then this is a difference of degree, not of type.*

⁓

Modi and Kejriwal are populist leaders who go head to head in the good governance arena in India. They moralize good governance in their own ways—the former as suraj, sushashan and "minimum government, maximum governance," and the latter as swaraj—as they invoke mythical and historical pasts, or create them anew, to guide India's present. Where one works to establish a xenophobic, fascist Hindu dictatorship, the other envisions a decentralized and participatory form of rule in common with everyone. Indeed, Kejriwal offers himself as a more liberal democratic alternative to Modi. As different as these two leaders seem, however, their populist strategies show uncanny resemblances.

Both men construct an unsullied and wronged us against a vile them. Their politics shares a proclivity to switch from being a reaction against someone or something (the Muslim other or the establishment, for instance), to turning into reactionary majoritarianism and authoritarianism. This can take the shape of ethnonationalist domination inflected with overt and violent communal, casteist, and patriarchal fervor, as in the case of Modi. Or it can turn out to be a politics that has Hindutva undercurrents but presents itself as formally secular and attempts to bridge social divides by hailing all ordinary citizens equally, as in Kejriwal's case. The commonality that Kejriwal summons, as I have suggested in this book, fails to suture the social fractures comprising the us and the them. His strategy is fraught, if more subtly than Modi's, in terms of its gender, class, and religious implications; and like the latter, it fails to account for the inequalities that underlie state structures and citizenship in practice.

In this book, I have followed Kejriwal's tracks to illuminate how his style of good governance emboldens a technomoral populist politics that is as enabling as risky. On the one hand, it articulates an inclusive common agenda for any and every man. It does so by disavowing ideology and dirty party politics, and by summoning a movement spirit to serve people ethically and efficiently. Kejriwal's "whatever works" pragmatic righteousness has been effective where service delivery is concerned. His government has improved public education and health care in Delhi, and has kept electricity and water rates cheap, which makes a difference for underprivileged classes in particular. This is significant in how it challenges scandal- and corruption-ridden regimes and the conventional neoliberal wisdom of privatization and downsizing welfare provisioning. That said, however, the very accommodativeness of the virtuous commons that AAP relies on creates a vacuum that can be filled with anything that appears good for the public and nation as long as it is dictated by trustworthy men. Like other projects undertaken in the name of the greater common good that produce violent effects—be they civilizational, developmental, or infrastructural[2]—Kejriwal's progressive reform agenda also carries dangers.

The AAP's antipolitical and postideological emptiness, or what I have called an alternative politics of *not*, leaves it open to converging with precisely the kind of nondemocratic and unethical agendas that it positions itself against—like the one that Modi stands for. The troubling overlap between these two apparently oppositional political stances has emerged clearly on many occasions. For example, AAP supported BJP's cleanliness mission (swachh bharat abhiyan) and yoga initiatives. Kejriwal also declared, even if rhetorically, that he would help garner votes for the BJP in the 2019 state elections in Maharashtra and Haryana if the party would match AAP's promise of providing free electricity to people using less than 200 units per month.[3] Because AAP disclaims ideology, it is able to hitch its wagon to various causes that promote nationalism and development. As long as the BJP designs policies that serve the nation, its exclusionary Hindutva politics and attacks on democratic freedom of speech and media can be overlooked.

This became obvious when AAP supported BJP's nontransparent decision to revoke Article 370, a constitutional provision that gave special autonomous status to the state of Jammu and Kashmir, and to convert the state into union territories in August 2019. Even though AAP has repeatedly demanded that Delhi, a national capital territory, be granted complete statehood in the interest of local self-governance, it backed BJP's move to wrest statehood from Jammu and Kashmir by arguing that the latter, unlike Delhi, is a militarized border region at risk of foreign-sponsored terror. In a statement, AAP conveyed that "whenever there is a national interest or a policy of public interest, we have supported it."[4] Thus, the sacredness of swaraj, democracy, and constitutional legality could be sacrificed for a higher nationalist cause.

In this context, AAP's celebration of seventy years of the Indian constitution barely two weeks after the Kashmir decision seemed ironic. As part of this commemoration, the party announced a new *desh bhakti* (national devotion) curriculum for schools in Delhi "to inculcate values of liberty, equality and fraternity"[5] among students and to teach them about love and respect for the nation. While this may well be an important initiative on civic citizenship and constitutionalism, its coding in the language of nationalism is disquieting when the BJP government uses similar terms to disenfranchise and attack anyone it deems antinational. AAP not only ignores these perils but also seeks to outdo its political rival. Indeed, in a move to reiterate its patriotic alignment and mettle in 2021, the party presented a 690,000-million-rupee *desh bhakti* budget, which included installing five hundred flag masts and initiating programs about the lives of nationalist leaders and freedom fighters.[6]

The danger in playing by the BJP's nationalist rules is that they are ineluctably tied to a patriarchal Hindutva ideology. The nation of BJP's imagination is unquestionably Hindu. When AAP toes the BJP's line, it cannot ignore the Hindutva sentiment and must embrace it. And it has. During a speech at the Delhi assembly in March 2021, for instance, Kejriwal openly declared himself a Hanuman devotee and reiterated his commitment to building Ram Rajya, referencing the very kingdom of Ram that Modi also promises to manifest as a good governance ideal:

> All of us worship Lord Rama. Personally, I worship Lord Hanuman who was a devotee of Lord Rama. Hence, I am a devotee of both Lord Rama and Hanuman. Lord Rama was the emperor of Ayodhya. During his rule, it is said, people were content, with no sorrows in life as they had access to all basic facilities. This was called the "Ram Rajya." . . . This . . . cannot be paralleled by us humans. However, even if we draw inspiration from this model of "Ram Rajya" and seek to try and establish a similar society, we would be successful in life. Hence, we have been constantly striving to establish this model of "Ram Rajya" in Delhi for the past six years based on ten principles.[7]

Kejriwal went on to describe AAP's modern developmentalist version of good governance as Ram Rajya, which included guaranteeing food, electricity, water, education, health, employment, and housing for people, as well as promoting respect for women and the elderly. Lest this largely service-delivery list sound too secular, in the same speech, Kejriwal promised that he would make sure that Delhi's Hindu senior citizens would be able to travel "free of cost" to the "magnificent" Ram temple in Ayodhya once it is built. This is the very temple that has been at the forefront of BJP's politics—the very temple for which Hindu right-wing groups razed the sixteenth-century Babri Masjid (a mosque) in 1992 because, they alleged, it stood on the same spot as Ram's birthplace, and sparked nationwide riots that left around two thousand people dead; the very temple whose construction began after it received the go-ahead from the Supreme Court of India in 2019. By promising free pilgrimages for elderly Hindus to this charged site of Hindutva politics, AAP was clearly coddling Hindutva sentiment.

This happened again in October 2022, as AAP campaigned for assembly elections in Modi's home state of Gujarat, which is also the site of a Hindutva-led, state-abetted pogrom against Muslims that left over a thousand dead and tens of thousands displaced in 2002.[8] At the time of the election campaign, eleven men convicted of gang-raping Bilkis Bano and murdering fourteen members of her family during the Gujarat riots were released for good behavior in prison with the help of the Modi government.[9] Yet AAP chose to remain silent. When questioned about why they had not made a statement regarding this obviously unjust, pro-Hindutva move, Manish Sisodia, then AAP's second in command, replied, "We are on the track of education, schools, hospitals and jobs. These things matter to us. People speak about what matters to them."[10] Neither deadly violence against Muslims nor the undermining of justice or secular constitutional principles, it appears, are worth attending to when national(ist) development, done efficiently, is the overriding motive.

Kejriwal's style of technomoral good governance is not "clean." Rather than offering a meaningful challenge to BJP's virulent, illiberal rule, AAP is taking a page out of the former's playbook to win elections. It has not yet shown itself to be capable of changing the terms of the political discourse; and using the master's tools does not, cannot, an alternative construct. As Hamraaz, a one-named online poet, exhorts in "A Suggestion,"[11]

Patriotic schools, large flags—
prayers and promises;
our CM[12] studied Gandhiji;
says Ram Rajya is his goal.
Let's study Ravidas, Kabir,
Phule and Ambedkar;[13]
instead of "soft Hi[n]dutva," friends,
let's learn to live together.

What started out for Kejriwal as a well-intentioned, judicialized effort for systemic political reform in the liberal democratic vein and a struggle against neoliberal privatization and antiwelfarism has morphed into something more checkered. This is what makes AAP's technomoral swaraj project risky. Its mission of participatory, improved, and accountable governance ends up narrowing the field of political action to moralism, administration, legalism, and service delivery. While claiming commonness and inclusivity, it also leans toward a kinder, gentler version of the communal and authoritarian politics associated with the BJP. The irony of Kejriwal using BJP's undemocratic, tainted tactics to defeat them at the polls, when he has previously asserted that winning elections is not the point for a party like his, is all too apparent. Disturbingly, Kejriwal's good governance strategy can further shrink spaces for democratic politics and dissent at a time when they are already terrifyingly imperiled.

That India has experienced a serious erosion of democratic institutions and principles under the BJP regime is by now well known. Global indexes, while problematic as normalizing measures, ratify this decline. According to the *Economist*'s Democracy Index, India's ranking decreased from 35 in 2015 to 42 in 2017, and to 46 out of 167 countries in 2022.[14] While the *Economist* categorizes India under "flawed democracies," the Freedom in the World Index, published by U.S.-based Freedom House, classifies it as "partly free." Its Global Freedom Score put India at 66 of 100 in 2023, down from 77 of 100 in 2017, when the country was categorized as "free."[15] India is not alone in the field of democratic backsliding. According to the Freedom House's 2022 report, entitled "The Global Expansion of Authoritarian Rule," sixty countries showed such a decline and were part of a consistent, sixteen-year trend of democratic undoing across the world. The report raised an alarm:

Global freedom faces a dire threat. Around the world, the enemies of liberal democracy... are accelerating their attacks. Authoritarian regimes have become more effective at co-opting or circumventing the norms and institutions meant to support basic liberties.... In countries with long-established democracies, internal forces have exploited the shortcomings in their systems, distorting national politics to promote hatred, violence, and unbridled power. Those countries that have struggled in the space between democracy and authoritarianism, meanwhile, are increasingly tilting toward the latter. The global order is nearing a tipping point, and if democracy's defenders do not work together to help guarantee freedom for all people, the authoritarian model will prevail.[16]

Warnings about the danger that the rise of authoritarianism globally poses to liberal democracy are common today in scholarly circles as much as in the public sphere. This illiberal wave is broadly characterized as populist, and the reasons given for it range from the economic to the cultural, or a mix of the two (Bilgrami 2018; Mishra 2017; Inglehart and Norris 2016). Some see it as a reaction against the inequality and precarity caused by globalization and austerity measures. "If we do not radically transform the present economic system to make it less inegalitarian," warns Thomas Piketty (2020), "xenophobic 'populism' could well triumph at the ballot box" (2); and it has, in many places. Others view the populist upsurge, in Western nation-states especially, as a cultural backlash against progressive, pluralist, cosmopolitan, liberal values by entrenched traditionalists who see their power and status being eroded (Inglehart and Norris 2016). Pankaj Mishra (2017), meanwhile, uses the Nietzschean term *ressentiment* to describe the anger fomented by the widespread betrayal of the liberal promise of equality as well as that of capitalist modernity on the one hand, and an unraveling of older bonds of tradition, family, faith, and community on the other. "The new horizons of individual desire and fear opened up by the neoliberal world economy do not favor democracy and human rights," he argues (271), as people seek out dictatorial saviors in places as varied as Turkey, the United States, Thailand, and India.

Neoliberal economic policies and cultural factors undoubtedly have a role to play in the authoritarian populist upswing and the concomitant unraveling of democracy we observe today. My book points to another dimension of this phenomenon, which has not gotten as much attention: the post–Cold War drive for political liberalization by powerful international institutions, who were also acting as democracy's defenders of sorts when pushing good governance globally. Perhaps this omission is not surprising. After all, good governance is commonly understood as expanding liberal democratic values and mechanisms, not undercutting them. Moreover, democratic good governance is defined as the other of populism, where the former is a rational, liberal ideal (never mind its illiberal underside) and the latter is an irrational, emotional, and deviant phenomenon. How could these opposing forces possibly go hand in hand? Yet this is exactly what my analysis points toward.

The very mechanisms put in place in the 1990s by the neoliberal development regime to globalize democratic norms and weaken populist authoritarianism may well abet the latter in the name of improving and cleaning up rule. Is it mere coincidence that as good governance policy mechanisms are put in place to expand and secure liberal democracy around the world, the latter actually suffers a setback? How is it that as more and more countries have enacted constitutions and put in place other legal and administrative measures to ensure the rule of law and to make governance transparent, clean, accountable, and participatory over the past three decades, the political field has become less, not more, democratic, as the Freedom House and others document? What, indeed, is the relationship between good governance as a dominant neoliberal policy mandate, the expansion of a dangerous tide of populism, and the reversal of democratic fortunes? To be clear, I am not suggesting causality here. Rather, the questions I raise point to a striking conjuncture that begs more investigation.

Good governance, as I have argued, offers a convenient vehicle for a majoritarian populist politics. Its malleability synchronizes with the imprecision of populism, both as a concept and practical strategy. Good governance is, in a sense, a stance of refusal. Its core becomes elaborated through what it is not—a loosely defined "bad" governance. This mode of refusal is a powerful tactic for crafting populist appeal. Furthermore, good governance offers ready ground for moralistic right-versus-wrong and us-versus-them framings that populism also feeds on. Good governance is not merely a package of technical policies but a complex technomoral assemblage, as I have argued. Moored in the liberal Western worldview that it normalizes, good governance also leaves room for local reconstruction of this hegemonic worldview. As a translocal, technomoral ensemble, good governance carries expertise as much as affective-moral force; it can be easily appropriated by populist demagogues who vernacularize this discourse differently to construct and rile up publics against enemies—be they the system, the elite, the other within or without, or the political classes—and to position themselves as trustee-saviors of the nation as it should be.

Good governance populism is a dangerous technomoral coupling. It can as easily serve neoliberal statecraft as challenge it. Although it can take the shape of egalitarian popular protest (Frank 2018), it can also a "slide into blood-and-soil purity politics" (Mazzarella 2019, 49) that normalizes dictatorship, even if of a benevolent kind. Whether this blending is redemptive or cruelly optimistic, and for whom, is not given—and hence the urgent need to explore both its unfolding potential and its limits.

Notes

Introduction

1. Transcription of "Shri Narendra Modi's Keynote Address at the 'Suraj Sankalp' National Convention," Mumbai, June 5, 2010, https://www.narendramodi.in/%E2%80%9Csuraj-sankalp%E2%80%9D-national-convention-keynote-address-by-hon%E2%80%99ble-cm-2679; accessed June 20, 2017.

2. Ram Rajya refers to the kingdom of the Hindu god Ram and is popularly understood to mean an ideal form of rule. The *Bhagavad Gita* is part of the *Mahabharata*.

3. He also invoked Gandhi's idea of swaraj (self-rule) and the ancient Sanskrit treatise, the *Arthshastra,* to reinforce the indigenous ethical lineage of good governance.

4. Jethwa was gunned down outside Gujarat's high court after filing a PIL against illegal limestone mining in the state's protected forests, which implicated Dinu Solanki, a local parliamentarian. See "Gujarat RTI Activist's Murder: Former BJP M.P. Solanki, Six Others Convicted," *Indian Express,* July 7, 2019, https://indianexpress.com/article/india/rti-activist-amit-jethwa-murder-former-bjp-mp-dinu-bogha-solanki-convicted-5818304/; accessed March 5, 2021. Solanki and six others were convicted of Jethwa's killing in 2019. See Press Trust of India, "Ex-BJP Lawmaker Dinu Solanki, 6 Others Guilty of Killing RTI Activist," NDTV, July 6, 2019, https://www.ndtv.com/india-news/amit-jethwa-murder-case-dinu-solanki-6-others-guilty-of-killing-amit-jethwa-rti-activist-2065408; accessed March 5, 2021.

5. J. Balaji, "Eight RTI Activists Killed in Seven Months," *Hindu,* July 25, 2010, updated November 28, 2021, https://www.thehindu.com/news/national/eight-rti-activists-killed-in-seven-months/article532051.ece; accessed March 5, 2021.

6. Himanshi Dhawan, "Activists Close Ranks to Protest Jethwa's Murder," *Times of India,* July 24, 2010, https://timesofindia.indiatimes.com/india/activists-close

-ranks-to-protest-jethwas-murder/articleshow/6206830.cms; accessed March 5, 2021.

7. "Inclusion of RTI Act in School Curriculum Mooted," *Deccan Herald*, last updated December 7, 2009, https://www.deccanherald.com/content/40044/inclusion-rti-act-school-curriculum.html; accessed July 15, 2022.

8. The idea of technomoral politics emerges from collaborative conversations with Erica Bornstein and was first explored in a coauthored article (Bornstein and Sharma 2016).

9. The report on structural adjustment in Africa declared that "underlying the litany of Africa's development problems is a crisis of governance" (World Bank 1989, 60), which needed "not just less government but better government" (5).

10. There were proposals to "strengthen public administration . . . build institutional capacity . . . promote institutional pluralism by promoting local government, NGOs, and grassroots organizations, . . . promote . . . respect for human rights . . . , [and] promote honest government by channeling funds in a way that reduce the chances of corruption" (Landell-Mills and Serageldin 1992, 316).

11. Klitgaard (1992) criticized anthropologists' propensity to "multiply the questions rather than to help with answers" and their calls to "critique our own culture first" (345).

12. Goodale (2022a) argues that the language of universal human rights replaced anticapitalist political struggles in the post–Cold War era, but it has been waning since the 2007–8 financial crisis. Rather than jettison it, he makes a case for its radical reformulation away from universality to translocality.

13. Goodale (2002b) makes a provocative case for the dejuridification of politics after 2008, arguing for a global decline in the reliance on law and (human) rights as means for accessing justice. India's experience of a growing basket of rights and new laws since 2005 largely because of pressure from social movements, does not quite square with Goodale's contention. Even the right-wing Modi government has relied as much on changing laws, such as those governing citizenship (Citizenship Amendment Act), NGOs, and corporations (Bornstein, n.d.), as on extralegal means, like Hindutva mob violence, to consolidate its fascist rule.

14. Gandhi (1997), who was trained as a lawyer, embodied this antagonism: "It is contrary to our manhood if we obey laws repugnant to our conscience," he wrote. "If I were a passive resister, I would say to [the government] that I would have nothing to do with their law" (91–92).

15. Ornit Shani (2022) argues that the making of the constitution itself was more than an elite project and involved diverse publics.

16. The court's judgment in a habeas corpus case (A. D. M. Jabalpur v. Shivkant Shukla, 1976 2 SCC 521) upheld the Emergency's lawfulness (Baxi 1980).

17. Activists involved in the movements against the Narmada dam and for food rights, and environmental groups, among others, filed PILs.

18. Webb (2010) looks at RTI dynamics through the lens of a Delhi NGO.

19. Anders's (2010) ethnographic study of good governance efforts in Malawi also focuses on bureaucrats and civil service reforms.

20. Fassin (2012) makes a similar point about other subfields, including medical anthropology, which probe morality without calling themselves moral anthropology.

1. The Indian Right to Information

1. The Official Secrets Act has not been formally withdrawn.

2. The covenant came into force in 1976. Article 19 (2) states: "Everyone shall have the right to freedom of expression; this right shall include freedom to seek, receive and impart information and ideas of all kinds." See "International Covenant on Civil and Political Rights, Adopted by the General Assembly of the United Nations on 19 December 1966," United Nations Treaty Series, https://treaties.un.org/doc/publication/unts/volume%20999/volume-999-i-14668-english.pdf; accessed February 19, 2022.

3. This is based on Transparency International, "Corruption Perceptions Index," 2007, https://www.transparency.org/en/cpi/2007; accessed January 13, 2018.

4. Goodale (2007) problematizes easy local/global dualism with respect to transnational human rights discourses.

5. Transparency International, "Research," https://www.transparency.org/en/research; accessed February 19, 2022.

6. United Nations, Department of Economic and Social Affairs, Sustainable Development, "Transforming Our World: The 2030 Agenda for Sustainable Development," https://sustainabledevelopment.un.org/post2015/transformingourworld; accessed February 17, 2022.

7. Unesco, "Unesco Launches SDG Survey on Access to Information at the U.N.," July 18, 2019, https://en.unesco.org/news/unesco-launches-sdg-survey-access-information; accessed February 13, 2022.

8. Mazdoor Kisan Shakti Sangathan (MKSS), http://mkssindia.org.

9. The local state is difficult to distinguish from local power brokers who are not officially part of the state (Sharma 2008). The Hindi term *sarkar,* which references the state or government, is also used to name local bigwigs belonging to dominant castes and classes (see also Mathur 2016). Indeed, state power and projects are often used to abet social hierarchies, which leads the marginalized to assert that the state is owned by the upper castes and the landed.

10. Butler (2015) discusses the publics and political possibilities shaped by the occupation of Tahrir Square. See Graeber (2013a) and Juris (2012) on occupations of public spaces during Occupy Wall Street.

11. For ethnographic insights on NREGA and its bureaucratic implementation, see Mathur (2016).

12. Although not restricted to transparency specifically, Anna Tsing writes about a similar conjuncture in late Suharto-era Indonesia where activists used the logging-based destruction of national forests to challenge authoritarianism.

13. Commonwealth Human Rights Initiative, "State Level RTI," https://www.humanrightsinitiative.org/content/state-level-rti; accessed August 20, 2019.

14. Singh told me that the detractors of the right to livelihood, including the World Bank, saw NREGA, a public employment and works program, as a potential cauldron of corruption. "The only way one could counter the argument that the NREGA would create a huge corruption machinery, was the RTI," he said, emphasizing the mutuality between the two rights.

15. They tried to delimit the transparency mandate to the federal government alone, exempting state governments from such requirements, and fought over whether bureaucratic notes on project files ought to be included in the law; the latter issue would continue to stoke contention well after the passage of the RTI Act (see chapter 3).

16. For a discussion of these advocacy efforts and Sonia Gandhi's role in the passage of the RTI Act, see Roy (2018), Sharma (2015), and Singh (2010).

17. Activists also rued Gandhi's weakening support for the RTI Act, as her party pushed for amendments to the law after it passed.

18. State of U.P. v. Raj Narain, AIR 1975 SC 865, SCC (4) 428 SCR (3) 333, https://www.right2info.org/resources/publications/case-pdfs/india_state-of-uttar-pradesh-v.-raj-narain; accessed July 22, 2019.

19. S. P. Gupta v. Union of India case, AIR 1982 SC 149, 1981 Supp. (1) SCC87, 1982 2 SCR 365, 66–67, https://indiankanoon.org/doc/1294854/; accessed October 22, 2017. The case concerned the disclosure of correspondence between the law minister, the chief justice of Delhi, and the chief justice of India on the appointment and transfer of judges. The Supreme Court argued that this correspondence was not privileged and in the public interest, and was therefore not legally protected from disclosure.

20. This chest thumping on the part of the BJP is not unlike the authoritarian nationalist stance it took in 2014, when it commenced canceling the registration of NGOs receiving foreign funds and modifying the Foreign Contributions (Regulation) Act to thwart political dissent (Bornstein and Sharma 2016).

21. World Bank, "Results Briefs: Supporting India's Transformation," October 15, 2019, https://www.worldbank.org/en/results/2019/10/15/supporting-indias-transformation; accessed June 13, 2020.

22. According to the World Bank and Organisation for Economic Co-operation and Development data, the net overseas development assistance received by India in 2018 was 0.1 percent of its gross national income (GNI). See World Bank, "Net ODA Received (% of GNI)," https://data.worldbank.org/indicator/DT.ODA.ODAT.GN.ZS; accessed June 12, 2020. See also Jonathan Glennie, "If India Doesn't 'Need' Aid, Why Do Foreign Governments Still Give It?," *Guardian,* November 8, 2010, https://www.theguardian.com/global-development/poverty-matters/2010/nov/08/india-aid-economic-development; accessed June 12, 2020.

23. Commonwealth Human Rights Initiative, "RTI Spurs Debate on World Bank Involvement in Delhi Water Deal," 2005, https://humanrightsinitiative.org/

programs/ai/rti/india/states/delhi/rti_spurs_debate_on_world_bank_delhi_water_project.pdf; accessed June 17, 2020.

24. Randeep Ramesh, "World Bank Rebuked over Water Deal," July 28, 2005, https://www.theguardian.com/world/2005/jul/29/india.randeepramesh2; accessed June 17, 2020.

25. Commonwealth Human Rights Initiative, "RTI Spurs Debate."

26. The initial slogan stated that the village council *(panchayat)* and money *(paisa)* "is ours, and not anyone's private property," and was expanded to include the "state" and the "nation."

2. Rightfully Worded

1. The right to food has since been established under the National Food Security Act of 2013.

2. The terms "camp" and "slum" are used interchangeably in Delhi to refer to urban shanties that are distinguished from middle- and upper-class residential "colonies."

3. Filed in the aftermath of starvation deaths following a drought in Rajasthan, the PIL expanded to include other states in India. For details on the 2001 PIL and the subsequent events leading up to the passage of the National Food Security Act in 2013, see the Right to Food campaign, http://www.righttofoodcampaign.in/home; accessed July 14, 2018.

4. "The Right to Information Act, 2005," http://www.rti.gov.in/rti-act.pdf; accessed December 12, 2016.

5. These organizations include the Intelligence Bureau, the Research and Analysis Wing of the Cabinet Secretariat, the Central Reserve Police Force, and the Central Economic Intelligence Bureau (Government of India 2005, 21).

6. These definitions are contested; citizens and state officials struggle over their meanings through the application and appeals process, and in courts. For a discussion of important RTI-related court cases, see Jaipuriar and Satpute (2009). The Commonwealth Human Rights Initiative also maintains a rich archive of information on RTI-related public debates and court proceedings at http://www.humanrightsinitiative.org/publication-access-to-information.

7. As a government-owned company, MTNL is a "public authority" under the RTI law.

8. The relationship between orality and writing as modes of communication and their reliability as conveyers of truth have long preoccupied philosophers. Socrates and other Greek philosophers argued that writing lacked the living presence of memory and the authenticity and enchantment of oratory; they saw the scripting of Homer's epics as a fall from grace because writing was dull and less certain compared to orality (Havelock 1986). Much later, Lévi-Strauss (1961) rued the destructive consequences of writing, while Derrida (1997) critiqued Western philosophy's privileging of speech over writing.

9. The structure of domination and rule in colonial India included officials, landowners, and moneylenders, who exerted power through bureaucratic and customary means; subaltern subjects struggled against all three.

10. Governmentality, in the Foucauldian perspective, includes various social institutions and bodies as nodes of rule; the state is positioned as one key "conductor" of governmental projects (Barry, Osborne, and Rose 1996; Foucault 1991). For more on the connections between writing, records, and bureaucratic state power, see Das (2004), Feldman (2008), Guha (1983), Saumerez-Smith (1996), and Scott (1998, 2009).

11. Tulsidas's version of the *Ramayana* is called the *Ramcharitmanas*.

12. I do not mean to separate academic and bureaucratic worlds, or to privilege the former over the latter. Academic anthropologists complete many routine bureaucratic tasks given the spread of audit cultures (Strathern 2000), such as filling in recommendation forms (Brenneis 2006) and writing departmental mission statements in keeping with managerial best practices (Strathern 2006). Yet we tend to create a discursive distinction between academic and bureaucratic work, bracketing off creative thinking, research, writing, and teaching from mind-numbing, unavoidable administrative duties. Perhaps this semantic differentiation between meaningful work and bullshit-job busywork, to modify David Graber (2013b), makes us feel less automaton-like and helps secure our social status.

13. I discuss PIO responses to such serial users or "habitual complainers" in chapter 3.

14. Bornstein (2019) makes a similar point about "the report" written by NGOs that must speak the language of the state in order to be legible.

3. Where the State Goes to Hide

1. Public sector undertakings, or PSUs, are majority state owned, although they enjoy different degrees of autonomy regarding financial decision-making.

2. Manmohan Singh, "P.M.'s Speech at the Annual Convention of Information Commissioners," New Delhi, October 12, 2012, https://archivepmo.nic.in/drmanmohansingh/speech-details.php?nodeid=1234; accessed February 15, 2021.

3. Supreme Court of India, 2011, Civil Appeal No. 6454 [Arising Out of SLP [C] No. 7526/2009]. Central Board of Secondary Education and Anr. v. Aditya Bandopadhyay and Ors, 1–54, at 53, https://cic.gov.in/sites/default/files/court%20orders/CBSEAndAnr-Vs-AdityaAndOrs.pdf; accessed February 15, 2021. This judgment states that "the RTI Act provides access to all information *that is available and existing*. . . . But where the information sought is not a part of the record of a public authority . . . the Act does not cast an obligation upon the public authority, to collect or collate such non-available information and then furnish it to an applicant. . . . It is also not required to . . . obtain and furnish any 'opinion' or 'advice' to an applicant" (49).

4. See Das (2004), Hull (2003), and Tarlo (2003); see also Foucault (1995), Gupta (2008), Messick (1993), Riles (2006), and Saumerez-Smith (1996).

5. On the everyday materialization and imaginations of the state, see Gupta (1995), Hansen and Stepputat (2001), Hull (2003), Riles (2006), and Scott (2009).

6. Aruna Roy and Nikhil Dey, "Taking the Life Out of the Right to Information," *Hindu,* July 24, 2006, http://www.hindu.com/2006/07/24/stories/2006072402411000.htm; accessed July 24, 2013.

7. The materiality and portability of government records also give rise to an informal paper economy of counterfeit state documents. Das (2004) shows how these documents reify modes of state power but also undermine the originary authority of the state's signature.

8. Roy and Dey, "Taking the Life Out of the Right to Information."

9. Orality is not just a powerful mode of antistate resistance and horizontality, as Scott (2009) asserts in his study of anarchic Southeast Asian hill societies; it can also serve to enforce hierarchy and subvert democratization when used by the powerful.

10. Hull (2003), writing about the Pakistani bureaucracy, discusses practices such as using passive voice and quotations from previous notes (rather than naming these notes' individual authors), which obscure the identities of decision makers (304–7).

11. Arendt (2000) criticizes the cog-in-a-wheel mentality that Eichmann used in his defense. She accuses him of thoughtlessness: he had the power to do things differently and he chose not to, and therein lay his agency and his evil.

12. While phone records can be retrieved, the content of phone or in-person conversations is inaccessible unless they are recorded through deception.

13. Weber was ambivalent about this disenchanting yet perfect monstrosity—an iron cage at once necessary for modern life and a shackle on creativity.

14. See Aloke Tikku, "Government Puts Limits on your Right to Info," *Hindustan Times,* August 10, 2012, https://www.hindustantimes.com/delhi/govt-puts-limits-on-your-right-to-info/story-igPLYOonpURXacHlHVthcK.html; accessed March 21, 2024. In the same year, Maharashtra pushed an amendment restricting RTI applications to 150 words. Vinita Deshmukh, "RTI Act: How Successive Government [sic] Have Tried to Maim the Transparency Law," Moneylife, July 19, 2018, https://www.moneylife.in/article/rti-act-how-successive-government-have-tried-to-maim-the-transparency-law/54738.html; accessed January 10, 2021.

15. Commonwealth Human Rights Initiative, "Hall of Shame: Mapping Attacks on RTI Users," http://attacksonrtiusers.org; accessed October 13, 2023.

4. Whose Law Is It Anyway?

1. Laxman's rendering of the history of postcolonial India through the moniker of the common man was meant to provoke laughter rooted in cynicism. "A sense of humor," he stated during an interview, "does not give hope. It has nothing to do with it" (Khanduri 2012, 310).

2. *Wagle Ki Duniya* was a popular TV series in the late 1980s that was revived by Sony in 2021.

3. In my previous work (Sharma 2008), I discuss the contentions between feminist, neoliberal, and radical uses of the term "empowerment."

4. See also Hart (2015), Nigam (2011), and Gudavarthy (2012).

5. He was referring to the protests surrounding the 1996 rape and murder of Priyadarshini Mattoo and the 1999 murder of Jessica Lall.

6. Ghertner (2011a) and Srivastava (2015) discuss RWA participation in the Bhagidari scheme.

7. These were the findings of a study conducted by the RTI Assessment and Analysis Group in collaboration with the NCPRI (RAAG 2009, 7–8).

8. Kalahandi is resource-rich region in Odisha that has been impoverished by extractive capitalism.

9. Considerable literature exists on the relation between the state and the Indian middle class. For colonial middle-class formation, see Chatterjee (1993) and Joshi (2001); for the preliberalization postcolonial era, see Deshpande (1997, 2003); and for the "new" middle class of postliberalization India, see Baviskar and Ray (2011), Fernandes (2006), and Srivastava (2015).

10. Srivastava (2015) and Baviskar (2011) analyze the remaking of Delhi into a "world-class city" as a classed project that removes the poor from the public sphere and view.

11. Ghertner (2011b) argues that during the lead-up to the 2010 Commonwealth Games in Delhi, the courts established new norms for removing slums based on modernist, middle-class aesthetic norms such that a "shopping mall, even if in violation of planning law, is legal because it looks legal" and a "slum, even if its residents have formalized at their current location, is illegal because it looks like a nuisance" (288).

12. Satark Nagrik Sangathan (Society for Citizens Vigilance Initiatives) maintains a website at https://snsindia.org.

13. The colonial state outlawed sati in 1829. After the Kanwar incident, male leaders from her Rajput community and their supporters argued that sati was an important, defendable tradition and that Kanwar's act was voluntary. Feminists and legal activists, however, referenced the impossibility of determining free will in a patriarchal context and agitated successfully for a new law that criminalized commissioning, abetting, and glorifying sati (Mani 1998).

14. Webb (2012) discusses how RTI NGOs serve as brokers for camp dwellers in Delhi, training them in civil society modes of engagement with the state.

15. Private schools in Delhi are required to reserve 25 percent of their seats for people belonging to economically and socially disadvantaged groups, but this measure is often ill-enforced.

16. Anand (2012, 2017) and others working on what water infrastructures tell us about unequal citizenship, neoliberal privatization, and racialized capitalism make this argument. For a discussion on urban South Africa, see von Schnitzler (2016); on the United States, see Ranganathan (2016).

17. Bornstein (2012) analyzes the meanings and practices of *daan* in the Indian humanitarian landscape.

18. Latin American indigenous ideas about *buen vivir* (the good life) as an alternative to the mainstream development logic have now been constitutionally institutionalized in some countries (Gudynas 2011). Sylvia Tidey (2022) shows how the global developmentalist ethos of good governance works against local moral ideas about the good life and care in contemporary Indonesia—small wonder, then, that anticorruption reforms make governance worse, not better.

19. See Holston (2008) on insurgent citizenship in the urban peripheries of Brazil.

20. Brown (1995), MacKinnon (1989), and Fraser (1989) explore the feminization of the welfare arena and masculinization of the liberal public sphere of rights in the U.S. context.

21. "Dolenomics" is a pejorative term used to criticize welfare policies in India that allegedly drain money and do no good; Dreze and Khera (2014) challenge this dismissal.

22. India Today Conclave, "Sibal Asks Raje: Does Anybody Know What Modinomics Means?," YouTube, March 8, 2014, video, 44:40, https://www.youtube.com/watch?v=K_HPSshwDsc; accessed March 21, 2019.

5. "A River That Starts Small and Grows Big"

1. "Gujarat RTI Activist's Murder."

2. AAP, "Why Are We Entering Politics?," http://www.aamaadmiparty.org/why-are-we-entering-politics; accessed July 5, 2016.

3. Das (2015) argues that the urban poor steal electricity to survive but do not see themselves as corrupt. Indeed, Bollywood films celebrate Robin Hood–like outlaw-savior figures, highlighting the complicated relationship between illegal acts and personal virtue.

4. Chakrabarty (1992) and Kaviraj (1997) discuss the difficulty of distinguishing public from private spheres in colonial India.

5. Buur (2001) discusses the bureaucratic work that goes into maintaining the separation between the onstage and backstage, the public and private, and the visible and invisible.

6. Dirks (2006) argues that state "scandal" was essential to colonial rule in India (Kripalani 2008). Low-paid functionaries indulged in private commerce, extractive financial deals, and gift exchanges to supplement their earnings. Top officials condoned and participated in these practices, as Warren Hastings's impeachment trial revealed.

7. Gary S. Becker, "If You Want to Cut Corruption, Cut Government," *Bloomberg*, December 11, 1995, https://www.bloomberg.com/news/articles/1995-12-10/if-you-want-to-cut-corruption-cut-government; accessed March 10, 2021.

8. Postcolonial and postsocialist countries rank lower on these indexes, given that they are considered imperfectly modern when measured against Western

benchmarks. India ranked 85th on Transparency International's 2022 Corruption Perception Index, sharing that position with Guyana and Tunisia, among others. Transparency International, "Corruption Perceptions Index," 2022, https://www.transparency.org/en/cpi/2022/index/ind; accessed October 9, 2023.

9. Speech given by Prime Minister Manmohan Singh at the 19th Conference of CBI and State Anti-corruption Bureaus, on October 10, 2012, http://pib.nic.in/newsite/erelease.aspx?relidp88292; accessed March 10, 2014.

10. "The Kejriwal School of Politics," NDTV, November 11, 2012, video, 44:51, http://www.ndtv.com/video/player/ndtv-special-ndtv-24x7/the-kejriwal-school-of-politics/254484; accessed November 11, 2012.

11. Hawala references the underground system of money transfers that works alongside formal banking, which relies on kin and nonkin networks of trust to move cash anywhere.

12. Basu (2011), then India's chief economic advisor, argued that giving bribes should be decriminalized, while accepting them should remain illegal.

13. The *rationwalas* I spoke to saw themselves as cogs in an unjust system. I invoke "evil" here in the sense used by Arendt (2000): banal, but conscious and not innocent.

14. Many saw the IAC as a middle-class movement (Das 2015; Dhume 2011; Varshney 2011; Yardley 2011).

15. Modi's Swachh Bharat Abhiyan (Clean India Mission) has similar objectives, including preventing open defecation and building toilets.

16. Chatterjee (1989) contends that the outside was masculine and Western, whereas the inside was feminine and native. For nationalists, India was superior to the West in the inside sphere but inferior in the outside sphere, making it necessary for patriarchal leaders to navigate colonial modernity and to compete with colonizers on their terms.

17. Today, 60 percent of the questions must be answered correctly.

18. Singh's Anti-corruption Bureaus speech, October 10, 2012.

19. See the Official Secrets Act of 1923, http://www.archive.india.gov.in/allimpfrms/allacts/3314.pdf; accessed February 9, 2017.

6. On Good Governance Populism

1. This mirrors the mainstream Western academic criticism of populism (Laclau 2005).

2. This law was in keeping with the 74th constitutional amendment, which dictated that power must be devolved to local bodies. Civil society organizations, like Janaagraha in Bangalore, played an important role in the push for decentralizing urban governance (Ramanathan 2007). For a critical look at such middle-class experiments, see Harriss (2007).

3. Urban development is a state responsibility. The federal government stipulated that states would have to enact this law to access National Urban Renewal Mission funding.

Notes to Chapter 6   243

4. Kejriwal (2012) writes, "There was democracy when people passed resolutions and kings vacated their castles" (33).

5. See Kishwar (1986) and Lal (2008) on Gandhi's relationship with women.

6. Mobilizing swaraj through the law was awkward, given Gandhi's (1997) contentious relationship with modern law.

7. See Paley (2001) on "marketing democracy."

8. Ram Rajya, or Ram-raj, refers to Hindu god Ram's rule, a divine form of good governance that Gandhi idealized in his writings on enlightened anarchy (Chatterjee 1986). The BJP invokes a Hindutva-laced Ram Rajya.

9. A Congress minister accused Kejriwal of hijacking the aam aadmi symbol, which had been central to Congress's vision since 1885. "Congress Objects to 'Aam Aadmi' in Kejriwal's Party," *Hindustan Times,* November 24, 2012, https://www.hindustantimes.com/delhi/congress-objects-to-aam-aadmi-in-kejriwal-s-party/story-07T9b00KdAV3UnxcRXpDGI.html; accessed October 3, 2016.

10. Kaur (2016) discusses how the BJP has mobilized the common man discourse, celebrating his ability to forgo state dependency and survive by innovating and making do—*jugaad* in Hindi.

11. This is unlike Modi's chaste oratory in sanitized Hindi.

12. "Mufflerman Returns: AAP's Kejriwal Embraces His Inner Superhero," Scroll.in, November 21, 2014, https://scroll.in/article/690875/Mufflerman-returns-AAPs-Kejriwal-embraces-his-inner-superhero; accessed June 22, 2017.

13. "Nayak 2: The Common Man Rises," Daily Motion, 2014, video, 4:45, https://www.dailymotion.com/video/x5s838v; accessed June 9, 2020. All India Bakchod dissolved in 2019.

14. Simon Denyer and Rama Lakshmi, "Anna Hazare Inspires Middle-Class Awakening in India," *Washington Post,* August 19, 2011, https://www.washingtonpost.com/world/asia-pacific/anna-hazare-inspires-young-middle-class-awakening-in-india/2011/08/19/gIQA1NaCQJ_story.html; accessed June 16, 2021.

15. See Chatterjee (2011), Giridhardas (2011), Patnaik (2011), Sainath (2011), Varshney (2011), and Yardley (2011).

16. Feminist analyses of Western state policies with insights for postcolonial settings include Brown (1995), Gordon (1990), and Butler and Scott (1992).

17. Feminist literature on the intersections of nationalism, patriarchy, and state building is substantial and regionally diverse (Alexander and Mohanty 1997; Kaplan, Alarcón, and Moallem 1999; Sangari and Vaid 1989).

18. Cohen (2022) notes that the aam aadmi has been conjured as an "Old Woman"—an ideal voter or an abject subject of governmental care—in the context of specific political projects.

19. Arvind Kejriwal (@ArvindKejriwal), "Main hoon Aam Aadmi. Main laoonga swaraj," X (formerly Twitter), November 24, 2012, 12:50 AM, https://twitter.com/ArvindKejriwal/status/272215688138063872.

20. @ArvindKejriwal, "Main hoon Aam Aadmi. Main laoonga poorn azadi," 12:49 AM, https://twitter.com/ArvindKejriwal/status/272215312244559872.

21. @ArvindKejriwal, "Main hoon Aam Aadmi. Main banaoonga Jan Lokpal," 12:48 AM, https://twitter.com/ArvindKejriwal/status/272215030123077632.

22. @ArvindKejriwal, "Main hoon Aam Aurat. Main door karungi mengai," 12:48 AM, https://twitter.com/arvindkejriwal/status/272215187573051393.

23. AAP, "Constitution of the Aam Aadmi Party as on 28.01.2021," https://aamaadmiparty.org/about/constitution/; accessed June 21, 2022.

24. The party's constitution lays out that its national executive body shall have at least seven women out of a total of thirty members. AAP, "National Executive," https://aamaadmiparty.org/about/national-executive/; accessed June 21, 2022.

25. AAP, "Political Affairs Committee," https://aamaadmiparty.org/political-affairs-committee/; accessed June 21, 2022.

26. See the statement by Women Against Sexual Violence and State Repression (2014). Bharti was acquitted of assault charges in 2020; see "Delhi Court Acquits AAP MLA Somnath Bharti in 2014 Assault Case," Wire, October 14, 2020, https://thewire.in/law/aap-mla-somnath-bharti-2014-assault-african-national; accessed October 23, 2021.

27. "Arvind Kejriwal: The Mastermind," NewsXLive Channel, September 4, 2012, YouTube, https://www.youtube.com/watch?v=-a3fEDU1b5c; accessed January 20, 2014.

28. "Will Team Anna's Party Achieve What the Movement Couldn't?," NDTV, August 3, 2012, http://www.ndtv.com/video/player/left-right-centre/will-team-anna-s-party-achieve-what-movement-couldn-t/241568; accessed January 20, 2014.

29. See the party's constitution. AAP, "Why We Are Different," https://aamaadmiparty.org/about/why-we-are-different/; accessed July 8, 2021.

30. "Hum Log: Kejriwal versus the People," NDTV, October 7, 2012, video, http://www.ndtv.com/video/player/hum-log/video-story/249766?hphin, posted July 2, 2014; accessed January 20, 2014.

31. "Hum Log."

32. "Hum Log."

33. AAP resigned after forty-nine days in office.

34. AAP, "How Are We Different?," http://www.aamaadmiparty.org/how-are-we-different; accessed July 20, 2017.

35. Available at https://www.youtube.com/watch?v=yEucUVLhuiI; accessed November 9, 2019. This video has since been deleted.

36. Jayant Sriram, "AAP Expels Yogendra Yadav, Prashant Bhushan," *Hindu*, April 21, 2015, updated November 16, 2021, https://www.thehindu.com/news/cities/Delhi/AAP-expels-four-rebel-leaders/article60328892.ece; accessed October 23, 2021.

37. Neerja Chowdhury, "Arvind Kejriwal's Four Mistakes: Why the AAP Leader Lost the Plot So Quickly," Scroll.in, April 30, 2017, https://scroll.in/article/836084/arvind-kejriwals-four-mistakes-why-the-aap-lost-the-plot-so-quickly; accessed October 23, 2021.

38. Scholarship on affect theory examines various social sites, such as labor (Hardt 1999); publics, politics, and digital activism (Papacharissi 2015); populism (Mishra 2017); non-Western geographies and genealogies (Navaro-Yashin 2017); and everyday life, emotions, and subjectivity (Ahmed 2004; Stewart 2007). See also Berlant (2011) and Massumi (2015).

39. I created three composite characters from the more than twenty people I spoke to in August 2014.

Epilogue

1. Pheroze L. Vincent, "AAP's Silence on Release of Rapists 'Reflects Narrow Outlook,'" *The Telegraph,* October 25, 2022, https://www.telegraphindia.com/india/aaps-silence-on-release-of-rapists-reflects-narrow-outlook/cid/1893992; accessed September 14, 2023.

2. For example, see Roy's discussion of the Narmada dam project: Arundhati Roy, "The Greater Common Good." *Frontline,* 1999, http://web.cecs.pdx.edu/~sheard/course/Design&Society/Readings/Narmada/greatercommongood.pdf; accessed March 15, 2024.

3. "Kejriwal Challenges BJP to Make Power Free in Poll-Bound Maharashtra, Haryana," *Business Standard,* August 4, 2019, https://www.business-standard.com/article/pti-stories/kejriwal-challenges-bjp-to-make-power-free-in-poll-bound-maharashtra-haryana-119080400430_1.html; accessed October 26, 2019.

4. "Kashmir and Delhi Opposite, Can't Be Compared: AAP," *India Today,* August 5, 2019, https://www.indiatoday.in/india/story/kashmir-and-delhi-opposite-can-t-be-compared-aap-1577608-2019-08-05; accessed October 25, 2019.

5. "Delhi Govt. Launches 'Constitution at 70' campaign for students of class 6 to 11," *India Today,* August 28, 2019, https://www.indiatoday.in/education-today/news/story/delhi-govt-launches-constitution-at-70-campaign-for-students-of-class-6-to-11-1592714-2019-08-28; accessed October 25, 2019.

6. Sidharth Mishra, "Ram Rajya in Kejriwal's Delhi," *New Indian Express,* May 10, 2021, https://www.newindianexpress.com/cities/delhi/2021/may/10/ram-rajya-in-kejriwals-delhi-2300512.html; accessed September 9, 2023.

7. Gaurav Vivek Bhatnagar, "Delhi Govt. Trying to Establish 'Ram Rajya' for Last Six Years: Kejriwal," March 10, 2021, https://thewire.in/politics/arvind-kejriwal-ram-rajya-delhi-government; accessed September 9, 2023.

8. "2002: Godhra Riots," *Hindu,* August 15, 2022, https://frontline.thehindu.com/the-nation/india-at-75-epochal-moments-2002-godhra-riots/article65725940.ece; accessed September 9, 2023.

9. Geeta Pandey, "Bilkis Bano: India P.M. Modi's Government Okayed Rapists' Release," BBC, October 18, 2022, https://www.bbc.com/news/world-asia-india-62574247; accessed September 9, 2023.

10. Vincent, "AAP's Silence on Release of Rapists."

11. "A Suggestion," Hamraaz, https://hamraazpoems.org/a-suggestion/; accessed September 9, 2023.

12. CM, or chief minister, refers to Kejriwal.

13. Ravidas and Kabir are important fifteenth- and sixteenth-century poet-saints and mystics. Jyotirao Phule was a nineteenth-century anticaste social reformer whose work inspired B. R. Ambedkar, the framer of India's constitution and a twentieth-century Dalit leader.

14. Economist Intelligence Unit (EIU), "Democracy Index 2022," https://www.eiu.com/n/campaigns/democracy-index-2022/; accessed September 21, 2023.

15. Freedom House, "Freedom in the World, 2023: India," https://freedomhouse.org/country/india/freedom-world/2023; accessed September 21, 2023.

16. Freedom House, "Freedom in the World, 2022: The Global Expansion of Authoritarian Rule," https://freedomhouse.org/report/freedom-world/2022/global-expansion-authoritarian-rule; accessed September 23, 2023.

Bibliography

Abrahamsen, Rita. 2000. *Disciplining Democracy: Development Discourse and Good Governance in Africa.* New York: Zed.

Abu-Lughod, Lila. 1986. "Guest and Daughter." In *Veiled Sentiments: Honor and Poetry in a Bedouin Society,* 1–35. Oakland: University of California Press.

Abu-Lughod, Lila. 1990. "The Romance of Resistance: Tracing Transformations of Power through Bedouin Women." *American Ethnologist* 17 (1): 41–55.

Abu-Lughod, Lila. 1991. "Writing against Culture." In *Recapturing Anthropology: Working in the Present,* edited by Richard Fox, 137–62. Santa Fe, N.M.: SAR Press.

Agamben, Giorgio. 1998. *Homo Sacer: Sovereign Power and Bare Life.* Translated by D. Heller Roazen. Stanford, Calif.: Stanford University Press.

Ahmed, Sara. 2004. *The Cultural Politics of Emotion.* New York: Routledge.

Alexander, Jacqui, and Chandra Talpade Mohanty, eds. 1997. *Feminist Genealogies, Colonial Legacies, Democratic Futures.* New York: Routledge.

Althusser, Louis. 2005. *For Marx.* Translated by Ben Brewester. New York: Verso.

Anand, Nikhil. 2012. "Municipal Disconnect: On Abject Water and Its Urban Infrastructures." *Ethnography* 13 (4): 487–509.

Anand, Nikhil. 2017. *Hydraulic City: Water and the Infrastructures of Citizenship in Mumbai.* Durham, N.C.: Duke University Press.

Anand, Rita. 2009. "RTI and the Middle Class." *Civil Society* 6 (6): 38. https://www.civilsocietyonline.com/static/media/static/2016/12/27/April_2009.pdf, accessed October 21, 2023.

Anders, Gerhard. 2010. *In the Shadow of Good Governance: An Ethnography of Civil Services Reform in Africa.* Leiden: Brill.

Anderson, Warwick. 1995. "Excremental Colonialism: Public Health and the Poetics of Pollution." *Critical Inquiry* 21 (3): 640–69.

Arendt, Hannah. 1958. "The Decline of the Nation State and the End of the Rights of Man." In *The Origins of Totalitarianism,* 267–302. New York: Meridian.

Arendt, Hannah. 2000. "Eichmann in Jerusalem." In *The Portable Hannah Arendt,* edited by Peter Baehr, 313–38. New York: Penguin.

Ballestero, Andrea S. 2012. "Transparency in Triads." *Political and Legal Anthropology Review* 35 (2): 160–66.

Barry, Andrew, Thomas Osborne, and Nikolas Rose. 1996. Introduction to *Foucault and Political Reason: Liberalism, Neo-liberalism, and Rationalities of Government,* edited by Andrew Barry, Thomas Osborne, and Nikolas Rose, 1–18. Chicago: University of Chicago Press.

Basu, Kaushik. 2011. "Why, for a Class of Bribes, the Act of Giving a Bribe Should Be Treated as Legal." MPRA Paper 50335. University Library of Munich, Munich, Germany. https://ideas.repec.org/p/pra/mprapa/50335.html, accessed October 21, 2023.

Baviskar, Amita. 2004. *In the Belly of the River: Tribal Conflicts over Development in the Narmada Valley.* 2nd ed. Oxford: Oxford University Press.

Baviskar, Amita. 2007. "Is Knowledge Power? The Right to Information Campaign in India." Sussex Institute of Development Studies. http://rtiworkshop.pbworks.com/f/2006-00-IN-Is-Knowledge-Power-The-Right-to-Information-Campaign-in-India-Amita-Baviskar.pdf, accessed March 30, 2013.

Baviskar, Amita. 2011. "Cows, Cars, and Cycle-Rickshaws: Bourgeois Environmentalists and the Battle for Delhi's Streets." In *Elite and Everyman: The Cultural Politics of the Indian Middle Classes,* edited by Amita Baviskar and Raka Ray, 391–418. New Delhi: Routledge.

Baviskar, Amita, and Nandini Sundar. 2008. "Democracy versus Economic Transformation?" *Economic and Political Weekly* 43 (46): 87–89.

Baviskar, Amita, and Raka Ray, eds. 2011. *Elite and Everyman: The Cultural Politics of the Indian Middle Classes.* New Delhi: Routledge.

Baxi, Upendra. 1980. *The Indian Supreme Court and Politics.* Lucknow, India: Eastern Book Company.

Bear, Laura, and Nayanika Mathur. 2015. "Remaking the Public Good: A New Anthropology of Bureaucracy." *Cambridge Journal of Anthropology* 33 (1): 18–34.

Benjamin, Walter. 2007. "The Storyteller: Reflections on the Works of Nikolai Leskov." In *Illuminations: Essays and Reflections,* edited by Hannah Arendt and translated by Harry Zohn, 83–110. New York: Schocken.

Bennett, Jane. 2001. *The Enchantment of Modern Life: Attachments, Crossings, and Ethics.* Princeton, N.J.: Princeton University Press.

Berlant, Lauren. 2008. "Introduction: Intimacy, Publicity, and Femininity." In *The Female Complaint: The Unfinished Business of Sentimentality in American Culture,* 1–32. Durham, N.C.: Duke University Press.

Berlant, Lauren. 2011. *Cruel Optimism.* Durham, N.C.: Duke University Press.

Bhabha, Homi. 1997. "Of Mimicry and Man: The Ambivalence of Colonial Discourse." In *Tensions of Empire: Colonial Cultures in a Bourgeois World,* edited by Ann L. Stoler and Frederick Cooper, 152–60. Berkeley: University of California Press.

Bhatia, Varuni. 2011. "Pranayam Revolution and the Baba." *Humanities Underground,* June 9, 2011. https://humanitiesunderground.org/pranayam-revolution-the-baba/, accessed July 13, 2021.

Bhushan, Bharat. 2021. "Citizens, Infiltrators, and Others: The Nature of Protests against the Citizenship Amendment Act." *South Atlantic Quarterly* 120 (1): 201–8.

Bhuwania, Anuj. 2016. *Courting the People: Public Interest Litigation in Post-Emergency India.* Cambridge: Cambridge University Press.

Bilgrami, Akeel. 2018. "Reflections on Three Populisms." *Philosophy and Social Criticism* 44 (4): 453–62.

Boeninger, Edgardo. 1992. "Governance and Development: Issues and Constraints." In Summers and Shah 1992, *Proceedings of the World Bank Annual Conference,* 267–87.

Bonilla, Yarimar. 2020. "Postdisaster Futures: Hopeful Pessimism, Imperial Ruination, and *La Futura Cuir.*" *Small Axe* 62:147–62.

Bornstein, Erica. 2012. *Disquieting Gifts: Humanitarianism in Delhi.* Stanford, Calif.: Stanford University Press.

Bornstein, Erica. 2019. "The Report: A Strategy and Non Profit Public Good." *Humanity* 10 (1): 109–31.

Bornstein, Erica, and Aradhana Sharma. 2016. "The Righteous and the Rightful: The Technomoral Politics of NGOs, Social Movements, and the State in India." *American Ethnologist* 43 (1): 76–90.

Bornstein, Erica. n.d. "A Revolution of Rules: The Regulatory Reform of India's Nonprofit Sector." Unpublished manuscript.

Bourdieu, Pierre. 1984. *Distinction: A Social Critique of the Judgement of Taste.* Translated by Richard Nice. Cambridge, Mass.: Harvard University Press.

Bourdieu, Pierre. 1998. *Practical Reason: On the Theory of Action.* Stanford, Calif.: Stanford University Press.

Brenneis, Don. 2006. "Reforming Promise." In *Documents: Artifacts of Modern Knowledge,* edited by Annelise Riles, 41–70. Ann Arbor: University of Michigan Press.

Brown, Wendy. 1995. "Finding the Man in the State." In *States of Inquiry: Power and Freedom in Late Modernity,* 166–96. Princeton, N.J.: Princeton University Press.

Brown, Wendy. 2015. *Undoing the Demos.* Chicago: Haymarket.

Butler, Judith. 2015. *Notes Toward a Performative Theory of Assembly.* Cambridge, Mass.: Harvard University Press.

Butler, Judith, and Joan W. Scott, eds. 1992. *Feminists Theorize the Political.* New York: Routledge.

Buur, Lars. 2001. "The South African Truth and Reconciliation Commission: A Technique of Nation-state Formation." In *States of Imagination: Ethnographic Explorations of the Postcolonial State,* edited by Thomas Blom Hansen and Finn Stepputat, 149–81. Durham, N.C.: Duke University Press.

Chakrabarty, Dipesh. 1992. "Of Garbage, Modernity and the Citizen's Gaze." *Economic and Political Weekly* 27 (10/11): 541–47.
Chakrabarty, Dipesh. 2000. *Provincializing Europe: Postcolonial Thought and Historical Difference.* Princeton, N.J.: Princeton University Press.
Chakravartty, Paula, and Srirupa Roy. 2015. "Mr. Modi Goes to Delhi: Mediated Populism and the 2014 Indian Elections." *Television and New Media* 16 (4): 311–22.
Chakravartty, Paula, and Srirupa Roy. 2017. "Mediatized Populisms: Inter-Asian Lineages. Introduction." *International Journal of Communication* 11:4073–92.
Chalfin, Brenda. 2010. *Neoliberal Frontiers: An Ethnography of Sovereignty in West Africa.* Chicago: University of Chicago Press.
Chandoke, Neera. 2005. "The Taming of Civil Society." *Seminar* 545 (January). https://www.india-seminar.com/2005/545/545%20neera%20chandhoke1.htm, accessed October 21, 2023.
Chatterjee, Partha. 1986. "The Moment of Manoeuvre: Gandhi and the Critique of Civil Society." In *Nationalist Thought and the Colonial World: A Derivative Discourse,* 85–130. Minneapolis: University of Minnesota Press.
Chatterjee, Partha. 1989. "Colonialism, Nationalism, and Colonialized Women: The Contest in India." *American Ethnologist* 16 (4): 622–33.
Chatterjee, Partha. 1993. *The Nation and Its Fragments: Colonial and Postcolonial Histories.* Princeton, N.J.: Princeton University Press.
Chatterjee, Partha. 2004. *The Politics of the Governed: Reflections on Popular Politics in Most of the World.* New York: Columbia University Press.
Chatterjee, Partha. 2008. "Democracy and Economic Transformation in India." *Economic and Political Weekly* 43 (16): 53–62.
Chatterjee, Partha. 2011. "Against Corruption = Against Politics." *Kafila,* August 28, 2011. https://kafila.online/2011/08/28/against-corruption-against-politics-partha-chatterjee/, accessed June 16, 2021.
Chatterjee, Partha. 2014. "Introduction: Postcolonial Legalism." *Comparative Studies of South Asia, Africa, and the Middle East* 34 (2): 224–27.
Chopra, Anuj. 2011. "Fatal Corruption: Why India's Problems Are Too Broad for Even a Jasmine Revolution to Root Out." *Foreign Policy,* May 3, 2011. http://www.foreignpolicy.com/articles/2011/05/03/fatal_corruption.
Chowdhury, Shovon. 2013. *The Competent Authority.* New Delhi: Rupa.
Clarke, John. 2010. "Of Crises and Conjunctures: The Problem of the Present." *Journal of Communication Inquiry* 34 (4): 337–54.
Cody, Francis. 2013. *The Light of Knowledge: Literacy Activism and the Politics of Writing in South India.* Ithaca, N.Y.: Cornell University Press.
Cody, Francis. 2015. "Populist Publics: Print Capitalism and Crowd Violence beyond Liberal Frameworks." *Comparative Studies of South Asia, Africa, and the Middle East* 35 (1): 50–65.
Cohen, Lawrence. 2010. "Ethical Publicity: On Transplant Victims, Wounded Communities and the Moral Demands of Dreaming." In *Ethical Life in South*

Asia, edited by Anand Pandian and Daud Ali, 253–74. Bloomington: Indiana University Press.

Cohen, Lawrence. 2022. "Old Woman." In *The People of India: New Indian Politics in the 21st Century,* edited by Ravinder Kaur and Nayanika Mathur, 98–116. Gurugram: Penguin Random House India.

Cohn, Bernard. S. 1987. "The Census, Social Structure and Objectification in South Asia." In *An Anthropologist among the Historians and Other Essays,* 224–54. Delhi: Oxford University Press.

Coleman, Gabriella. 2014. *Hacker, Hoaxer, Whistleblower, Spy: The Many Faces of Anonymous.* New York: Verso.

Couso, Javier A., Alexandra Huneeus, and Rachel Sieder. 2010. *Cultures of Legality: Judicialization and Political Activism in Latin America.* Cambridge: Cambridge University Press.

Cowen, Michael, and Robert Shenton. 1995. "The Invention of Development." In *The Power of Development,* edited by Jonathan Crush, 27–43. London: Routledge.

Das, Veena. 2004. "The Signature of the State: The Paradox of Illegibility." In *Anthropology in the Margins of the State,* edited by Veena Das and Deborah Poole, 225–52. Santa Fe, N.M.: SAR Press.

Das, Veena. 2011. "State, Citizenship, and the Urban Poor." *Citizenship Studies* 15 (3–4): 319–33.

Das, Veena. 2012. "Ordinary Ethics." In *A Companion to Moral Anthropology,* edited by Didier Fassin, 133–49. Malden, Mass.: Wiley-Blackwell.

Das, Veena. 2015. "Corruption and the Possibility of Life." *Contributions to Indian Sociology* 49 (3): 322–43.

De, Rohit. 2014. "Rebellion, Dacoity, and Equality: The Emergence of the Constitutional Field in Postcolonial India." *Comparative Studies of South Asia, Africa, and the Middle East* 34 (2): 260–78.

De, Rohit. 2018. *A People's Constitution: The Everyday Life of Law in the Indian Republic.* Princeton, N.J.: Princeton University Press.

De, Rohit, and Robert Travers. 2019. "Petitioning and Political Cultures in South Asia: Introduction." *Modern Asian Studies* 53 (1): 1–20.

de Sardan, J. P. Olivier. 1999. "A Moral Economy of Corruption in Africa?" *Journal of Modern African Studies* 37 (1): 25–52.

Deshpande, Satish. 1997. "From Development to Adjustment: Economic Ideologies, the Middle Class and 50 Years of Independence." *Review of Development and Change* 2 (2): 294–318.

Deshpande, Satish. 2003. "The Centrality of the Middle Class." In *Contemporary India: A Sociological View,* 125–50. New Delhi: Viking Penguin India.

Derrida, Jacques. 1997. *Of Grammatology.* Translated by Gayatri Chakravorty Spivak. Baltimore, Md.: Johns Hopkins University Press.

Dery, David. 1998. "'Papereality' and Learning in Bureaucratic Organizations." *Administration and Society* 29:677–89.

Dhume, Sadanand. 2011. "Gandhi's Revenge." *Foreign Policy,* August 22, 2011. https://foreignpolicy.com/2011/08/22/gandhis-revenge/, accessed May 30, 2022.

Dirks, Nicholas B. 2006. *The Scandal of Empire: India and the Creation of Imperial Britain.* Cambridge, Mass.: Harvard University Press.

Doornbos, Martin. 2001. "'Good Governance': The Rise and Decline of a Policy Metaphor?" *Journal of Development Studies* 37 (6): 93–108.

Douglas, Mary. 2002. *Purity and Danger: An Analysis of Concepts of Pollution and Taboo.* New York: Routledge.

Douzinas, Costas. 2009. "What Are Human Rights?" *Guardian,* March 18, 2009. https://www.theguardian.com/commentisfree/libertycentral/2009/mar/18/human-rights-asylum, accessed July 22, 2022.

Douzinas, Costas. 2013. "The Paradoxes of Human Rights." *Constellations* 20 (1): 51–67.

Dreze, Jean, and Reetika Khera. 2014. "Water for the Leeward India." *Outlook Magazine,* March 15, 2014. https://www.im4change.org/latest-news-updates/water-for-the-leeward-india-jean-dreze-and-reetika-khera-24521.html, accessed January 23, 2022.

Eckert, Julia. 2011. "Introduction: Subjects of Citizenship." *Citizenship Studies* 15 (3–4): 309–17.

Eckert, Julia, Brian Donahoe, Christian Strümpell, and Zerrin Özlem Biner. 2012. "Introduction: Law's Travels and Transformations." In *Law Against the State: Ethnographic Forays into Law's Transformations,* edited by Julia Eckert, Brian Donahoe, Christian Strümpell, and Zerrin Özlem Biner, 1–22. Cambridge: Cambridge University Press.

Escobar, Arturo. 1995. *Encountering Development: The Making and Unmaking of the Third World.* Princeton, N.J.: Princeton University Press.

Fassin, Didier. 2012. "Introduction: Toward a Critical Moral Anthropology." In *A Companion to Moral Anthropology,* edited by Didier Fassin, 1–18. Malden, Mass.: Wiley-Blackwell.

Feldman, Ilana. 2008. *Governing Gaza: Bureaucracy, Authority, and the Work of Rule (1917–1967).* Durham, N.C.: Duke University Press.

Ferguson, James. 1994. *The Anti-Politics Machine: "Development," Depoliticization, and Bureaucratic Power in Lesotho.* Minneapolis: University of Minnesota Press.

Ferguson, James. 2006. *Global Shadows: Africa in the Neoliberal World Order.* Durham, N.C.: Duke University Press.

Ferguson, James. 2015. *Give a Man a Fish: Reflections on the New Politics of Distribution.* Durham, N.C.: Duke University Press.

Ferguson, James, and Akhil Gupta. 2002. "Spatializing States: Toward an Ethnography of Neoliberal Governmentality." *American Ethnologist* 29 (4): 981–1002.

Fernandes, Leela. 2006. *India's New Middle Class: Democratic Politics in an Era of Economic Reform.* Minneapolis: University of Minnesota Press.

Fernandes, Leela. 2011. "Hegemony and Inequality: Theoretical Reflections on India's 'New' Middle Class." In *Elite and Everyman: The Cultural Politics of the Indian Middle Classes,* edited by Amita Baviskar and Raka Ray, 58–82. New Delhi: Routledge.

Fortun, Kim. 2001. *Advocacy after Bhopal: Environmentalism, Disaster, New Global Orders.* Chicago: University of Chicago Press.

Foucault, Michel. 1972. *The Archaeology of Knowledge and the Discourse on Language.* Translated by A. M. Sheridan Smith. New York: Pantheon.

Foucault, Michel. 1982. "On the Genealogy of Ethics: An Overview of a Work in Progress." In *Michel Foucault: Beyond Structuralism and Hermeneutics,* edited by Hubert L. Dreyfus and Paul Rabinow, 229–52. Chicago: University of Chicago Press.

Foucault, Michel. 1991. "Governmentality." In *The Foucault Effect: Studies in Governmentality,* edited by Graham Burchell, Colin Gordon, and Peter Miller, 87–104. London: Harvester-Wheatsheaf.

Foucault, Michel. 1995. *Discipline and Punish: The Birth of the Prison.* Translated by Alan Sheridan. New York: Vintage.

Foucault, Michel. 2003. "Eleven: 17 March 1976 (Lecture on Biopower)." In *Society Must Be Defended: Lectures at the College de France, 1975–1976,* edited by Arnold I. Davidson, translated by David Macey, 239–63. New York: Picador.

Frank, Jason. 2018. "Populism Isn't the Problem." *Boston Review,* August 15, 2018. https://www.bostonreview.net/articles/jason-frank-populism-not-the-problem/, accessed September 14, 2023.

Fraser, Nancy. 1989. "Women, Welfare, and the Politics of Need Interpretation." In *Unruly Practices: Power, Discourse, and Gender in Contemporary Social Theory,* 144–60. Minneapolis: University of Minnesota Press.

Fuller, Christopher, and Véronique Bénéï, eds. 2000. *The Everyday State and Society in Modern India.* New Delhi: Social Science Press.

Gandhi, M. K. 1997. *"Hind Swaraj" and Other Writings.* Edited by Anthony J. Parel. Cambridge: Cambridge University Press.

Gandolfo, Daniella, and Todd Ramon Ochóa. 2017. "Ethnographic Excess." In *Crumpled Paper Boat: Experiments in Ethnographic Writing,* edited by Anand Pandian and Stuart McLean, 185–88. Durham, N.C.: Duke University Press.

Ghertner, Asher. 2008. "Analysis of New Legal Discourse behind Delhi's Slum Demolitions." *Economic and Political Weekly* 43 (20): 57–66.

Ghertner, Asher. 2011a. "Gentrifying the State, Gentrifying Participation: Elite Governance Programs in Delhi." *International Journal of Urban and Regional Research* 35 (3): 504–32.

Ghertner, Asher. 2011b. "Rule by Aesthetics: World-Class City Making in Delhi." In *Worlding Cities: Asian Experiments and the Art of Being Global,* edited by Ananya Roy and Aihwa Ong, 279–306. Malden, Mass.: Blackwell.

Gibson-Graham, J. K. 2006. "Affects and Emotions for a Postcapitalist Politics." In *A Postcapitalist Politics,* 1–22. Minneapolis: University of Minnesota Press.

Giridhardas, Anand. 2011. "The Middles Found Their Voice in 2011." *New York Times,* December 30, 2011. https://www.nytimes.com/2011/12/31/world/asia/31iht-currents31.html, accessed June 16, 2021.

Goodale, Mark. 2007. "Introduction: Locating Rights, Envisioning Law between the Global and the Local." In *The Practice of Human Rights: Tracking Law between the Global and the Local,* edited by Mark Goodale and Sally Engle Merry, 1–38. Cambridge: Cambridge University Press.

Goodale, Mark. 2022a. *Reinventing Human Rights.* Stanford, Calif.: Stanford University Press.

Goodale, Mark. 2022b. "Translocal Dilemmas: Social Mobilization and Justice-Seeking Beyond the Boundaries of Law." Paper presented at After Law: Mobilization, Injustice, and Confrontation in the Post-juristocratic Transition, University of Lausanne, Lausanne, Switzerland, June 6–10, 2022.

Goody, Jack. 1986. *The Logic of Writing and the Organization of Society.* Cambridge: Cambridge University Press.

Gordon, Linda, ed. 1990. *Women, the State, and Welfare.* Madison: University of Wisconsin Press.

Government of India. 2005. "The Right to Information Act, 2005." *Gazette of India,* June 21, 2005.

Graeber, David. 2013a. *The Democracy Project: A History, a Crisis, a Movement.* New York: Spiegel and Grau.

Graeber, David. 2013b. "On the Phenomenon of Bullshit Jobs: A Work Rant." *Strike! Magazine* 3 (August). https://www.strike.coop/bullshit-jobs/, accessed August 18, 2020.

Graeber, David. 2015. *The Utopia of Rules: On Technology, Stupidity, and the Secret Joys of Bureaucracy.* London: Melville House.

Gramsci, Antonio. 1971. *Selections from the Prison Notebooks.* Edited and translated by Quintin Hoare and Geoffrey Nowell Smith. New York: International.

Greenhouse, Carol. 2012. "Law." In *A Companion to Moral Anthropology,* edited by Didier Fassin, 432–48. Malden, Mass.: Wiley-Blackwell.

Gregory, Steven. 1998. "Globalization and the 'Place' of Politics in Contemporary Theory: A Commentary." *City and Society* 10 (1): 47–64.

Gudavarthy, Ajay, ed. 2012. *Re-framing Democracy and Agency in India: Interrogating Political Society.* London: Anthem.

Gudynas, Eduardo. 2011. "*Buen Vivir:* Today's Tomorrow." *Development* 54 (4): 441–47.

Guha, Ranajit. 1982. "On Some Aspects of the Historiography of Colonial India." In *Subaltern Studies I: Writings on South Asian History and Society,* edited by Ranajit Guha, 1–8. Oxford: Oxford University Press.

Guha, Ranajit. 1983. *Elementary Aspects of Peasant Insurgency in Colonial India.* Oxford: Oxford University Press.

Guha, Ranajit, and Gayatri Chakravorty Spivak, eds. 1988. *Selected Subaltern Studies*. Oxford: Oxford University Press.
Gupta, Akhil. 1992. "The Song of the Nonaligned World: Transnational Identities and the Reinscription of Space in Late Capitalism." *Cultural Anthropology* 7 (1): 63–79.
Gupta, Akhil. 1995. "Blurred Boundaries: The Discourse of Corruption, the Culture of Politics, and the Imagined State." *American Ethnologist* 22 (2): 375–402.
Gupta, Akhil. 2008. "Literacy, Bureaucratic Domination, and Democracy." In *Democracy: Anthropological Approaches,* edited by Julia Paley, 167–92. Santa Fe, N.M.: SAR Press.
Gupta, Akhil. 2012. *Red Tape: Bureaucracy, Structural Violence, and Poverty in India*. Durham, N.C.: Duke University Press.
Gupta, Akhil, and James Ferguson. 1997. "Beyond 'Culture': Space, Identity, and the Politics of Difference." In *Culture Power Place: Explorations in Cultural Anthropology,* edited by Akhil Gupta and James Ferguson, 33–51. Durham, N.C.: Duke University Press.
Hacking, Ian. 1982. "Biopower and the Avalanche of Printed Numbers." *Humanities in Society* 5 (3–4): 279–95.
Hall, Stuart. 1985. "Signification, Representation, Ideology: Althusser and the Poststructuralist Debates." *Critical Studies in Mass Communication* 2 (2): 91–114.
Haller, Dieter, and Cris Shore. 2005. *Corruption: Anthropological Perspectives*. London: Pluto.
Hansen, Thomas Blom, and Finn Stepputat, eds. 2001. *States of Imagination: Ethnographic Explorations of the Postcolonial State*. Durham, N.C.: Duke University Press.
Hardt, Michael. 1999. "Affective Labor." *Boundary 2* 26 (2): 89–100.
Harriss, John. 2007. "Antinomies of Empowerment: Observations on Civil Society, Politics and Urban Governance in India." *Economic and Political Weekly* 42 (26): 2716–24.
Hart, Gillian. 2015. "Political Society and Its Discontents: Translating Passive Revolution in India and South Africa Today." *Economic and Political Weekly* 50 (43): 43–51.
Harvey, David. 1989. *The Condition of Postmodernity: An Enquiry into the Origins of Cultural Change*. Oxford: Basil Blackwell.
Harvey, David. 2005. *A Brief History of Neoliberalism*. Oxford: Oxford University Press.
Havelock, Eric. 1986. *A Muse Learns to Write: Reflections on Orality and Literacy from Antiquity to the Present*. New Haven, Conn.: Yale University Press.
Hess, Linda. 1988. "The Poet, the People, and the Western Scholar: Influence of a Sacred Drama and Text on Social Values in North India." *Theater Journal* 40 (2): 236–53.
Herzfeld, Michael. 1992. *The Social Production of Indifference: Exploring the Symbolic Roots of Western Bureaucracy*. Chicago: University of Chicago Press.

Hetherington, Kregg. 2008. "Populist Transparency: The Documentation of Reality in Rural Paraguay." *Journal of Legal Anthropology* 1 (1): 45–69.

Hetherington, Kregg. 2011. *Guerrilla Auditors: The Politics of Transparency in Neoliberal Paraguay.* Durham, N.C.: Duke University Press.

Hindess, Barry. 2004. "Liberalism—What's in a Name?" In *Global Governmentality: Governing International Spaces,* edited by Wendy Larner and William Walters, 23–39. New York: Routledge.

Holston, James. 2008. *Insurgent Citizenship: Disjunctions of Democracy and Modernity in Brazil.* Princeton, N.J.: Princeton University Press.

Horton, Lynn. 2012. "Is World Bank 'Good Governance' Good for the Poor? Central American Experiences." *Comparative Sociology* 11:1–28.

Hull, Matthew S. 2003. "The File: Agency, Authority, and Autography in an Islamabad Bureaucracy." *Language and Communication* 23:287–314.

Hurston, Zora Neale. 1969. *Mules and Men.* New York: Negro University Press.

Inglehart, Ronald, and Pippa Norris. 2016. "Trump, Brexit, and the Rise of Populism: Economic Have-nots and Cultural Backlash." Harvard Kennedy School Faculty Research Working Paper RWP16-026, August 2016.

Jackson, Michael. 2017. "After the Fact: The Question of Fidelity in Ethnographic Writing." In *Crumpled Paper Boat: Experiments in Ethnographic Writing,* edited by Anand Pandian and Stuart McLean, 48–67. Durham, N.C.: Duke University Press.

Jaipuriar, Divya Jyoti, and Jayshree Satpute. 2009. *Leading Cases on Right to Information.* New Delhi: Human Rights Law Network.

James, Erica Caple. 2012. "Witchcraft, Bureaucraft, and the Social Life of US(Aid) in Haiti." *Cultural Anthropology* 27 (1): 50–75.

Jeelani, Mehboob. 2011. "The Insurgent." *Caravan Magazine,* August 31, 2011. https://caravanmagazine.in/reportage/insurgent, accessed June 11, 2021.

Jodhka, Surinder. 2021. "Why Are the Farmers of Punjab Protesting?" *Journal of Peasant Studies* 48 (7): 1356–70.

John, Gemma. 2015. "Ways of Knowing: Freedom of Information, Access to Persons and 'Flexible' Bureaucracy in Scotland." *Cambridge Journal of Anthropology* 33 (1): 65–80.

Joseph, Manu. 2012. "Indian Revolution Born in Farce Ends in One." *New York Times,* January 4, 2012. https://www.nytimes.com/2012/01/05/world/asia/05iht-letter05.html?pagewanted=all, accessed June 16, 2021.

Joshi, Sanjay. 2001. *Fractured Modernity: Making of a Middle Class in Colonial North India.* Oxford: Oxford University Press.

Juris, Jeffrey. 2012. "Reflections on #Occupy Everywhere: Social Media, Public Space, and Emerging Logics of Aggregation." *American Ethnologist* 39 (2): 259–79.

Kaplan, Caren, Norma Alarcón, and Minoo Moallem, eds. 1999. *Between Woman and Nation: Nationalisms, Transnational Feminisms, and the State.* Durham, N.C.: Duke University Press.

Kaur, Ravinder. 2016. "The Innovative Indian: Common Man and the Politics of Jugaad Culture." *Contemporary South Asia* 24 (3): 313–27.
Kaviraj, Sudipta. 1997. "Filth and the Public Sphere: Concepts and Practices about Space in Calcutta." *Public Culture* 10 (1): 83–113.
Kaviraj, Sudipta. 2011. *The Enchantment of Democracy and India: Politics and Ideas*. Ranikhet, India: Permanent Black.
Keck, Margaret, and Kathryn Sikkink. 1998. *Activists beyond Borders: Advocacy Networks in International Politics*. Ithaca, N.Y.: Cornell University Press.
Kejriwal, Arvind. 2011. Interview conducted by Sheela Bhatt. Rediff.com, December 9, 2011. http://www.rediff.com/news/slide-show/slide-show-1-interview-with-arvind-kejriwal-on-lokpal-bill/20111209.htm, accessed March 30, 2015.
Kejriwal, Arvind. 2012. *Swaraj*. New Delhi: HarperCollins.
Kejriwal, Arvind. 2013. "*Swaraj*: Redefining Indian Political History—Reforms and Roadmap for Democratic Revolution." Keynote address, Fourth Annual India Leadership Conclave and Indian Affairs Business Leadership Awards, Mumbai, India, June 21, 2013. http://www.youtube.com/watch?v=hn99ic9mqcs, accessed November 3, 2019.
Khagram, Sanjeev. 2002. "Restructuring the Global Politics of Development: The Case of India's Narmada Valley Dams." In *Restructuring World Politics: Transnational Social Movements, Networks, and Norms*, edited by Sanjeev Khagram, James V. Riker, and Kathryn Sikkink, 206–30. Minneapolis: University of Minnesota.
Khanduri, Ritu G. 2012. "Picturing India: Nation, Development and the Common Man." *Visual Anthropology* 25 (4): 303–23.
Kirk, Jason A. 2011. *India and the World Bank: The Politics of Aid and Influence*. London: Anthem.
Kirmani, Nida. 2007. "Struggling for Transparency: The Campaign for the India's 2005 Right to Information Act." Paper written for ESRC's Non-governmental Public Action Programme in collaboration with the Institute of Commonwealth Studies.
Kishwar, Madhu. 1986. *Gandhi and Women*. Delhi: Manushi Prakashan.
Klein, Naomi. 2007. *The Shock Doctrine: The Rise of Disaster Capitalism*. New York: Metropolitan Books.
Klitgaard, Robert. 1992. Comment on "The Cultural Dimensions of Governance," by Martin (1992). In Summers and Shah 1992, *Proceedings of the World Bank Annual Conference*, 343–48.
Klitgaard, Robert. 1998. "International Cooperation against Corruption." *Finance and Development*, March 1998. https://www.imf.org/external/pubs/ft/fandd/1998/03/pdf/klitgaar.pdf, accessed October 13, 2017.
Kothari, Rajni. 1984. "The Non-party Political Process." *Economic and Political Weekly* 19 (5): 216–24.
Kripalani, J. B. 2008. "Deep Roots." *Seminar* 590 (October). https://www.india-seminar.com/2008/590/590_j_b_kripalani.htm, accessed October 21, 2023.

Laclau, Ernesto. 2005. *On Populist Reason*. New York: Verso.
Laidlaw, James. 2002. "For an Anthropology of Ethics and Freedom." *Journal of the Royal Anthropological Institute* 8 (2): 311-32.
Lal, Vinay. 2008. "The Gandhi Everyone Loves to Hate." *Economic and Political Weekly* 43 (40): 55-64.
Lama-Rewal, Stephanie T. 2007. "Neighborhood Associations and Local Democracy." *Economic and Political Weekly* 42 (47): 24-30.
Landell-Mills, Pierre, and Ismail Serageldin. 1992. "Governance and the External Factor." In Summers and Shah 1992, *Proceedings of the World Bank Annual Conference*, 303-20.
Latour, Bruno. 1992. "Where Are the Missing Masses? The Sociology of a Few Mundane Artifacts." In *Shaping Technology/Building Society: Studies in Sociotechnical Change*, edited by W. E. Bijker and J. Law, 225-58. Cambridge, Mass.: MIT Press.
Latour, Bruno. 2005. *Reassembling the Social: An Introduction to Actor-Network-Theory*. Oxford: Oxford University Press.
Latour, Bruno. 2010. *The Making of Law: An Ethnography of the Conseil d'Etat*. Cambridge: Polity Press.
Laxman, R. K. 1998. *The Tunnel of Time: An Autobiography*. New Delhi: Penguin.
Lévi-Strauss, Claude. 1961. *Tristes Tropiques*. Translated by John Russell. New York: Criterion.
Lewis, Oscar. 1969. "Culture of Poverty." In *On Understanding Poverty: Perspectives from the Social Sciences*, edited by Daniel P. Moynihan, 187-220. New York: Basic.
Liang, Lawrence. 2005. "Porous Legalities and Avenues of Participation." In *Sarai Reader 05: Bare Acts*, edited by Monica Narula, Shuddhabrata Sengupta, Jeebesh Bagchi, and Geert Lovink, 6-17. Delhi: Sarai Programme; Centre for the Study of Developing Societies.
Lomnitz, Larissa Adler. 1988. "Informal Exchange Networks in Formal Systems: A Theoretical Model." *American Anthropologist* 90 (1): 42-55.
Lorde, Audre. 2007. "The Master's Tools Will Never Dismantle the Master's House." In *Sister Outsider: Essays and Speeches*, 110-13. Berkeley, Calif.: Crossing.
Lutgendorf, Philip. 1991. *The Life of a Text: Performing the Ramcaritmanas of Tulsidas*. Berkeley: University of California Press.
MacKinnon, Catharine A. 1989. *Toward a Feminist Theory of the State*. Cambridge, Mass.: Harvard University Press.
MacPherson, C. B. 1962. *The Political Theory of Possessive Individualism: Hobbes to Locke*. Oxford: Clarendon.
Mahmood, Saba. 2001. "Feminist Theory, Embodiment, and the Docile Agent: Some Reflections on the Egyptian Islamic Revival." *Cultural Anthropology* 16 (2): 202-36.
Mahmood, Saba. 2005. *Politics of Piety: The Islamic Revival and the Feminist Subject*. Princeton, N.J.: Princeton University Press.

Mander, Harsh, and Abha Joshi. n.d. "The Movement for the Right to Information in India: People's Power for the Control of Corruption." Commonwealth Human Rights Initiative. http://www.humanrightsinitiative.org/programs/ai/rti/india/articles/The%20Movement%20for%20RTI%20in%20India.pdf, accessed July 24, 2013.

Mani, Lata. 1998. *Contentious Traditions: The Debate on Sati in Colonial India.* Berkeley: University of California Press.

Martin, Denis-Constant. 1992. "The Cultural Dimensions of Governance." In Summers and Shah 1992, *Proceedings of the World Bank Annual Conference,* 325–41.

Massumi, Brian. 2015. *Politics of Affect.* Cambridge: Polity Press.

Mathur, Nayanika. 2012. "Transparent-making Documents and the Crisis of Implementation: A Rural Employment Law and Development Bureaucracy in India." *Political and Legal Anthropology Review* 35 (2): 167–85.

Mathur, Nayanika. 2016. *Paper Tiger: Law, Bureaucracy and the Developmental State in Himalayan India.* Cambridge: Cambridge University Press.

Mathur, Nayanika. 2019. "A Petition to Kill: Efficacious Arzees against Big Cats in India." *Modern Asian Studies* 53 (1): 278–311.

Mattingly, Cheryl, and Jason Throop. 2018. "The Anthropology of Ethics and Morality." *Annual Review of Anthropology* 47:475–92.

Mauss, Marcel. (1925) 1990. *The Gift: The Form and Reason for Exchange in Archaic Societies.* Translated by W. D. Halls. London: Norton.

Mazzarella, William. 2019. "The Anthropology of Populism: Beyond the Liberal Settlement." *Annual Review of Anthropology* 48:45–60.

McGranahan, Carole. 2015. "Anthropology as Theoretical Storytelling." *Savage Minds,* October 19, 2015. https://savageminds.org/2015/10/19/anthropology-as-theoretical-storytelling/, accessed July 22, 2022.

Mehta, Pratap Bhanu. 2003. *The Burden of Democracy.* New Delhi: Penguin India.

Mehta, Pratap Bhanu. 2011. "Of the Few, by the Few." *Indian Express,* April 7, 2011. https://indianexpress.com/article/opinion/columns/of-the-few-by-the-few/, accessed July 13, 2021.

Menon, Nivedita. 2004. *Recovering Subversion: Feminist Politics beyond the Law.* New Delhi: Permanent Black.

Menon, Nivedita. 2010. Introduction to *Empire and Nation: Selected Essays,* edited by Partha Chatterjee, 1–30. New York: Columbia University Press.

Menon, Nivedita. 2013. "New Social Movements, New Perspectives." 33rd J. P. Memorial Lecture, Gandhi Peace Foundation, New Delhi, India, March 23, 2013. https://www.outlookindia.com/national/us-versus-them-news-284639, accessed July 6, 2024.

Merry, Sally Engle. 2006. *Human Rights and Gender Violence: Translating International Law into Local Justice.* Chicago: University of Chicago Press.

Merry, Sally. 2011. "Measuring the World: Indicators, Human Rights, and Global Governance." *Current Anthropology* 52 (3): S83–S95.

Messick, Brinkley. 1993. *The Calligraphic State: Textual Domination and History in a Muslim Society.* Berkeley: University of California Press.

Mishra, Pankaj. 2017. *Age of Anger: A History of the Present.* New York: Farrar, Straus and Giroux.

Moore, Sally Falk. 1978. *Law as Process: An Anthropological Approach.* London: Routledge.

Moore, Sally Falk. 2005. "Certainties Undone: Fifty Turbulent Years of Legal Anthropology, 1949–1999." In *Law and Anthropology: A Reader,* edited by Sally Falk Moore, 346–67. Malden, Mass.: Wiley-Blackwell.

Morgan, Lewis Henry. (1877) 1985. *Ancient Society.* Tucson: University of Arizona Press.

Morris, Rosalind. 2004. "Intimacy and Corruption in Thailand's Age of Transparency." In *Off Stage/On Display: Intimacy and Ethnography in the Age of Public Culture,* edited by Andrew Shryock, 225–43. Stanford, Calif.: Stanford University Press.

Mouffe, Chantal. 2005. *On the Political.* London: Routledge.

Moyn, Samuel. 2014. "A Powerless Companion: Human Rights in the Age of Neoliberalism." *Law and Contemporary Problems* 77 (4): 147–69.

Mudde, Cas. 2007. *Populist Radical Right Parties in Europe.* Cambridge: Cambridge University Press.

Mudde, Cas. 2015. "The Problem with Populism." *Guardian,* February 17, 2015. https://www.theguardian.com/commentisfree/2015/feb/17/problem-populism-syriza-podemos-dark-side-europe, accessed May 31, 2021.

Muir, Sarah, and Akhil Gupta. 2018. "Rethinking the Anthropology of Corruption: An Introduction to Supplement 18." *Current Anthropology* 59 (suppl. 18): S4–S15.

Mukhopadhyay, Amitabh. 2007. "File Notings and Governmentality." *Seminar* 569 (January). http://www.india-seminar.com/semframe.html, accessed January 15, 2021.

Nader, Laura. 1974. "Up the Anthropologist: Perspectives Gained from Studying Up." In *Reinventing Anthropology,* edited by Dell Hymes, 284–311. New York: Vintage.

Narayan, Kirin. 2012. *Alive in Writing: Crafting Ethnography in the Company of Chekhov.* Chicago: University of Chicago Press.

Navaro-Yashin, Yael. 2012. *The Make-Believe Space: Affective Geography in a Postwar Polity.* Durham, N.C.: Duke University Press.

Navaro-Yashin, Yael. 2017. "Diversifying Affect." *Cultural Anthropology* 32 (2): 209–14.

Nelson, Joan M. 1992. Comment on "Governance and Development" by Boeninger (1992). In Summers and Shah 1992, *Proceedings of the World Bank Annual Conference,* 289–94.

Nigam, Aditya. 2011. "In the Ruins of Political Society—A Response to Partha Chatterjee." *Kafila,* August 28, 2011. https://kafila.online/2011/08/28/in-the-ruins

-of-political-society---a-response-to-partha-chatterjee/, accessed December 20, 2021.
Nigam, Aditya. 2012. "Politics, 'Political Society' and 'the Everyday.'" *Kafila,* March 31, 2012. https://kafila.online/2012/03/31/politics-political-society-and-the-every day/, accessed November 25, 2021.
Nye, J. S. 1967. "Corruption and Political Development: A Cost–Benefit Analysis." *American Political Science Review* 61 (2): 417–27.
Ong, Aihwa. 2006. *Neoliberalism as Exception: Mutations in Citizenship and Sovereignty.* Durham, N.C.: Duke University Press.
Ong, Aihwa, and Stephen J. Collier. 2005. *Global Assemblages: Technology, Politics, and Ethics as Anthropological Problems.* Malden, Mass.: Blackwell.
Osanloo, Arzoo. 2020. *Forgiveness Work: Mercy, Law, and Victims' Rights in Iran.* Princeton, N.J.: Princeton University Press.
Osborne, David, and Ted Gaebler. 1993. *Reinventing Government: How the Entrepreneurial Spirit Is Transforming the Public Sector.* New York: Penguin.
Paley, Julia. 2001. *Marketing Democracy: Power and Social Movements in Postdictatorship Chile.* Berkeley: University of California Press.
Paley, Julia, ed. 2008. *Democracy: Anthropological Approaches.* Santa Fe, N.M.: SAR Press.
Pandian, Anand, and Stuart McLean, eds. 2017. *Crumpled Paper Boat: Experiments in Ethnographic Writing.* Durham, N.C.: Duke University Press.
Papacharissi, Zizi. 2015. *Affective Publics: Sentiment, Technology, and Politics.* Cambridge: Cambridge University Press.
Pardo, Italo. 2018. "Corrupt, Abusive, and Legal: Italian Breaches of the Democratic Contract." *Current Anthropology* 59 (suppl. 18): S60–S71.
Patnaik, Prabhat. 2011. "Afterword on a Movement." *Monthly Review Online,* September 12, 2011. https://mronline.org/2011/09/12/afterword-on-a-movement/, accessed June 16, 2021.
Petryna, Adriana. 2003. *Life Exposed: Biological Citizens after Chernobyl.* Princeton, N.J.: Princeton University Press.
Piketty, Thomas. 2020. *Capital and Ideology.* Translated by Arthur Goldhammer. Cambridge, Mass.: Harvard University Press.
Prakash, Gyan. 2019. *Emergency Chronicles: Indira Gandhi and Democracy's Turning Point.* Princeton, N.J.: Princeton University Press.
RAAG (RTI Assessment and Analysis Group). 2009. *Safeguarding the Right to Information: Report of the People's RTI Assessment.* New Delhi: RAAG and National Campaign for People's Right to Information.
Ramanathan, Ramesh. 2007. "Federalism, Urban Decentralisation and Citizen Participation." *Economic and Political Weekly* 42 (8): 674–81.
Rancière, Jacques. 2014. *Hatred of Democracy.* Translated by S. Corcoran. London: Verso.
Rancière, Jacques. 2017. "Attacks on 'Populism' Seek to Enshrine the Idea that There Is No Alternative." Verso Books (blog), May 2, 2017. https://www.versobooks

.com/blogs/3193-attacks-on-populism-seek-to-enshrine-the-idea-that-there-is-no-alternative, accessed November 15, 2017.
Randeria, Shalini. 2003. "Cunning States and Unaccountable International Institutions: Legal Plurality, Social Movements and Rights of Local Communities to Common Property Resources." *European Journal of Sociology* 44 (1): 27–60.
Randeria, Shalini, and Ciara Grunder. 2009. "The (Un)making of Policy in the Shadow of the World Bank: Infrastructure Development, Urban Resettlement and the Cunning State in India." AAS Working Papers in Social Anthropology 6. http://hw.oeaw.ac.at/0xc1aa500e_0x00206f3f.pdf, accessed October 15, 2017.
Ranganathan, Malini. 2016. "Thinking with Flint: Racial Liberalism and the Roots of an American Water Tragedy." *Capitalism, Nature, Socialism* 27 (3): 17–33.
Reed, Adam. 2006. "Documents Unfolding." In *Documents: Artifacts of Modern Knowledge,* edited by Annelise Riles, 158–77. Ann Arbor: University of Michigan Press.
Redfield, Peter. 2013. *Life in Crisis: The Ethical Journey of Doctors Without Borders.* Berkeley: University of California Press.
Riles, Annelise. 1998. "Infinity within the Brackets." *American Ethnologist* 25 (3): 378–98.
Riles, Annelise, ed. 2006. *Documents: Artifacts of Modern Knowledge.* Ann Arbor: University of Michigan Press.
Robbins, Joel. 2013. "Beyond the Suffering Subject: Toward an Anthropology of the Good." *Journal of the Royal Anthropological Institute* 19 (3): 447–62.
Roy, Aruna, with the MKSS Collective. 2018. *The RTI Story: Power to the People.* New Delhi: Roli.
Roy, Arundhati. 2011. "When Corruption Is Viewed Fuzzily." *Indian Express,* April 30, 2011. http://www.indianexpress.com/news/when-corruption-is-viewed-fuzzily/783688/0, accessed July 9, 2013.
Roy, Srirupa. 2014. "Being the Change: The Aam Aadmi Party and the Politics of the Extraordinary in Indian Democracy." *Economic and Political Weekly* 49 (15): 45–54.
Sainath, P. 2011. "The Discreet Charm of Civil Society." *Hindu,* June 17, 2011, updated August 18, 2016. https://www.thehindu.com/opinion/columns/sainath/the-discreet-charm-of-civil-society/article2110433.ece, accessed July 11, 2024.
Samet, Robert. 2013. "The Photographer's Body: Populism, Polarization, and the Uses of Victimhood in Venezuela." *American Ethnologist* 40 (3): 525–39.
Samet, Robert, and Naomi Schiller. 2017. "All Populisms Are Not Created Equal." *Anthropology News,* May 8, 2017. https://doi.org/10.1111/AN.432.
Sampson, Steven. 2015. "The Anticorruption Package." *Ephemera: Theory and Politics in Organization* 15 (2): 115–23.
Sanders, Todd, and Harry G. West. 2003. "Power Revealed and Concealed in the New World Order." In *Transparency and Conspiracy: Ethnographies of Suspicion in the New World Order,* edited by Harry G. West and Todd Sanders, 1–37. Durham, N.C.: Duke University Press.

Sangari, Kumkum, and Sudesh Vaid, eds. 1989. *Recasting Women: Essays in Colonial History.* New Delhi: Kali for Women.

Saumerez Smith, Richard. 1996. *Rule by Records: Land Registration and Village Custom in Early British Panjab.* Oxford: Oxford University Press.

Scott, James. 1969. "The Analysis of Corruption in Developing Nations." *Comparative Studies in Society and History* 11 (3): 315–41.

Scott, James. 1998. *Seeing Like a State: How Certain Schemes to Improve the Human Condition Have Failed.* New Haven, Conn.: Yale University Press.

Scott, James. 2009. "Orality, Writing, and Texts." In *The Art of Not Being Governed: An Anarchist History of Upland Southeast Asia,* 220–37. New Haven, Conn.: Yale University Press.

Sengupta, Shuddhabrata. 2011. "At the Risk of Heresy, Why I Am Not Celebrating with Anna Hazare." *Kafila,* April 9, 2011. https://kafila.online/2011/04/09/at-the-risk-of-heresy-why-i-am-not-celebrating-with-anna-hazare/, accessed September 27, 2019.

Shani, Ornit. 2022. "The People and the Making of India's Constitution." *Historical Journal* 65 (4): 1102–23.

Sharma, Aradhana. 2008. *Logics of Empowerment: Development, Gender, and Governance in Neoliberal India.* Minneapolis: University of Minnesota Press.

Sharma, Aradhana. 2013. "State Transparency after the Neoliberal Turn: The Politics, Limits, and Paradoxes of India's Right to Information Law." *Political and Legal Anthropology Review* 36 (2): 308–25.

Sharma, Aradhana. 2014. "Epic Fasts and Shallow Spectacles: The 'India Against Corruption' Movement, Its Critics, and the Re-making of 'Gandhi.'" *South Asia: Journal of South Asian Studies* 37 (3): 365–80.

Sharma, Aradhana. 2018. "New Brooms and Old: Sweeping Up Corruption in India, One Law at a Time." *Current Anthropology* 59 (suppl. 18): S72–S82.

Sharma, Aradhana. 2022. "Good Governance." In *The People of India: New Indian Politics in the 21st Century,* edited by Ravinder Kaur and Nayanika Mathur, 170–81. Gurugram: Penguin Random House India.

Sharma, Aradhana, and Akhil Gupta. 2006. "Introduction: Rethinking Theories of the State in an Age of Globalization." In *The Anthropology of the State: A Reader,* edited by Aradhana Sharma and Akhil Gupta, 1–41. Malden, Mass.: Blackwell.

Sharma, Prashant. 2015. *Democracy and Transparency in the Indian State: The Making of the Right to Information Act.* New York: Routledge.

Sheth, D. L., and Harsh Sethi. 1991. "The NGO Sector in India: Historical Context and Current Discourse." *Voluntas* 2 (2): 49–68.

Sieder, Rachel. 2020. "Revisiting the Judicialization of Politics in Latin America." *Latin American Research Review* 55 (1): 159–67.

Sieder, Rachel, Line Schjolden, and Alan Angell. 2005. Introduction to *The Judicialization of Politics in Latin America,* edited by Rachel Sieder, Line Schjolden, and Alan Angell, 1–20. New York: Palgrave Macmillan.

Singh, Shekhar. 2010. "The Genesis and Evolution of the Right to Information Regime in India." Paper presented at regional workshop Towards a More Open and Transparent Governance in South Asia. New Delhi, India, April 27–29, 2010. http://rtiworkshop.pbworks.com/f/2010-04-IN-Country-Paper-Shekhar-Singh.pdf, accessed July 24, 2013.

Sneath, David. 2006. "Transacting and Enacting: Corruption, Obligation and the Use of Monies in Mongolia." *Ethnos* 71 (1): 89–112.

Srivastava, Sanjay. 2015. *Entangled Urbanism: Slum, Gated Community, and Shopping Mall in Delhi and Gurgaon*. Oxford: Oxford University Press.

Stewart, Kathleen. 2007. *Ordinary Affects*. Durham, N.C.: Duke University Press.

Stiglitz, Joseph. 2007. *Making Globalization Work*. New York: Norton.

Strathern, Marilyn. 2006. "Bullet-Proofing: A Tale from the United Kingdom." In *Documents: Artifacts of Modern Knowledge*, edited by Annelise Riles, 181–205. Ann Arbor: University of Michigan Press.

Strathern, Marilyn, ed. 2000. *Audit Cultures: Anthropological Studies in Accountability, Ethics and the Academy*. London: Routledge.

Summers, Lawrence H., and Shekhar Shah, eds. 1992. *Proceedings of the World Bank Annual Conference on Development Economics, 1991*. Washington, D.C.: World Bank.

Sundar, Nandini. 2011. "Sparring Partners." Blog, June 29, 2011. http://nandinisundar.blogspot.com/2011/06/sparring-partners.html#more, accessed November 25, 2021.

Sunder Rajan, Rajeswari. 2003. *The Scandal of the State: Women, Law, and Citizenship in Postcolonial India*. Durham, N.C.: Duke University Press.

Tarlo, Emma. 2003. *Unsettling Memories: Narratives of the Emergency in Delhi*. New Delhi: Permanent Black.

Thompson, E. P. 1966. *The Making of the English Working Class*. New York: Vintage.

Ticktin, Miriam. 2006. "Where Ethics and Politics Meet: The Violence of Humanitarianism in France." *American Ethnologist* 33 (1): 33–49.

Tidey, Sylvia. 2022. *Ethics or the Right Thing? Corruption and Care in the Age of Good Governance*. Chicago: Hau.

Tsing, Anna. 2005. *Friction: An Ethnography of Global Connection*. Princeton, N.J.: Princeton University Press.

Ulysse, Gina. 2007. *Downtown Ladies: Informal Commercial Importers, a Haitian Anthropologist, and Self-Making in Jamaica*. Chicago: University of Chicago Press.

Valverde, Mariana. 2012. *Everyday Law on the Street: City Governance in an Age of Diversity*. Chicago: University of Chicago Press.

Valverde, Mariana, and Aaron Moore. 2019. "The Performance of Transparency in Public–Private Infrastructure Project Governance: The Politics of Documentary Practices." *Urban Studies* 56 (4): 689–704.

Varshney, Ashutosh. 2011. "Has Urban India Arrived?" *Indian Express,* August 25, 2011. https://indianexpress.com/article/opinion/columns/has-urban-india-ar rived/, accessed June 16, 2021.

Visvanathan, Shiv. 2008. "The Necessity of Corruption." *Seminar* 590 (October). http://www.india-seminar.com/2008/590/590_shiv_visvanathan.htm, accessed March 13, 2014.

Visvanathan, Shiv. 2011. "The Return of the Political." *Seminar* 625 (September). http://www.india-seminar.com/2011/625/625_comment.htm, accessed July 18, 2016.

von Schnitzler, Antina. 2016. "Performing Dignity: Human Rights and the Legal Politics of Water." In *Democracy's Infrastructure: Techno-politics and Protest after Apartheid,* 168–95. Princeton, N.J.: Princeton University Press.

Walley, Christine. 2013. *Exit Zero: Family and Class in Postindustrial Chicago.* Chicago: University of Chicago Press.

Webb, Martin. 2010. "Success Stories: Rhetoric, Authenticity, and the Right to Information Movement in North India." *Contemporary South Asia* 18 (3): 293–304.

Webb, Martin. 2012. "Activating Citizens, Remaking Brokerage: Transparency Activism, Ethical Scenes, and the Urban Poor in Delhi." *Political and Legal Anthropology Review* 35 (2): 206–22.

Weber, Max. 1978. *Economy and Society.* Edited by Guenther Roth and Claus Wittich. Berkeley: University of California Press.

Weber, Max. 2006. "Bureaucracy." In *The Anthropology of the State: A Reader,* edited by Aradhana Sharma and Akhil Gupta, 49–70. Malden, Mass.: Blackwell.

Widlok, Thomas. 2016. *Anthropology and the Economy of Sharing.* London: Routledge.

Williams, Raymond. 1977. *Marxism and Literature.* Oxford: Oxford University Press.

Women against Sexual Violence and State Repression. "Letter to Arvind Kejriwal: Women against Sexual Violence and State Repression." *Kafila,* January 21, 2014. https://kafila.online/2014/01/21/letter-to-arvind-kejriwal-women-against -sexual-violence-and-state-repression/, accessed October 23, 2021.

World Bank. 1989. *Sub-Saharan Africa: From Crisis to Sustainable Growth.* Washington, D.C.: World Bank.

World Bank. 1992. *Governance and Development.* Washington, D.C.: World Bank.

Yardley, Jim. 2011. "Protests Awaken a Goliath in India." *New York Times,* October 29, 2011. https://www.nytimes.com/2011/10/30/world/asia/indias-middle -class-appears-to-shed-political-apathy.html?pagewanted=all, accessed May 30, 2022.

Index

Page numbers in italic refer to illustrations.

aam aadmi, 3, 120, 122, 133, 150, 169, 199, 201, 202, 207, 213; corrupt, 168; discourse, 197; empowered, 150; as Old Woman, 243n18. *See also* common man

Aam Aadmi Party (AAP), 17, 20, 122, 155, 195, 196, 203, 213, 216, 221, 223; antipolitics and, 204; BJP and, 225, 226; campaign by, 220, 227; common good and, 225; elitism and, 205; empowerment and, 215; founding of, 3, 14; IAC and, 206; identification of, 204; Indian constitution and, 226; internal challenges of, 212; joining, 214; *kaabil* trustees and, 208; leadership of, 201, 207, 211–12; nationalism and, 198, 200, 202, 225, 226; patriarchy and, 201; populism and, 197; as social movement/political revolution, 204; swaraj and, 206; volunteers and, 209, 210–20, 217–18

AAP. *See* Aam Aadmi Party

accountability, 9, 16, 23, 31, 35, 37, 39, 40, 42, 90, 102, 106, 107, 111, 112, 114, 120, 124, 153; democratic, 44, 51, 113; governmental, 13; public, 96; transparency and, 115

activism, 16, 17, 43, 81, 113, 126, 127; good governance, 159, 184; grassroots, 25, 28; judicialized, 12, 13, 15, 18, 43, 52, 54, 111, 178; movement, 6, 16; RTI, 57, 130, 143; transparency, 14, 48, 52, 62

affectscape, 209, 221

Alliance Française, 177

All India Bakchod, 198

Ambedkar, B. R., 228, 246n13

Anand, Nikhil, 240n16

Anand, Rita, 119, 120, 121

Anders, Gerhard, 235n19

Anna movement, 202, 215

Anonymous, researching, 87

anthropology, 14, 15–16, 18; medical, 235n20; moral, 15, 16, 22, 235n20; political/legal, 13

anticorruption, 5, 153, 195, 216, 217; good governance and, 14; law, 155, 160, 200; movement, 4, 14, 154, 162, 181

antipolitics, 189, 203, 204

267

Area Sabhas, 190
Arendt, Hannah, 239n11, 242n13
Arthshastra, 233n3
Article 370, revoking, 225
Asian Development Bank, 1, 45
authoritarianism, 126, 132, 151, 208, 218, 224, 235n12; benevolent, 205–6; democracy and, 135, 229; excesses of, 20; good governance and, 187; populism and, 4, 187
autoethnography, 22
AVAM (AAP Volunteer Action Manch), 207, 208, 209, 210, 216; empowerment and, 215; organization of, 212; purge of, 218

Babri Masjid, 227
Bahawalpur, 66, 67
Bano, Bilkis, 227
Barkha Dutt, Anchor, 164, 167, 171
Basu, Kaushik, 165, 242n12
Bear, Laura, 87, 88
Beawar, 36, 37, 39
Becker, Gary, 158
Benjamin, Walter, 18, 55, 63, 67; neoliberal capitalism, and, 64; storytelling and, 65, 68, 85
Berlant, Lauren, 220, 221
Bhagavad Gita, 27, 233n2
Bhagidari scheme, 127, 128, 240n6
Bharatiya Janata Party (BJP), 46, 151, 194, 195, 206, 216, 223, 236n20, 243n8, 243n10; AAP and, 225, 226; convention of, 1; nationalist rules of, 226; politics of, 227, 228
Bharat Mata, 202
Bharti, Somnath, 201
Bhawan, Rashtrapati, 94–95
Bhopal, 39, 44
Bhushan, Prashant, 164, 165, 213
Bihar, 78, 143, 179
BJP. *See* Bharatiya Janata Party
Bolsonaro, Jair, 185

Bornstein, Erica, 234n8, 238n14, 241n17
bribes, 164, 165, 167, 168, 173, 175, 176, 242n12; drive against, 160
Brown, Wendy, 64, 241n20, 243n16
bureaucracy, 4, 13, 14, 17, 18, 21, 58, 75, 87–88, 99, 102, 104, 112, 121; anthropological studies of, 16; conformity and, 84; democracy and, 114; departmental, 106; empty language and, 111; governmental, 16, 71–72; health, 61, 70; insensitivity of, 183; Kafkaesque, 145; law and, 157; logics of, 156; rational, 177; RTI and, 83; storytelling and, 68; structures/procedures and, 115; struggling with, 70; transparency and, 92, 93, 103, 114–17; utopian nature of, 83
bureaucraft, 82, 93, 104, 106, 108–9, 112, 113–14, 115, 117, 157, 182; procedural, 107; routine, 111
bureaucratese, 18, 21, 70, 99, 111, 176
Butler, Judith, 235n10, 243n16
Buur, Lars, 241n5

Cabinet Secretariat, Research and Analysis Wing of, 237n5
camps. *See* slums
capitalism, 16, 39, 49, 179, 203; crony, 165; extractive, 240n8; media and, 64; neoliberal, 64, 65; racialized, 240n16; scientific, 6
castes, 142, 178, 235n9
Central Bureau of Investigation, 155
Central Economic Intelligence Bureau, 237n5
Central Government Health Scheme, 60
Central Information Commission, 58, 120
Central Reserve Police Force, 237n5
Central Vigilance Commission, 153

centrism, ideological, 203, 204
Chakrabarty, Dipesh, 182, 241n4
Chatterjee, Partha, 19, 145, 148, 242n16; political society and, 123, 124
Chavez, Hugo, 5, 185
Chernobyl disaster, 40
Chopra, Anuj, 168; corruption and, 167, 171, 172–73
citizenship, 4, 5, 16, 17, 21, 22, 39, 85, 113, 122, 128, 144, 147, 168, 202, 226; abstract, 123, 201; civic, 173; democratic, 23; differential, 148; enlightened, 151; generic, 84; imagination of, 148; as labor, 144, 148; layered, 149; liberal, 84, 124; meanings of, 13; patterned, 18; politics of, 124, 149; proprietary, 148; reshaping, 55; self-reliant, 151; statehood and, 29
Citizenship Amendment Act, 4, 234n13
civil servants, 45, 55, 95, 101
civil society, 27, 123, 132, 135, 148, 151, 153; control of, 191; organizations, 5, 10, 42; political society and, 124; rule-bending and, 125
Cohen, Lawrence, 35, 243n18
Cold War, 6, 26, 90, 187
Coleman, Gabriella, 87
colony-wallahs, 142, 143
common man, 3, 19, 198, 200; discourse of, 202; symbol of, 201; term, 123
Common Man (character), 121–22, 199, 200
commonness, 200–201, 202, 208
commons: fractured, 147–52; inverted, 183; moral, 196–205; populist, 209; public, 53, 106
Commonwealth Games, 162, 240n11
Commonwealth Human Rights Initiative, 116, 237n5
common woman, 200, 201
communication, 85, 107; imperatives of, 70; improving, 218; information and, 64; orality/writing and, 237n8; styles of, 81; written, 63
Communist Party of India, 37
Congress Party, 40, 41, 47, 122, 155, 194, 216; corruption and, 163; RTI and, 42
consumer court, 56
Consumer Protection Act, 56
corruption, 5, 13, 14, 15, 17, 19, 22, 32, 35, 90, 93, 122, 126, 162; beyond culture/law, 177–80; celebratory view of, 183; centralization and, 194; complexity of, 180–81; conundrum of, 155–59; corporate, 153; as cultural pathology, 167–77; culture and, 173, 177–80; discourse on, 158, 159, 180; ending, 3, 31, 76, 157, 164, 169, 170, 181, 182, 184, 206; ethnography of, 158; lack of consensus on, 156–57; law and, 19–20, 157; legal reform and, 159; middle class and, 161, 168, 173; proliferation of, 168; social acceptance of, 154; social life of, 182; state, 26, 60, 159–67; transparency and, 21, 178
Corruption Perception Index, 31, 242n8
cruel optimism, 221, 222
culture, 6, 229; audit, 64; bureaucratic, 102; changing, 104; corruption and, 173, 177–80; oral, 63; political, 188; popular, 192; state and, 8; VIP, 204

Das, Veena, 146, 239n7, 241n3; on citizenship, 149; corruption and, 156
Delhi, 67, 94, 95, 98, 194; as national microcosm, 16–17; as world-class city, 240n10
Delhi Development Authority, 108
Delhi Metro, 11
Delhi Public School, workshop at, 72
Delhi Transport Corporation (DTC), 213

Delhi University, 161, 178
democracy, 22, 32, 38, 122, 131, 133, 135, 147; authoritarianism and, 229; bureaucracy and, 114; centralized, 16; democratic transformation, 43, 84, 152; economistic view on, 216; as fantasy, 219; formal, 189; homogeneity and, 132; internal, 195; liberal, 6, 30, 187, 188, 203, 220, 229, 230; participatory, 211–12; sacredness of, 226; secrecy and, 114; subversion of, 151; swaraj and, 220; transparency and, 114–15
democratic participation, 4, 9, 38, 96, 114, 207
Department for International Development, 46
Department of Commerce, RTI and, 101
Department of Personnel and Training, 74
Derrida, Jacques, 237n8
de Sardan, J. P. Olivier, 156
development, 31, 32, 122, 180, 225; aid, 45; economic, 7, 31; global capitalist, 30; international, 49, 185; legal framework for, 31; loans, 46; measures, 47; neoliberal, 11; organizations, 16–17; outcomes, 49–50; sustainable, 187; urban, 190, 242n3
Dhawan, Tulsi Das, 62, 66, 68
dictatorship, benevolent, 218, 219, 220
Dirks, Nicholas B., 241n6
Dixit, Sheila, 127
dolenomics, 151, 241n21
Doornbos, Martin, 188
Douzinas, Costas, 10
Dreze, Jean, 241n21
due process, 9, 147

Eckert, Julia, 10, 147
Economist Democracy Index, 228

Eichmann, Adolf, 239n11
elites, 124–25, 131, 133, 143, 146, 147, 151
Emergency Supreme Court, 12
entanglements, 7, 12, 88, 208; colonial, 11; global, 51; illiberal, 13; neoliberal, 13; translocal, 29
entitlements, 10, 144; temporary, 124; transforming, 151; welfare, 13
environmental concerns, 39, 40, 44, 50
Erdogan, Tayyip, 185
ethics, 49–50, 51, 52, 66, 132
ethnography, 5; dynamics of, 21; strong theory and, 22

FAAs. *See* first appellate authorities
Fair Price Shop, 165, 166
famine relief, 33, 36
Fassin, Didier, 15, 235n20
Feldman, Ilana, 92
Ferguson, James, 146–47
files, 105–14
first appellate authorities (FAAs), 57–58, 100
First Information Report (FIR), 76
food rations, 56, 142
Food Security Act, 220
Ford, Henry, 220
Foreign Contributions (Regulation) Act, 236n20
Foucault, Michel, 18, 63, 64–65, 84
Fraser, Nancy, 241n20
freedom, 9, 15; liberal, 27; self-government and, 208
Freedom House, 228, 230
Freedom in the World Index, 228
freedom of speech, 26, 44, 72, 225
free markets, 31, 219
French Revolution, 26

Gaebler, Ted, 1
Gandhi, Indira, 122, 139, 197, 211; state of emergency and, 12, 43

… Index …

Gandhi, Mahatma, 52, 54, 189, 202, 206, 228, 243n5, 243n8; good governance and, 3; on repugnant laws, 234n14; self-rule and, 3; swaraj and, 3, 10, 191, 192, 200, 233n3
Gandhi, Sonia, 243n6; RTI Act and, 41, 42, 46, 236n16, 236n17
Gandolfo, Daniella, 21
Gazette of India, 41, 57
gender, 21, 22, 43; citizenship and, 151; corruption discourse and, 159; patriarchal state and, 150
Ghertner, Asher, 240n11
Gibson-Graham, J. K., 21
Global Corruption Barometer, 31
"Global Expansion of Authoritarian Rule, The" (Freedom House), 228
Global Freedom Score, 228
globalization, 54, 96, 229; capitalist, 30; post-Fordist, 64
Goodale, Mark, 234n12, 234n13, 235n4
good governance, 19, 45, 122, 125, 128, 149, 150, 160–61, 183, 203, 217–18; accountability for, 37; anticorruption and, 14; (anti)politics of, 30–32; culture and, 9; decentralized, 190; defining, 1–2, 7, 8, 31; democratic, 16, 17, 31, 32, 38, 42, 44, 123, 126, 185, 189, 205, 208, 230; developmentalist version of, 227; dewelfarized, 205; discourse, 13, 14, 157, 181; dominance of, 50; economistic view on, 216; establishing, 5, 6, 201; as exercise of power, 205; global development ethos of, 241n18; human rights and, 11; improving, 4, 20, 123, 144; laws, 151, 200; local roots for, 9; moral goodness and, 9, 14; municipal, 126; neoliberal, 4, 10, 11, 15, 46, 158; planning and, 134–35; poor, 129, 186; populism and, 4, 5, 13, 20, 163, 185, 186–89, 199, 201, 205, 209, 221, 230, 231; public welfare and, 186; style of, 5, 224; technomoral, 15, 20, 23, 163, 186, 197, 227; transforming, 135, 205; transparency and, 108, 114, 117; urban, 14, 190
Google Hangout, 207
Google Maps, 213
Gordon, Linda, 243n16
governmentality, 15, 238n10
Graeber, David, 83, 238n12
grassroots organizations, 33–39, 234n10
Gregory, Steven, 28
Gujarat, 1, 2, 78, 233n4; riots in, 227

Hacker, Hoaxer, Whistleblower, Spy: The Many Faces of Anonymous (Coleman), 87
Hamraaz, poetry of, 227–28
Hanuman, Lord, 226
Harvey, David, 30
Hastings, Warren, 241n6
Hazare, Anna, 3, 154, 155, 197; nationalism of, 198
Herzfeld, Michael, 111
Hess, Linda, 68
Hetherington, Kregg, 14, 108
hierarchy, 93, 110, 204, 208, 220, 239n9; administrative, 92; bureaucratic, 89, 93, 100, 104, 138; class and gender, 52, 63; global-local, 28; rational, 103; transparency and, 94–117
Hindess, Barry, 32, 208
Holi gaali, secret literature of, 122
Holston, James, 241n19
Homer, 237n8
Hull, Matthew S., 239n10
human rights, 10, 15, 33, 38, 40, 43, 48, 229, 234n10; campaign, 44; good governance and, 11; transnational, 235n4; universal, 234n12
hunger strikes, 34, 54, 155, 196

IAC. *See* India Against Corruption
IAS. *See* Indian Administrative Services
ideology, 40, 185; beyond, 201–5; good governance, 17; Hindutva, 226; idealism and, 4; repudiating, 196; smoke screen, 203
illegality, 145, 153, 156, 157, 170, 241n3
illiberalism, 13, 17, 84, 115, 117, 185, 205
IMF. *See* International Monetary Fund
India Against Corruption (IAC), 154, 155, 160, 161, 162, 168, 169, 171, 195, 196, 199–200, 202, 203, 204, 216; AAP and, 206; campaign of, 3, 5, 158, 167, 213; corruption and, 180–81; elitism and, 205; Jan Lokpal bill and, 163; middle class and, 181, 242n14; populism and, 197; techno-moral mission of, 181
India International Centre, 153
Indian Administrative Services (IAS), 33, 89, 94, 111
Indian Coffee House, 154
Indian Constitution, 57, 124, 147, 171, 226
Indian Evidence Act (1872), 108–9
Indian Institute of Technology, 100, 198
Indian National Congress, 122, 197
Indian Penal Code, 163
Indian Revenue Service, 3, 159, 198
Indian Spring, 3, 155
Indian Supreme Court, 12, 26, 39, 56, 103, 171, 227; freedom of information and, 44; RTI law and, 72
inequalities, 15, 123, 159, 229; class, 156; economic, 156; gender, 201; material conditions of, 63; political, 156; social, 147, 156; structural, 158, 169, 177
informality, 145, 157; network of, 176, 177

information, 11, 38, 59, 61–65, 101, 103, 107; accessibility of, 77; censuses/statistics and, 65; centrality of, 64; denial of, 91; disclosure of, 76, 81; freedom of, 44, 45, 48, 50, 77–78; political value of, 30; public, 31, 107; public good and, 218; public interest and, 58; requesting, 3, 116; right to, 33, 36, 90, 125; sharing, 39, 43, 45, 91, 100, 102
Information Commission, 74, 75, 120
infrastructure, 46, 59, 190, 207; bureaucratic/legal, 184; public-private, 112; water, 142, 146
International Covenant on Civil and Political Rights (1966), 26
International Monetary Fund (IMF), 6, 11, 31

Jackson, Michael, 70
Jagdamba camp, 137, 139
Jal Board, 49, 50
James, Erica, 93, 109
Jan Lokpal bill, 2, 150, 154, 155, 161, 163, 167, 198; campaign for, 202; enacting, 3. *See also* People's Ombuds bill
Jethwa, Amit, 2, 3, 153, 233n4
judicialization, 10, 12, 13, 15, 16, 18, 54, 78, 111, 184; neoliberalism and, 11
justice, 9, 15, 38, 50; economic, 40; redistributive, 12; social, 52; vigilante, 201

Kabir, 228, 246n13
Kanwar, Roop, 137, 240n13, 241n13
Kaur, Ravinder, 243n10
Kaviraj, Sudipta, 241n4
Kejriwal, Arvind, 2, 21, 102, 121, 162, 163, 164, 165, 166, 169, 178, 185, 193, 194, 201, 206, 213, 214, 220, 226; aam aadmi discourse and, 197; AAP and, 3, 20, 211, 223, 227; anticorruption

movement and, 154; antipolitics and, 204; autocratic actions of, 208; BJP and, 228; common man and, 198; corruption and, 73, 159–60, 202–3; as corruption hunter, 199; cult of personality and, 221; dictatorship and, 219; on Gandhi, 204; good governance and, 23, 160–61, 205, 221, 224–25, 227; IAC and, 155, 199–200; leadership of, 5; on media/civil society, 191; Modi and, 186, 189; moral antipolitics and, 204; moral commons and, 196, 202; Nagar Raj law and, 189–90; patriarchal monarchy and, 191–92; populist indeterminacy and, 203; public service and, 204–5; reform agenda of, 225; RTI law and, 49, 72, 153; RWAs and, 119; swaraj and, 4, 186, 189, 192, 195, 207, 209, 213, 221; volunteers and, 207, 211, 212
Khera, Reetika, 241n21
Khirki village, raid in, 201
Klein, Naomi, 48
Klitgaard, Robert, 8, 234n11
Kot Kirana, public hearing in, 34, 35
Krishan, Lord, 1
Kumar, Renu, 42, 43, 47, 48, 49

Laclau, Ernesto: populism and, 187, 188, 196
Lall, Jessica: murder of, 240n5
Latour, Bruno, 92
law, 17, 21, 131, 150; anthropology of, 15; bureaucracy and, 157; corruption and, 19–20, 157, 177–80; morality and, 15; nationalist leaders and, 12; proliferation of, 11; social life of, 4; transparency, 27, 92
Laxman, R. K., 122, 197, 239n1
legalism, 179, 228
legal norms, 11, 31, 103, 123
Lévi-Strauss, Claude, 237n8

Liang, Lawrence, 145
liberalism, 6, 13, 84, 229; bourgeois, 52, 53; tactical, 29, 51–54; transnational, 52; undemocratic, 188
liberalization, 26, 45, 49, 169; economic, 20, 30, 31, 90; political, 7, 9, 11, 20, 31, 230
Lomnitz, Larissa Adler, 177
Lorde, Audre, 83

MacKinnon, Catharine, 241n20
Madras Coffee House, described, 209–10
Mahabharata, 233n2
Maharashtra, 225, 239n14
marginalization, 11, 29, 180
masculinism, 144, 158, 159
Mathur, Nayanika, 14, 88
Mattoo, Priyadarshini, 240n3
Mazdoor Kisan Shakti Sangathan (MKSS), 27, 28, 29, 32, 33, 44, 47; Beawar dharna of, 39; campaign by, 43; canvassing by, 37; corruption and, 38; establishment of, 34; information and, 90; public hearings by, 35; role of, 35, 39, 42; slogan by, 53; strategic positioning of, 52; transparency and, 40; wage justice/information freedom and, 50
media, 99, 191; analysis, 21; capitalism and, 64; commentaries, 19; national, 132
Mehta, Pratap Bhanu, 147, 164, 167
Menon, Nivedita, 125
Merry, Sally, 10
middle class, 125, 126, 127, 128, 129, 130, 133, 135, 143, 151, 159; awakening of, 200; corruption and, 161, 168, 173; formation of, 203; ordinariness and, 199; poor governance and, 134; RTI and, 121, 131, 132; state and, 240n9; swaraj and, 193; transforming governance and, 132

Mill, John Stuart, 205
Mishra, Pankaj, 229
MKSS. *See* Mazdoor Kisan Shakti Sangathan
MLAs, 112, 140, 142, 154, 161, 216
modernity, 129, 172; capitalist, 63, 229; colonial, 242n16; liberal, 157
Modi, Narendra, 23, 185, 198, 223–24, 227; BJP and, 223; good governance and, 1–2, 4, 20, 224, 226; Kejriwal and, 186, 189; maximum governance and, 5; oratory of, 243n11; regime of, 186; Swachh Bharat Abhiyan and, 242n15
Mohallas, 190
Moore, Sally Falk, 112
moral commons, cobbling, 196–205
morality, 9, 16, 60, 147, 161, 202–3, 228; anthropology of, 15; law and, 15
MTNL telephone service, 59, 237n7
Mukhopadhyaya, Amitabh, 110

Nagar Raj law, 3, 150, 189–90, 192, 195
Narmada dam, 234n17; movement, 44, 215, 245n2
National Advisory Council, 41
National Campaign for People's Right to Information (NCPRI), 39, 41, 111, 240n7; formation of, 40
National Democratic Alliance, 41
National Food Security Act (2013), 237n1, 237n3
nationalism, 2, 52, 198, 202, 225, 243n17; patriarchal, 205
National Political Affairs Committee (AAP), 201
National Registry of Citizens, 4
National Rural Employment Guarantee Act (NREGA), 36, 38, 73, 122, 179, 235n11, 236n14
National Urban Mission Renewal, 242n3

NCPRI. *See* National Campaign for People's Right to Information
NDTV, 164, 167, 171
Nehru, Jawaharlal, 42, 166
neoliberalism, 2, 6, 9, 13, 16, 30–32, 51, 52, 64, 65, 88, 181, 202, 230; global, 20; judicialization and, 11
neoliberal policies, 10, 47, 50
nongovernmental organizations (NGOs), 2, 5, 10, 11, 12, 16, 26, 28, 43, 55, 58, 78, 94, 132, 140, 141; protransparency, 20; RTI, 240n14
nonparty political formations, 12
NREGA. *See* National Rural Employment Guarantee Act

Ochóa, Todd Ramon, 21
officialdom, 101, 106, 110, 111
Official Secrets Act (1923), 2, 39, 42, 44, 48, 59, 107, 109, 183, 235n1
Old Woman, as aam aadmi, 243n18
opacity, 3, 83, 87, 93, 102, 104, 111, 113, 115
Open Society Institute (Open Society Foundation), 31
orality, 63, 106, 109, 176, 237n18, 239n9
Orban, Victor, 185
Organisation for Economic Co-operation and Development, 236n22
Osborne, David, 1

paperealities, 105–6
Parivartan, 2, 55, 71, 72, 119, 121, 159, 165, 189, 196; activists, 56, 57, 190–91; RTI Act and, 160
Patil, Paratibha, 139
Patkar, Medha, 213, 215
Patnaik, Prabhat, 181
patriarchy, 159, 178, 200, 201, 243n17
People's Ombuds bill, 3, 155, 206. *See also* Jan Lokpal bill
personhood, 18, 62, 81, 84, 172

petitioning, 82, 84, 180; described, 81. *See also* right to information petitions

Phule, Jyotirao, 228, 246n13

Piketty, Thomas, 229

PIOs. *See* public information officers

planned economies, collapse of, 186

Platinum PLUs, 135, 144–45, 146, 150, 151

pluralism: institutional, 234n10; moral, 8; normative, 8

political society, 123, 125, 135, 148, 151; civil society and, 124; negotiation tactics of, 145

political theory, 13, 186

politics, 5, 6, 11, 22, 124, 128, 134, 156, 171, 180, 185, 209; activist, 43; alternative, 225; blood-and-soil purity, 231; citizenship, 149; civil, 19; democratic, 50; ethical, 28, 204; governance, 7, 13–14, 15, 17, 30; grassroots, 12; Hindutva, 186, 224, 225; judicialized, 10, 178; liberal, 13, 52, 54; national, 23, 229; political society, 19, 144, 145–46; populist, 10, 15, 20, 185, 224; power, 205; transformation of, 196; translocal, 51–54; transparency, 14; urban subaltern, 146

populism, 5, 12, 14, 15, 21, 206, 224; AAP and, 197; authoritarian, 187, 229; described, 188; good governance, 20, 163, 185, 186–89, 199, 204, 205, 209, 221, 230, 231; IAC and, 197; ideological/class attachment and, 188; mediatized, 196; nationalist, 202; structural moments of, 196; technomoral, 196, 224; wave of, 10, 230

porous legalities, 145, 146

postcolonialism, 11, 13, 53, 104, 241n8

poverty, 33, 190, 197; corruption and, 73

power, 13, 15, 103, 106, 114; bureaucratic, 65, 83, 88, 110, 115, 238n10; corporate, 50; devolution of, 208; knowledge and, 65; moral, 206; political, 208; soft, 47; state, 50, 62, 83, 88, 114, 115, 145; transparency and, 88

Press Council of India, 41

Prevention of Corruption Act, 154, 164

PricewaterhouseCoopers (PwC), 49, 50

privatization, 31, 49, 127, 205, 225; neoliberal, 240n16

proceduralism, 48, 82, 110, 111, 113

public authority, 58–59, 91

Public Distribution System, 56, 165

public good, information and, 218

public information officers (PIOs), 57–58, 72, 73, 75, 76, 89, 90–91, 93, 94, 96, 98, 100, 101, 102, 103, 104, 108, 169–70; RTI queries and, 79; workloads of, 99

public interest, 61, 133; national interest and, 59

public interest litigation (PIL), 12, 13, 44, 56, 234n17, 237n3

public-private distinction, 19, 112, 128, 157, 159, 172, 173

public sector, 31; information in, 101

public sector undertakings (PSUs), 238n1

public services, 190; governance as, 204–5

public spaces, 60, 182, 183

public sphere, 37, 60; masculinization of, 241n10; power in, 106

Raghunandan, T. R., 173

Raje, Vasundhara, 151

Ram (Hindu god), 68, 226, 233n2, 243n8

Ramayana (Tulsidas), 67, 68, 238n11

Ramcharitmanas (Tulsidas), 238n11
Ramlila Maidan, 213
Ram Rajya (Ram-raj), 1, 195, 227, 228, 233n2, 243n8; building, 226
Rancière, Jacques, 188
rationwalas, 166, 242n13
Ravidas, 228, 246n13
Reed, Adam, 84
reform: bureaucratic, 22; civil service, 235n19; corruption and, 184; economic, 187; good governance, 4, 5, 6–13, 14, 200, 202; governance, 17, 30, 147, 203; legal, 14, 149; market, 26; political, 26, 228
Research and Analysis Wing (Cabinet Secretariat), 237n5
Resident Welfare Associations (RWAs), 74, 75, 119, 121, 123, 126, 127, 129, 130, 132, 144, 190; Bhagidari scheme and, 240n6; public interest litigation and, 134
restructuring, 29, 45; economic, 186; neoliberal, 50, 51; political, 31
rights, 4, 19, 21, 53, 122, 146, 148, 151; civil, 27; constitutional, 125; duties and, 128; educated, 151; entitlement-based, 151; expansion of, 149–50; fundamental, 12; gendered, 151; governance, 19, 151; political, 27, 124; universal, 53; welfare, 19, 51. *See also* human rights
Right to Food campaign, 237n3
Right to Information (RTI) Act, 2, 18–19, 26, 28, 32, 36, 38, 43, 44, 45, 46, 47, 55, 57, 59, 74, 76, 77, 78, 83, 88, 89, 91–92, 96, 97, 99, 100, 101, 103, 107, 113, 114, 119, 120, 125, 129; aam aadmi and, 121; amendments, 41, 71, 236n17; campaign for, 27; challenges of, 116; circulation of, 41; common man and, 123; corruption and, 56, 155, 158; economy of appearances and, 106; enactment of, 33, 51, 62; impact of, 80, 90; insider knowledge and, 111; middle class and, 121, 131, 132; neoliberal currents and, 48; passage of, 14, 17, 29, 236n16; penalty clause of, 75; right to speech and, 72; social/activist life of, 65; social divides and, 121; support for, 3, 131, 134; transparency and, 104; undoing of, 116, 153; using, 79–81, 149–50
right to information (RTI) activists, 54, 56, 57, 78, 82, 197
Right to Information (RTI) Assessment and Advocacy Group, 80, 240n7
right to information (RTI) movement, 4, 16, 40, 54, 112; social justice and, 52
right to information (RTI) petitions, 18, 31, 58, 59, 60, 61, 62, 63, 65, 68, 70, 71, 82, 84, 85, 97, 99; filing, 116, 136, 138, 140, 143–44; ideal, 72–81; PIOs and, 79; processing, 89
right to information (RTI) workshops, 25, 27, 45, 72, 74, 91, 97, 107
Roy, Aruna, 17, 21, 27, 34, 35, 36, 37, 38, 40, 41, 45, 50, 53, 54, 111, 121, 150, 245n2; liberal statism and, 52; MKSS and, 33, 37, 39, 44
rule of law, 11, 12, 31
RWAs. *See* Resident Welfare Associations

Sanders, Todd, 114–15
Satark Nagrik Sangathan (Society for Citizens Vigilance Initiatives) (SNS), 112, 135, 136, 137, 138, 240n12
satyagraha, 3, 10
Scott, James, 63, 81, 243n16
secrecy, 32, 116; administrative, 107; democracy and, 114; state, 44, 90, 101
Sedgwick, Eve, 21

Index

self-governance, 189, 190, 208, 225. *See also* swaraj
self-positioning, ethnographic craft and, 20–23
Shani, Ornit, 234n15
Sharma, Prashant, 14, 29
Sheikh Sarai, 135–36
Shekhawat, Bhairon Singh, 36
Shourie Committee, 41
Singh, Bhagat, 196, 202, 236n14; corruption and, 171, 172–73
Singh, Manmohan, 103, 164, 180
Singh, Shekhar, 21, 39, 41, 42, 47, 112, 114, 164, 165; antienvironmentalism and, 40; on officialdom, 31; on RTI law, 83; securitization and, 48; transparency and, 49
Singh, V. P., 41
Sisodia, Manish, 227
slums, 19, 56, 108, 123, 132, 135, 136, 137, 139, 141, 142, 143, 144, 145, 217; term, 237n2
Sneath, David, 156
SNS. *See* Satark Nagrik Sangathan
social media, 5, 20, 196
social movements, 4, 5, 10, 12, 45, 180, 195, 204
social relations, 64, 147
Socrates, 237n8
Solanki, Dinu, 233n4
Sori, Soni, 213
Soros, George, 31
Soros Foundation, 26
Southeast Asian hill people, 63, 239n9
sovereignty, 107; nation-state, 7, 30, 59; popular, 206; state, 18, 107
S. P. Gupta v. The Union of India, 44
Sreedharan, E., 161
state: corruption of, 159–67; patriarchal, 150; transformation, 10; verticality, 107, 113. *See also* power
State of Uttar Pradesh v. Raj Narain, 44

Storyteller, The (Benjamin), 55
storytelling, 18, 55, 65–72, 81, 85; art of, 72; bureaucracy and, 68; ethnographic, 21–22, 209; theoretical, 21; written information and, 65
Sundar, Nandi, 13
Sunil, 83; information freedom and, 77–78; RTI law and, 78
suraj, 1, 2, 4, 224
Swachch Bharat Abhiyan (Clean India Mission), 242n15
swaraj, 5, 17, 186, 196, 200, 213, 215, 219, 224, 228, 233n3; appeal of, 191; contradictions of, 209; corruption and, 195; demanding, 211–12; described, 214; dictating, 205–9; economistic view on, 216; Gandhian, 10; institutionalization of, 194; as institutionalized practice, 221; middle class and, 193; mission of, 189; model for, 207, 217; pitching, 189–95; populism and, 189; raising awareness about, 206; sacredness of, 226; self-governance and, 189

Tahrir Square, occupation of, 235n10
technology, 69; document, 84; governance, 17, 65
technomoral politics, 6, 10, 38, 114, 224, 234n8; analysis of, 22; dynamics of, 14, 189; idea of, vii; judicialized, 155–56; promoting, 4
Tidey, Sylvia, 14, 241n18
Times of India, 122
Torvalds, Linus, 218–19
transparency, 5, 9, 13, 17, 18, 22, 23, 26, 27, 28, 29, 35, 41, 47, 57, 87, 179, 198, 202; accountability and, 115; activism for, 14, 48, 52, 62; (anti)politics of, 30–32; bureaucracy and, 92, 93, 103; corruption and, 21, 178; democracy and, 30, 114–15, 117; enforcing, 62–63; hierarchy

and, 94–117; implementing, 112; importance of, 33, 40; information disclosure and, 76; laws, 17, 18, 27, 29, 39, 46, 58, 160; legalized, 45, 102, 103; limits of, 116; state, 44, 45, 65, 88, 92, 101; terrorism/security and, 49

Transparency International, 5, 26, 31, 159; Corruption Perception Index of, 242n8

Transport Department, 175, 176

Trump, Donald, 5, 185

Tsing, Anna, 10, 28, 52, 54, 235n12

Tulsidas, 67, 68, 238n11

Union Carbide, 39, 44

United Nations, 5, 31

United Nations Development Programme, 46

United Progressive Alliance (UPA), 41, 122

Universal Declaration of Human Rights (1948), 8, 26

utilitarian, 57, 64, 68, 82, 95

Valverde, Marianne, 14, 112

Vidyut (Electricity) Board, 159

vigilance bureaus, 153

village council, 35, 237n26

violence, 66, 144; neoliberal, 13; RTI-related, 116; structural, 145, 183

Visvanathan, Shiv, 167, 172, 183; baroquization and, 184

volunteers, 55, 217–18; class issues and, 217; expelling, 209, 211–12

Wagle Ki Duniya (television series), 239n2

water, 149, 217; access to, 142–43; poaching, 144; privatization of, 49

Webb, Martin, 234n18, 240n14

Weber, Max, 239n13; on administrative management, 157; bureaucracy and, 63, 92, 93, 99, 104, 114, 115, 116, 157, 177; on calculable rules, 99

welfare, 13, 116, 151, 205; downsizing, 225; feminization of, 241n20

welfare policies, 146–47, 241n21

West, Harry G., 114–15

Whistleblowers' Act, 150

whistleblowing, 11

Williams, Raymond, 103–4

World Bank, 1, 5, 6, 7–8, 26, 30, 31, 45, 47, 73, 186, 187, 203; borrowing from, 46; culture/politics and, 7; development economics and, 7; good governance and, 8, 50; liberal democracy and, 188; pressure from, 11, 25; RTI and, 49; water privatization scandal and, 49

Yashin, Yael Navaro, 88

You Said It, 121

ARADHANA SHARMA is associate professor of anthropology at Wesleyan University. She is author of *Logics of Empowerment: Development, Gender, and Governance in Neoliberal India* (Minnesota, 2008) and coeditor of *The Anthropology of the State: A Reader.*